THE EXACTING EAR

The Story of Listener-Sponsored
Radio, and an Anthology of
Programs from KPFA, KPFK, and WBAI

PANTHEON BOOKS

THE
EXACTING
EAR

EDITED BY ELEANOR McKINNEY

WITH A PREFACE BY ERICH FROMM

A Division of Random House • NEW YORK

CONTENTS

I
——————

ON PACIFICA
RADIO

I

1

Preface
by Erich Fromm

That radio offers one of the most splendid possibilities to bring to each citizen not only what art and science have to offer, but also orientation on social, philosophical, and political problems is a fact that no one will doubt. However, there is no denying another fact—that the tremendous role advertising plays in radio, as well as in television, makes a radio station to some degree dependent on the good will of its advertisers, and hence very cautious about presenting views that might be controversial or even shocking. Yet for the nation to have the full benefit of radio it is important to transcend these restrictive factors.

In a far-reaching insight Lewis Hill conceived the idea of a new kind of broadcasting institution, one supported directly by its listeners whose lives would be informed and enriched by its existence. Radio broadcasting created by individuals in direct relation to listeners could bypass the restrictions of advertising bias and vested interests, and be free to broadcast the full and uncensored range of political views in America and throughout the world. Such a radio station could explore responsibly any controversy, could communicate music, poetry, and examine in depth every concern vital to human beings.

Pacifica Radio and its three broadcasting stations on the

East and West coasts grew out of this idea. This original and daring experiment began in Berkeley, California, in 1949 at Radio Station KPFA. The new radio station appealed to individuals, not mass audiences. It did not seek to broadcast everything in order to please everyone, but to concentrate on a few subject areas done superbly well. Its aim was to supplement the existing forms of public communication, not to compete with them. KPFA expressed over the air its expectant trust in the responsibility of its listeners: that they would voluntarily subscribe to exceptional radio programs just as they subscribe to newspapers and magazines; that they would pay this voluntary fee even though they could hear the broadcasts for nothing.

Such a new concept appeared to be manifestly impossible, and leading periodicals reporting on the new radio experiment predicted the venture would last about six months. Seventeen years later, Pacifica Radio survives, with a history of radio broadcasting that defies analysis. Thousands of civic and political leaders, writers, composers, poets, folk singers, musicians, artists, thinkers with no public role, concerned citizens of ranging views —all have appeared on Pacifica Radio over the years, having a public platform unknown in America since the traditional Free Forums of pioneer days. Techniques now common in radio and television had their origin in Pacifica's informal, intensely personal, uncensored, and free-ranging discussions, interviews, conversations, and documentaries. Controversial subjects never before treated on radio were frequently heard on all Pacifica stations.

Struggling against perpetual economic shortages, with dedicated staff members devoting uncounted hours to the survival of the stations, Pacifica Radio continued to turn out programing unmatched in its consistent level of quality and diversity.

Readers of this anthology will discover why Pacifica Radio became a phenomenon not only in each local area of its broadcasting, but throughout the entire nation. Listener involvement extended far beyond the act of subscribing to support the stations—because these programs and the stations producing them became a symbol and a reality of the individual voice in a mass society. Listeners worked for the stations in dozens of volunteer jobs, from fund-raising to technical and clerical work. At times of economic crisis, or when threatened by outside pressures, the stations received listener support on every level from dollars to personal work at and for the stations.

Pacifica radio stations know nothing of the isolation common to broadcasting in America. They are personal: a two-way communication and a two-way responsibility. The current of contemporary life is reflected in its fullest range in these new institutions whose major contribution to American life is yet to be fully understood and fully appreciated.

May this volume serve to further that end.

2

Editor's Foreword

The continued existence of Pacifica Foundation and its three radio stations is a tribute to the men and women who created it and sustained it by their labor during its twenty-year history. To tell their story is beyond the scope of this book, which honors them all, though many who gave much are not mentioned here. When something wholly new is being created, the best of our human gifts and the worst of our failures often collide in dynamic intersection. It was so in Pacifica. And from time to time there were outside pressures so severe that headlines throughout the nation reported controversies threatening Pacifica's very existence. Some of these are reported within this book.

This is, however, an anthology of some of Pacifica's diverse radio broadcasts. It reflects only fragments of the spectacular range of uncommon radio programing that became known throughout the world. In selecting examples of the thousands of talents and views reflected in Pacifica broadcasts, it was our task to find programs—still on tape among the archives of KPFA in Berkeley, California, KPFK in Los Angeles, California, and WBAI in New York City—that would document the Pacifica idea. Many wonderful broadcasts had been permanently lost, erased from tapes urgently needed for current programing. Sometimes after laborious transcribing, we found that the subtle magic of oral communication had been lost between the recording and the printed page. The whole range of music, together with composers, commentators, and critics in lecture and discussion, had to be left out.

Each program in this anthology has been edited to condense, within the space limits imposed by the printed page, the leisurely thought and conversation encouraged on the air. First is a brief review of Pacifica's history, selected from a set of informal broadcasts given on WBAI in 1962, in response to listener requests for information about how Pacifica came into being.

About Pacifica Radio
Broadcast, 1962

This is Eleanor McKinney. Here in the WBAI studio before a microphone, I speak to you in the privacy of your home. On listener-sponsored radio somebody is always having his say about something-or-other. But today, since many of you have asked about Pacifica Radio and how it grew, we're going to take a brief look backward to the early days of this experiment in broadcasting.

It began in 1946 when Lewis Hill, a White House correspondent for a Washington, D.C., radio station, left his job and traveled to California with an extraordinary idea. Lew Hill envisioned a new use for this powerful and sensitive microphone through which you now hear my voice. Was it possible to bring into American radio the human being at his best—his music, thoughts, art, controversies, his ancient and modern accomplishments and conflicts? Was it possible that listeners, given the chance, would voluntarily assist in this adventurous experiment in communication?

With a few friends who shared the excitement and hope of this idea, Lewis Hill formed Pacifica Foundation. The name was chosen not for the Pacific coast, but for the aims of the new broadcasting institution—to explore the causes of strife between individuals and nations which plague mankind with war. The potent communicative instrument of radio broadcasting had never been used in the serious service of these problems. Nor had radio ever been able to provide an atmosphere of freedom and diversity which would attract serious writers, artists, and thinkers. Limited advertising was first envisaged as the means of supporting the new experiment, but by 1948 the concept of listener-sponsorship had evolved.

Pacifica Foundation was formed then, in the San Francisco Bay Area. It was incorporated as a nonprofit educational corporation. It had no money, no prestige, no impressive list of celebrities on a letterhead. It had no organization backing it. It was simply a small group of individuals with a vision, and the determination to see that vision become a practical reality.

The vision seemed at that time idealistic beyond that faculty so dear to the American heart—common sense. In the imagination and hope of these few ordinary people in the San Francisco Bay Area was a dream of radio stations in major metropolitan areas throughout the United States. Each would be supported, not through advertising, but voluntarily by its own local community of listeners. A quality of programing unprecedented in the history of radio would in time reach millions of listeners daily. The art and thought of contemporary and traditional times would be broadcast, along with the most thoughtful possible exploration into all issues affecting the individual in each community and in the nation as a whole. Individual talents and insights seldom heard in the public life of a community would be given a voice in an atmosphere of informality, candor, and freedom. And ultimately these stations would become production centers for the distribution of programs reflecting the best in American life to countries throughout the world.

This was a whopping and ambitious project for a few utterly unknown and unfinanced individuals. But there was one very important ingredient present in this high-flown idea. And that was, in fact, common sense. Lewis Hill combined very rare qualities, almost extremes, which are seldom brought together in one man—the radical ideals of a visionary and poet, and the practicality of a man of action. He believed most of all in *doing*, in putting to work and to the test any ideas he had. Pacifica Radio was designed to the most minute detail—its economic structure, its budget, its policies, even its program format. All this was put down in a bulky prospectus, and sent to people all over the United States, seeking contributions to obtain a radio channel, to build a station, and to begin the first experiment.

It took three years to raise the minimum for this purpose. From January, 1946, until January, 1949, the group evoked interest in this idea, and slowly funds were accumulated. They were placed in trust. If enough money could not be raised to begin the first station, all the funds would be returned to the donors. By November, 1948, enough money had been collected to apply to the Federal Communications Commission for an FM station of 1,000 watts.

The group had a critical decision to make. The $15,000 in the bank was enough to build a station and operate it for about a month. Yet there was little prospect of raising more money without an operating radio station to demonstrate what could actually be done. A meeting was held to decide whether to return the money to the donors and give up the project, or to take a leap in the dark and begin the experiment. The exciting prospect of creating the radio station we had all dreamed about was compelling. To be liberated from the tyrannies of the stop watch and the commercials, from typical radio's condescending concept of the audience, was an inducement of immense challenge. We were all convinced that the commercial notion of "all us bright people in here broadcasting to all you sheep-type masses out there" was completely false. We longed for a chance to produce programs to share with the many discriminating listeners we knew filled the community—to address them as people of intelligence instead of aiming for their pocketbooks. (I'll have more to say about the irony of this, later.)

Finally, Lewis Hill reminded us, "In a crisis—grow. That's the only creative possibility—take a risk and expand." The phrase was to become the key to many decisions in the future.

So we got to work.

The small radio station was built into existing offices on the sixth floor of an office building in Berkeley, California. The studios and control room were custom-built, mostly from used equipment. Friends and strangers heard about the new venture and came up to help stuff sound-proofing materials into studio walls, hammer on sound tile, help with carpentry and painting. The program schedule was designed, and the volunteer program talents so richly present in the San Francisco Bay Area were called upon.

The offices were jammed with different groups rehearsing programs, with carpenters, engineers, and three KPFA staff members trying to be everywhere at once.

One night the first signals of the new transmitter were tested. At home, in the early morning, we turned on a radio. There came the familiar voice of our engineer, testing. The thing actually worked. It seemed like a miracle. At three o'clock in the afternoon on April 15, 1949, Lew Hill stepped to a microphone, and the workmen, hammering down the carpet at the last moment, paused in their work. The rest of us were busy pounding out program copy and continuity on typewriters nearby. He announced for the first time: "This is KPFA, listener-sponsored radio in Berkeley." For a moment the typewriter copy blurred before our eyes—and the project was underway.

Soon there were delighted telephone calls from listeners, and cautious praise in the newspapers along with predictions that such an experiment, which depended on listeners for support, would have a short life. Visitors dropped in to "see for themselves" where such extraordinary radio programs came from. They were curious about the ideas behind the radical difference from ordinary radio. They enjoyed the absence of radio's conventions, hearing an announcer casually say, "The tape just got tangled up" or "The background music you hear is leaking from the other studio where they're rehearsing the next program." They never heard, "Technical difficulties beyond our control. . . ." There were no fanfares, no themes, no organ stings. Duration of programs was designed to fulfill natural content—not to be chopped off in regular segments by the stop watch. So that programs could begin at scheduled times, the spaces between the flexible endings were filled with bits of prose or poetry, or simply by silence when the mood or impact would have been jarred by a sudden shift to another subject. The spontaneity of staff and program participants sharing their best talents with each other and the listeners created an informality, a delighted enjoyment, that was communicated over the air.

In the first five months, six hundred program participants appeared in live programs, which ranged through drama, literature, public affairs, music, and children's programs. There was no attempt to please everybody or to be all things to all people. The aim was to do a few things very well. Listeners were invited to listen elsewhere if they were not interested in the immediate broadcast. We sometimes delighted in breaking the radio taboo about mentioning any other station's call letters and specifically recommended good programs on other stations. In commentary and panel discussion KPFA explored majority viewpoints and minority views seldom or never heard on radio; it stressed the basic ethical realities in human relationships that underlie all public problems. After all, why were we all engaged in this broadcasting experiment? At the root was concern and respect for human beings. It was really as simple as that.

As the days passed, curious visitors, attracted by the informality and personal address to the listener, wandered up to KPFA's offices and offered to help. Listeners found themselves voluntarily trapped once they set foot inside the station. They were taught to be announcers, or mimeographers, or engineer-helpers, or envelope-stuffers. A large volunteer staff soon participated in the work of the station.

For fifteen months the experiment continued. However, voluntary subscriptions sent in by listeners remained inadequate to relieve the difficult task of raising funds to meet operating costs each week. Although community response had far exceeded expectations, the station had to reach a larger audience if it was to survive. The Foundation decided to suspend broadcasting in order to make a full-time fund-raising effort.

When the staff announced over the air that KPFA was to stop broadcasting, the telephones began to ring and listeners came to plead that the station continue. At their suggestion, a public meeting of KPFA listeners was announced. To the discouraged staff it was an overwhelming experience to see the meeting place crowded with listeners who valued the station so much that they were determined to give their own energies and money to its survival. A working fund of $2,300 was raised immediately. Vigorous committees and volunteer workers plunged into fund-raising and getting subscription pledges for a new KPFA, and carried on an intensive campaign for nine months. Strangers to each other, but joined in the common bond of interest in KPFA, listeners worked together—some ten hours a day, six days a week during the nine months the station was silent.

KPFA had generated an intense loyalty in the large nucleus of its audience, and wide interest throughout the San Francisco Bay Area. The response in the community to the candid, the genuine, the original in radio programing was dramatically demonstrated in these months of hard work. That KPFA had communicated its goals was unmistakable. Its public-affairs programing had particularly affected its listening audience. Never before had American radio regularly broadcast old-fashioned free forums—with no subject or view precluded provided that the participants observed the responsibilities that go with freedom. To some of the public, merely airing a point of view signifies sympathy with it. Certainly KPFA was accused of every bias known to political theory, from far right to Communist. The reaction of the listening community to these charges was demonstrated at the first public meeting to save KPFA when someone accused the station of being "extreme left," which provoked nothing but laughter. The audience gave vigorous approval to the only radio station within its experience in which radically different points of view were aired in an atmosphere devoid of fear or censorship.

And so, after nine months of this community effort to bring back KPFA, it returned to the air with a much enlarged signal range. Community enthusiasm had given the project new life, which was renewed when a few months later the Fund for Adult Education of the Ford Foundation gave Pacifica Foundation a three-year grant of $150,000.

In testing whether listeners would voluntarily subscribe to a radio broadcasting service, the KPFA experiment was of unique importance. Newspapers and magazines, which had minced no words in predicting the early failure of a station expecting listeners to pay for a broadcast service they could hear for nothing, now continually wrote feature stories about KPFA. Its live concerts, premieres of composers' new works, no-holds-barred controversial discussions were news, not just radio-page notices. In time even the U.S. State Department began sending foreign dignitaries to KPFA to study this uniquely independent kind of broadcasting which Americans were voluntarily supporting. But always, like an ominous undertone to the delight and success of the work itself, was the problem of money, money, money.

Pacifica's founder, Lewis Hill, died in 1957. Dr. Gordon Agnew, Chairman of Pacifica Foundation, described his contribution in a broadcast on KPFA: "I regard Lewis Hill as one of the truly creative personalities of this generation. His contribution to the intellectual and cultural enrichment of our society is one of such dimensions as to defy adequate evaluation. Lewis Hill envisioned a pattern in which KPFA would be the pilot experiment of a movement ultimately extending nationally and internationally. He was a founder of the Broadcasting Foundation of America, which has already commenced exploratory activities in Europe and Asia. Lewis Hill needs no monument of stone to stand as a tribute to his life. Pacifica Radio constitutes a monument, and we share with you . . . this audacious and challenging adventure of the mind and of the heart."

In October, 1957, Dr. Harold Winkler became Pacifica's new President and Director of KPFA. He was a former member of Pacifica's Board of Directors, and had been a professor of government and political science at Harvard University and the University of California.

Just before the station's ninth birthday, the George Foster Peabody Award for Public Service, radio's highest award, was made to KPFA for "courageous venture into the lightly-trafficked field of thoughtful broadcasting, and for its demonstration that mature entertainment plus ideas constitute public service broadcasting at its best. . . ."

Then, after four years of planning and groundwork, Pacifica Foundation completed plans for a sister station in southern California, and KPFK began broadcasting in July, 1959, in Los Angeles.

One day, while struggling with the innumerable problems besetting Pacifica in its main office in Berkeley, California, Dr. Harold Winkler received a long distance call from New York. At the other end of the line was Louis Schweitzer, a remarkable man whose exceptional individuality expressed itself in his unusual philanthropies. Mr. Schweitzer said, "If Pacifica wants a station in New York, I'll give you one." Mr. Schweitzer, among his other activities, was owner of a commercial station, WBAI. During a newspaper strike he discovered that when the station had enough commercials to make it solvent his intelligent program policies were crowded out. "I realized right then, when we were most successful commercially, that was not what I wanted at all," Mr. Schweitzer reported. "I saw that if the station ever succeeded, it would be a failure." Mr. Schweitzer had long been an admirer of Pacifica Radio in California, and realized that it was doing exactly what he would have liked to do. And so, in 1960, Pacifica began broadcasting on the eastern seaboard.

With the conclusion of this capsule history, I return to this moment and the irony I mentioned earlier about working at Pacifica Radio, where audiences are not manipulated but are offered the fullest range of thought and information, where their intelligence, not their pocketbook, is addressed. The dilemma of Pacifica Radio always was, and is, how to communicate to the listener that if he is to keep this broadcasting service it must be his responsibility—that it cannot exist or survive without his support. Many interested people and foundations have from time to time given large sums of money to help it survive one crisis or another while listener subscriptions were growing toward the point of self-support. But they gave these funds precisely to help this new economic concept: listener-sponsored radio broadcasting. And all these years and three stations later, we're still communicating to you: Help provide for yourself this unique broadcasting service, even though you *can* hear it for nothing. Pacifica uses the radio instrument for the most meaningful purposes it has ever been used, and challenges you to recognize that responsible broadcasting is made possible only by responsible listeners.

E. McK.

3

The Theory of
Listener-Sponsored
Radio

by Lewis Hill (1951)

Listener sponsorship is an answer to the practical problem of getting better radio programs and keeping them. But it involves, as a theory of radio, an analysis of the problem as well as an answer to it. The theory advances not only an economic innovation for broadcasting but an interpretation of the facts of life in American radio. And actually it begins in a concern with some of the facts of life in general.

I imagine we can agree that if a sound is worth passing through the magnificent apparatus of a microphone, a transmitter, and your receiving set, it ought to convey some meaningful intelligence. There are innumerable ways of wasting time and generating nonsense, and there are also uncounted ways of making money, many of which may be pursued in broad daylight. But the elaborate machinery and the peculiar intimacy of the radio medium have better and more basic uses. The theory I want to discuss rests on two particular assumptions: first, that radio can and should be used for significant communication and art; and second, that since broadcasting is an act of communication, it ought to be subject to the same aesthetic and ethical principles as we apply to any communicative act, including the most personal. Of course we know that in American radio many obstacles stand in the way of these principles. When I have examined some of the obstacles, I shall try to indicate briefly how listener sponsorship offers a means of surmounting them.

What does stand in the way?

When we ask this question we usually think at once of the advertiser or of the mass audience. We feel that one or both of these demonological figures must account for the mediocrity and exploitation which on the whole signify radio in the United States. And since, as we know, no one can reform the advertiser or confer with the inscrutable mass, we are more or less accustomed to thinking of improvement as utopian.

We seem generally to ignore, when we criticize radio, the moment and situation in which someone actually broadcasts. I refer to the person who actually opens his mouth or plays his fiddle. I mean to include also the individual who holds the stop watch, the one who writes the script, and perhaps the man who controls the switch. And I am definitely referring to these individuals as individuals—for after all, willing or not, they have that dimension. Now these are the people who actually start the production that comes out at the other end. Even if someone else has decided why there should be a broadcast and what should be in it, these are the people who make it. Yet we never hear these people mentioned in any serious social or moral criticism of American radio. They do not appear in the demonologies of the advertiser and the mass. They constitute most of the radio industry, but are perhaps the last people we would think of in trying to place the fundamental responsibility for what radio does.

This curious fact reveals more about the problem than any number of surveys of public taste and advertising venality. And this is the point at which our theory has to begin. We start with the forgotten man of broadcasting—the man who broadcasts.

Let me instance the announcer, not only to seize the simplest case, but because he will serve as the gross symbol for the writer, the musician, and all who try to make a living in the program end of radio. You will recall without difficulty, I hope, this fellow's nightly solicitude toward your internal organs. In his baritone way he makes a claim on your attention and faith which few of your closest friends would venture. I know of no better explanation of this man's relation to you, to his utterances, his job, and his industry, than one of the time-honored audition tests given to applicants for announcing jobs at certain of the networks. The test consists of three or four paragraphs minutely constructed to avoid conveying any meaning. The words are familiar, and every sentence is grammatically sound but the text is gibberish. The applicant is required to read this text in different voices, as though it meant different things: with solemnity and heavy sincerity, with lighthearted humor, and of course with "punch." If his judges award him the job and turn him loose on you, he has succeeded on account of an extraordinary skill in simulating emotions, intentions, and beliefs which he does not possess. In fact the test was especially designed to assure that nothing in the announcer's mind except the sound of his voice—no comprehension, no value, no choice, and above all no sense of responsibility—could possibly enter into what he said or what he sounded like. This is the criterion of his job.

The significance of this situation is strangely neglected, as I have said, although the commonplaces of industrial life that best explain it are much discussed. We all know, for example, that the purpose of commercial radio is to induce mass sales. For mass sales there must be a mass norm, and the activity must be conducted as nearly as possible without risk of departure from the norm. But art and the communication of ideas—as most of us also appreciate—are risky affairs, for it can never be predicted in those activities just when the purely individual and abnormal may assert itself. Indeed to get any real art or any significant communication, one must rely entirely on individuals, and must resign himself to accept not only their uniqueness but the possibility that the individual may at any time fail. By suppressing the individual, the unique, the industry reduces the risk of failure (abnormality) and assures itself a standard product for mass consumption.

We know these commonplaces, but it is truly staggering to contemplate what they imply and cause in American radio. Should you inquire why there is no affinity between the serious arts and radio, you will find that this is the reason.

America is well supplied with remarkably talented writers, musicians, philosophers, and scientists whose work will survive for some centuries. Such people have no relation whatever to our greatest communication medium. I have been describing a fact at the level of the industry's staff; it is actually so notorious in the whole tradition and atmosphere of our radio that it precludes anyone of serious talent and reasonable sanity from offering material for broadcast, much less joining a staff. The country's best minds, like one mind, shun the medium unless the possessor of one happens to be running for office. Yet if we want an improvement in radio worth the trouble, it is these people whose talent the medium must attract. The basic situation of broadcasting must be such that artists and thinkers have a place to work—with freedom. Short of this, the suffering listener has no out.

It may be clearer why I indicated at the outset that listener sponsorship involves some basic concerns. This is the first problem it sets out to solve—to give the genuine artist and thinker a possible, even a desirable, place to work in radio.

Unfortunately it will not do to go halfway in the effort. Many have tried. The story of American radio is sprinkled with episodes in which some ambitious producer, momentarily out of touch with reality, has tried. These episodes remind me of someone's recent comment about purchasing a house under the Federal Housing Administration. This, he explains, is a system which makes it possible to convert an imaginary equity into a vested illusion. There are still in the industry many a frustrated idealist, many an embittered artist, whose last efforts foundered in the sales department, but who hope someday to own a program. Since our first object is to avoid that chronic industrial frustration, we have to give a somewhat elementary interpretation to the idea of freedom in radio.

The answer of the KPFA project on this point is not necessarily the only good answer, but it is explicit. It requires that the people who actually do the broadcasting should also be responsible for what and why they broadcast. In short, they must control the policy which determines their actions. If I may, I will emphasize that neither a "Public Be Damned" nor a "Down with Commerce" attitude enters into this formulation. The problem was, you remember, not whether you as a listener should choose what you like or agree with—as obviously you should and do—but how to get some genuinely significant choices before you. Radio which aims to do that must express what its practitioners believe to be real, good, beautiful, and so forth, and what they believe is truly at stake in the assertion of such values. For better or worse these are matters like the nature of the deity which cannot be determined by majority vote or a sales curve. Either some particular person makes up his mind about these things and learns to express them for himself, or we have no values or no significant expression of them. Since values and expressions as fundamental as this are what we must have to improve radio noticeably, there is no choice but to begin by extending to someone the privilege of thinking and acting in ways important to him. Whatever else may happen, we thus assign to the participating individual the responsibility, artistic integrity, freedom of expression, and the like, which in conventional radio are normally denied him. KPFA is operated literally on this principle.

Well, then, who in present-day America might be expected to permit such a broadcasting group to earn a living at it, and on what terms?

You already know the answer that KPFA proposes, and you

may have wondered why I choose to present it as a theory, as though there were alternatives to listener sponsorship. Certainly when we develop the idea of broadcasting to this point, the listener is the only one discernible who has a real stake in the outcome. But while that may be an adequate reason for a subscription plan, I think there is a better and more rewarding one.

I have already examined the problem of getting the creative product on radio before we worry about how it is to be evaluated. It must have occurred to you that such a principle could easily revert to the fabled ivory tower. Some self-determining group of broadcasters might find that no one, not the least minority of the minority audiences, gave a hang for their product, morally responsible or not. What then? Then, you will say, there would be no radio station—or not for long—and the various individualists involved could go scratch for a living. But it is the reverse possibility that explains what is most important about listener sponsorship. When we imagine the opposite situation, we are compelled to account for some conscious flow of influences, some creative tension between broadcaster and audience that constantly reaffirms their mutual relevance. Listener sponsorship will require this mutual stimulus if it is to exist at all.

KPFA's present air schedule is a modest example. It embraces four main categories—music, drama and literature, public affairs, and children's programs. The schedule has two sources in almost equal balance as to their importance and influence. On the one hand, these happen to be subjects of primary interest to people working at KPFA. On the other hand, they happen also to represent the articulate interests of well-defined minorities in the audience of the San Francisco Bay Area. The correspondence is not accidental. A constant exchange between the staff and the audience enriches the schedule with fresh judgment and new ideas, materials, and issues. Thus members of the staff work out their own ideas and, if you like, categorical imperatives, with some of the undistracted certitude one feels in deciding what he will have for dinner, subject to the menu. Listener sponsorship makes possible this extremely productive balance of interests and initiatives.

The fact that the subscription is voluntary merely enlarges the same point. We make a considerable step forward, it seems to me, when we use a system of broadcasting which promises that the mediocre will not survive. But the significance of what does survive increases in ways of the profoundest import to our times when it proceeds from voluntary action. Anyone can listen to a listener-sponsored station. Anyone can understand the rationale of listener sponsorship—that unless the station is supported by those who value it, no one can listen to it including those who value it. This is common sense. But beyond this, actually sending in the subscription, which one does not have to send in unless one particularly wants to, implies the kind of cultural engagement, as some French philosophers call it, that is surely indispensable for the sake of the whole culture. When we have a radio station fully supported by subscribers who have not responded to a special gift offer, who are not participating in a lottery, who have not ventured an investment at 3 per cent, but who use this means of supporting values that seem to them of basic and lasting importance —then we will have more than a subscription roster. It will amount, I think, to a new focus of action or a new shaping influence that can hardly fail to strengthen all of us.

We are concerned, of course, with a supplemental form of radio. Listener sponsorship is not a substitute for the commercial industry. But in every major metropolitan area of the country there is room for such an undertaking. I believe we may expect that if these theories and high hopes can be confirmed soundly in a pilot experiment, the idea will not be long in spreading.

KPFA happens to be the pilot experiment. No one there imagines he is the artist or thinker whose talent ultimately must be attracted to radio. KPFA is the beginning of a tradition to make that possible. The survival of this station is based upon the necessity of voluntary subscriptions from 2 per cent of the total FM audience in the area in which it operates. We are hoping to succeed for several reasons, not the least among which is the realization that our success may inspire others to experiment for the eventual betterment of the broadcast product.

4

The Problem of Balance
by Hallock Hoffman

Hallock Hoffman, President of Pacifica Foundation, spoke on the air during the investigation of Pacifica Foundation by the Senate Internal Security Subcommittee (see page 319). The following Commentary was delivered in January, 1963. Here, it incorporates brief excerpts from another of Hoffman's frequent Commentaries on Pacifica Radio.

As Pacifica began to be investigated by the Senate Internal Security Subcommittee, an old question was raised for the three Pacifica stations. It is the question of balance in programing. The Fund for the Republic, the American Civil Liberties Union (ACLU), and I suppose every agency with a public program of any kind must face this question sooner or later. It is hard to deal with even when the agency is not "on trial" before public opinion. It becomes harder in the atmosphere of an investigation.

The question can be asked in a variety of ways. Someone is always asking the ACLU why so many of the persons it defends seem to be connected with left-wing causes. The Fund for the Republic used to be charged with being "soft" on Communism, because its studies and the statements of its officers suggested that one should approach even Communists with an open mind about their recommendations. And on the other hand, radical left-wing groups often used to accuse liberals of being soft on Fascism or McCarthyism if they would not denounce every congressional investigation as witch-hunting or red-baiting.

Last week I talked about the impending appearance of Pacifia Foundation officials before the Senate Internal Security Subcommittee. The mail has brought a number of letters in response to my remarks. Two of them, both thoughtful and well written, exemplify this problem. One asks why I did not urge Pacifica to take its stand with the true defenders of liberty under the Bill of Rights, telling the Foundation officials to refuse to testify before the Eastland subcommittee on the ground that the subcommittee had no constitutional right to investigate anybody practicing free speech. The other letter, pointing out the courteous treatment of the Pacifica Foundation by the subcommittee and reminding me that the decision to hold closed hearings for preliminary inquiries was originally intended to protect witnesses from embarrassment or public discomfort, asked why I seemed so unconcerned about the problem of Communist totalitarianism and subversion.

The question of balance always brings up the question of the scale being used to find it. For example, one might take the position that the stations could allot their public-affairs time on a fair basis by giving every current political view equal time on the air. If it were possible to identify the currents of political thought, and to find commentators who represented each of them, there might be a right-wing Republican, a moderate Republican, a conservative Democrat, a liberal Democrat, a Socialist, a Communist, and so forth—each with exactly the same number of minutes each week to set forth his opinions. Or one might with equal logic suggest that the opinions offered by the station ought to reflect the distribution of opinion among the American electorate, allotting about 95 per cent of the time to Republican and Democratic views and dividing up the remaining 5 per cent among all the different, more extreme opinions that could be discovered—Fascist, Communist, Socialist, John Birch Society, or whatever.

Either of these schemes would of course pose difficulties as to the scheduling of broadcasts in the interest of balance. Should all speakers be scheduled at the same time of day on successive days? Or would balance imply that they should be broadcast on the same day, all together? Someone might be able to listen at 8:00 P.M. and not at 9:00—so the audience would change, and therefore the apparent balance of the station's programing might not work out even if the most meticulous apportionment of the broadcast day were made to each shade of opinion.

But even if these difficulties could be overcome, there would remain the question of whether the stations ought to seek balance within their own program schedules, or should rather try to achieve some proportion in respect to the spectrum of the whole broadcast media.

A strong argument can be made that the Pacifica stations should supply the program lacks resulting from the limitations of commercial radio. Commercial radio tends to aim at a steady, massive audience. It therefore reflects the most popular opinions, and the controversies it deals with tend to be of the kind that do not call attention to the broadcasters or their sponsors. A dramatic example of this tendency was to be seen during the Cuban crisis of 1962, when almost without exception the commercial broadcasting stations, both in their news coverage and their public affairs programs, became spokesmen for the Kennedy administration position on the Cuban blockade. Challenges to that position either were ignored or were treated in such a manner that audiences were prevented from learning there was any intellectually respectable opposition to it.

Under these circumstances, the Pacifica stations might legitimately conclude that they were serving the ideal of balance by presenting the "other" sides of issues on which public feeling runs high. To give a fair hearing to opposition views, within public affairs broadcasting as a whole, the Pacifica stations would become outlets for all the views not available on commercial stations —which would mean that the Pacifica public affairs programs would present a consistently high proportion of unpopular views.

A somewhat similar idea of balance would come from analyzing the Pacifica audience. No one knows exactly what kind of people listen to the three Pacifica stations, but the partial surveys all indicate that you are better educated, more intelligent, more interested in public affairs, and more oriented toward questioning popular myths than the average audiences for commercial radio. The balance of Pacifica programing would therefore, if it reflected your characteristics, be one that would seem threatening to the commercial radio audience. Since you do not so readily accept the myths about Communism, race, religion, economics, or politics, the opinions that would appeal to you as worthy of respect would sound radical or even dangerous to a majority of those who listen to public affairs programs on most radio stations. To take just one example: I would guess that cooperatives as a form of economic organization are much more familiar to Pacifica audiences than to most American audiences, and the standard stereotypes about the tax advantages of co-ops must seem foolish to you, while they sound like proper and respectable opinions to most radio listeners.

The implications of the Senate Internal Security Subcommittee inquiries to date appear to be similar to those disclosed by the House Committee on Un-American Activities inquiry into the Fund for the Republic's study of blacklisting in the entertainment industry. Back in 1954, when the blacklisting study was commissioned, the Fund believed that the argument about blacklisting in radio, television, and the motion picture industry would be on a better basis if it were determined whether blacklisting actually took place. The study showed that it did, that a sizable number of people were prevented from working for any employer in the entertainment field because they had been judged to be unsafe to employ by one or more groups within the industry.

The report of the study also showed that the investigations of the House Committee on Un-American Activities were at times a part of the process of determining both which persons should be blacklisted and which should be "cleared"—that is, removed from the list of unemployables. The Fund had naïvely hoped that once the question of whether there was blacklisting had been settled, a public discussion of whether blacklisting was good for the Republic would take place. That discussion did not begin; another occurred instead. It was devoted to finding out why the Fund had decided to investigate the blacklist, whether the authors of the study were sympathetic to Communism, and so forth. In the course of these arguments, John Cogley—the principal author of the report and the man who had charge of the study for the Fund —was subpoenaed to appear before the House Committee.

John testified for many hours, and much of the time in response to detailed questions about the political beliefs of his researchers or about the sources of his information. He conducted himself with scrupulous honesty and integrity. At the end of his appearance, when the committee had finished its list of questions for him, John was asked whether he wished to make a statement. He said that he wanted to ask the committee a question. It was "Why am I here?"

Mr. Walter, the committee chairman, replied, "We wanted to find out whether you had reached the same conclusions we would have reached if we had decided to make the study you made."

This statement was honest, but it got Mr. Walter into a lot of trouble with the newspapers of the country. It was, many editors wrote, none of Mr. Walter's business what conclusions any reporter reached upon preparing his report. The committee might have a charter to investigate un-American activities, but it had no right to tell reporters what to think about the facts they dug up.

The Senate Internal Security Subcommittee was careful in all its public statements to repeat that it was not in the least interested in the content of Pacifica programs. But many of its questions were aimed at finding out how decisions were reached as to which programs would be put on the air and at discovering who made those decisions. These questions may be separated in logic from questions of program content, but they cannot be distinguished in fact. In the end, the problem of balance has to be settled by a man who makes a decision for or against putting some program on the air. The decision is complex and involves many judgments about the quality of the program and the worth of its message. However guided he may be by statements of principle or policy, a program director has finally to decide on the basis of what he hears—or expects to hear—from the participants or performers. He believes either that the program is worth an audience's attention or that it is not. He will have in mind the other programs that have already been heard; he will have in mind the possibilities of future programs. But each program has to stand, in the main, on its own merits. And those merits are not a fit subject for congressional inquiry.

In one sense the intentions of the Pacifica Foundation are incredibly presumptuous. The Foundation takes as its mission the work of broadcasting in the public interest, convenience, and necessity, and accepts the responsibility of deciding whether that mission is fulfilled. But presumptuous as it may be, it is the same presumption that guides other broadcasting licensees. Periodically broadcasters are obliged to show the Federal Communications Commission that they have devoted substantial parts of their broadcast time to public purposes, and supposedly the failure to make such a showing is cause for their losing their right to broadcast.

Pacifica, because it is noncommercial, does not have the market system on its side. It cannot claim that businessmen have supported its program judgments by spending their advertising dollars with it. It cannot claim to be a persuasive salesman. It must appeal to a different standard, and its standard is less objective than audience ratings and sales. It must make a judgment not about what the people want, but about what a serious and thoughtful man, having at his disposal a remarkable instrument that permits him to listen to all sorts of people talking about all sorts of subjects, would find worth listening to.

In my opinion, Pacifica should lean toward programs that present either opinions or information not available elsewhere. Just as I feel little obligation to spend time on my broadcasts saying what is wrong with Communist governments, since everyone hears what is wrong with Communist governments from every side, I think Pacifica serves the ideal of balance if it spends little time reinforcing popular beliefs. Just as I feel much obligation to point out what seems to me true about the claims of Communists or other unpopular people, because so little attention is paid to these matters elsewhere, so I feel Pacifica should be on the lookout for information that is hard for people to get from other sources. Just as I feel a serious obligation to make my arguments as intelligent and honest as I can, so I believe Pacifica should regard its audiences as composed of mature, intelligent, and responsible adults, who can be trusted to make up their own minds when they have the materials to judge. I do not believe Pacifica should tell its audience what to think about the content of its programs— although I believe the stations have an obligation, as we all do, to identify insofar as possible the sources of the information or opinions expressed.

The Pacifica stations have many shortcomings, many limitations arising out of their scarce financial resources and some caused by the inadequacies of the people who man the stations or who, like myself, presume to offer commentaries. The stations depend upon volunteers, and not all the best things in life are free. Despite the weaknesses and shortcomings, the Pacifica stations represent a notable experiment and give promise of greater achievements in the future.

The Foundation has asked through KPFA for fourteen years, through KPFK for four years, and through WBAI for three: What is new? What is worth attending to? What is going on? in music, poetry, drama, literature—in all forms of expressing man's desire to know and make known what he knows. The range of our interest as listeners has been expanded, the range of our experience has been enlarged, the range of our freedom to know and apprehend and be open to the world of men's makings has grown. New composers and dramatists and critics and performers have had their first opportunity to be heard on Pacifica stations, and we, the fortunate listeners, have had a chance to hear them.

Pacifica's attitude of freedom has thus encompassed the whole striving of the human spirit for the exaltation of its humanity. It has been a sort of continuing encyclical, a letter to all mankind about mankind's visions and problems and glories and failures. It has been an exemplar of good citizenship, a model of the inquiring mind, and an inspiration to generosity of spirit.

The enemies of the stations, which are the enemies of all free minds, are fear and prejudice. The problem with charges of imbalance, as with the Senate investigation, is that they could become sources of fear or prejudice. It is up to us, as subscriber and listener custodians of this experiment in free communications, to guard Pacifica against these dangers. One of the best ways I can think of to safeguard the Foundation at this moment in its history is to show our support by renewing our subscriptions and signing up our friends as new subscribers.

This is Hallock Hoffman in Santa Barbara.

5

On Working at Pacifica
by Christopher Koch

A Pacifica radio station is a chaos of activity, some of it meaningful and much of it frenetic and useless. The offices of any of the three stations, whether in a rambling loft above a restaurant in Berkeley or in the formerly fashionable town house in Manhattan, are a cross between the temporary headquarters for the latest protest movement and a bohemian coffee shop. They certainly bear little resemblance to those of a radio station.

The rooms are piled high with old copies of the *New York Times,* dozens of stacks of magazines (some well known and national and some obscure mimeographed sheets), and odd-shaped boxes of tape. If you took the time to look through these tapes you might find a box from North Africa with a note attached to it with a rubber band saying something like this. "I had a chance to interview Ben Balthazar on my office dictaphone. The quality isn't too good, but this is one of the most inaccessible guerrilla leaders in Africa today."

More frequently, these unsolicited tapes are less exotic. "Attached is a tape recording of my thoughts on the graduated income tax. I have been systematically excluded from other radio stations, but I am told that you still believe in free speech." Nine times out of ten, such tapes are completely unintelligible. Some staff member has to listen to it, write a note, and mail it back. But once in a while it just may contain something significant. That, in a sense, has been the story of Pacifica.

Most of my work during the five years I spent with Pacifica as News Director, Public Affairs Director, and finally Program Director of New York's WBAI, was routine (as the work of most paid staff members is). We audition tapes, answer letters from pleased and irate listeners, and try to get some of the innumerable program ideas recorded. We argue on the phone or in the reception office with great numbers of people who seem destined to be prosecuted and denied their rights. "Do you know, Mr. Koch, the FBI has been sending radiation through my walls because of my criticisms of the Catholic church?" Or much more frequently, we are threatened, "You recently broadcast a commentary by the Socialist World Revolutionary Council. In the interests of equal time, we demand that you play our rebuttal as representatives of the Socialist Workers Classic Party. If you refuse, we plan to file a complaint with the FCC."

Then too, there is always a crisis—a major clash of personalities, a dispute over the purpose and function of the foundation, a key dismissal or resignation. And so hours must be spent in whispered conversations at the local bar or coffee shop, or late into the evening in messy offices, among used coffee cups and the stale smell of too many cigarettes. Pacifica's dynamic program policy, reflected in this volume, attracts some strong and creative people. She has not maintained a dynamic administrative formula within which such people can work successfully.

Pacifica stations normally operate with a core staff of between fourteen and twenty-one people who carry out the essential functions of broadcasting. Volunteers swirl around this core like satellites, typing letters, filing (and misfiling) notes, memos, and program material, or auditioning tapes and producing programs. The stations could not function without them. Some of these volunteers work very hard, and they include many talented and frequently well-known people. Among the volunteers, for example, are all of Pacifica's program participants and commentators, none of whom is paid. But there are others who are simply looking for a warm place to rest, and a variety of strange people are always lounging about Pacifica's offices. I do not want to belittle the enthusiasm of these sad wanderers from cause to cause. As tape girls rush by looking for a lost program due for broadcast in two minutes, or as an engineer yells for an announcer who ought to be on the air at that very moment, it is frequently these young men and women who argue most vehemently about program possibilities. "What about having a 'pot' party on the air, man?" Or one may say in great disgust, "You mean they took that out of Mailer's speech. And you call this 'free radio'!"

With volunteers as with programs it is sometimes difficult to tell the genuine from the fraudulent. Pacifica, more than most institutions, makes a virtue out of a necessity. Thus there is an assumption that if you hand someone a tape recorder and send him out into the world, great things will happen. I suppose they may, but more frequently the happening is a broken tape recorder. If someone without a regular job hangs around a Pacifica station long enough, it is fairly easy for him to get a chance at producing a program.

The desperate lack of money and hence of a trained and disciplined staff, make such theories of spontaneous creativity particularly attractive. The average staff member is harassed by innumerable details. Not only is he unable to produce half the programs he wants, but 75 per cent of those he can do are second-rate. He knows this far better than the audience. And so you have to be compulsive at Pacifica, and ignore your own, inner sense of judgment.

The staff member works under the pressure of a huge maw, the clock that eats up programs as greedily as a New York City garbage truck devours refuse. Most Pacifica stations broadcast something like 19 hours a day. About half of this time is devoted to talk programs. That amounts to the preparation and broadcast of a 270-page manuscript every day, or around 80,000 words. An hour interview takes from 10 to 20 hours to prepare, record, and complete for broadcast. An hour talk takes from 20 to 40 hours, and a good documentary may take anywhere from 60 to 240 hours to do well. Out of a paid staff of 21, no more than 5 will be directly involved with programing. Think about it. Control over quality is almost impossible.

That is why the stations put tape recorders into the hands of novices and why so much of the programing is inadequate. On the other hand, every once in a while something truly significant may happen. In the midst of all Pacifica's chaos Jack Levine walked into WBAI looking for someone to whom he could tell his story. No one else in broadcasting or journalism (with the exception of Carey McWilliams at *The Nation*) would touch him. Levine, the former FBI agent, talked to us; we played his tape to several prominent lawyers who told us it was in the public interest to program it, and Levine's attack on the FBI and J. Edgar Hoover was heard in the New York area and in northern and southern California. We knew the broadcast was rash. I recall one former executive mumbling, "We need this like a hole in the head." Levine warned us that we would be investigated. But no one suggested that we should not go ahead with it.

A young girl may walk into the station after getting out of a southern jail, and in the studio under the patient and incisive questioning of Elsa Knight Thompson her story suddenly comes alive and she and a good part of the audience weep. Someone may sit up all night for weeks mixing the sounds of people and things and came out with a sound montage that adds a new dimension to our experience of ourselves and each other. Someone may go out and raise the money to go to Mississippi, or Mexico, or to California's central valley and live with the people there for a while, recording their conversations and their music, and then come back and make beautiful programs out of it.

That is, finally, what makes it all worthwhile. Pacifica stations have been so casually administered that the truly creative could find resting place there, until they were worn down by the harassments of attempting to do the untenable. And the audience has been willing to listen through hours of dull lectures or badly recorded symposiums on the Biological Basis of Cross Fertilization, or the off-beat programs for tiny minorities who otherwise would have nothing for them on the mass media, waiting for something that brings a new area of life home to them.

This is, in a sense, often freedom by default. The great programs that have been broadcast have happened despite everything. They were produced by people in the midst of crises, on tape recorders that failed to work, with tape that was so old it crumbled to the touch. But they were, eventually, broadcast. Then, for a few moments, there was sudden intense relationship between people on the tape and the audience listening at home— a magic created by a program producer. At that moment, everything else was forgotten. There was communication. It never happens anywhere else on radio or television.

New York
November, 1965

II
―――――――

A PACIFICA
ANTHOLOGY

Interview with Ammon Hennacy

Byron Bryant, a teacher and writer, was one of KPFA's earliest commentators and a program producer for many years. A favorite visitor to KPFA was Ammon Hennacy, editor of Catholic Worker *and author of* Autobiography of a Catholic Anarchist. *Interviewed here by Byron Bryant in 1958, Mr. Hennacy speaks for himself.*

BRYANT: I understand you are making another one of your swings around the country. What is it that brings you to San Francisco this time?

HENNACY: I first came to Los Angeles for the wedding of my daughter Carmen. Last year I got as far as Las Vegas and I had to go right home in order to go to jail in the air-raid drill—I got there just in time, too. I did thirty days on that and I got out just in time to fast twelve days and do my picketing. It all just worked out nice so I think the Lord must be with me.

BRYANT: I understand that before you left for Los Angeles you had just completed your longest fast; was this the longest fast you ever tried?

HENNACY: No, I tried a thirteen-day fast last year—it was just thirteen years since we dropped the bomb so I did penance for that. I did penance for all the rest of you people, too. And before that I did fast from May 28th to July 6th in Washington in order to bring the attention, mostly of Catholics to waken them up. Protestants don't know much what penance is, but Catholics ought to know that we're doing penance for our sins—the sins of our country in dropping the bomb. I felt that although I wasn't much guilty, as I say, I felt like doing penance. The first seventeen days were a little rough. You lose your appetite before you start if you are a professional faster, but you get a little weak and you get a bad taste in your mouth. I lost twenty-five pounds the first seventeen days, but the next twelve days I didn't lose any. So I thought, 'What's the matter?' I went to other scales and they were all the same. I guess I was on holy ground.

BRYANT: You say you were fasting mainly to interest Catholics. To what extent do you think you managed to do that? Did Catholics in general across the country know about it?

HENNACY: Yes, it was in the *Catholic Worker* that I was going to do it. I had a Catholic anarchist from London fast with me for two days, I had a Catholic pacifist from Switzerland fast with me one or two days, I had a non-Catholic pacifist from New Zealand fast with me, and I had different priests and nuns fast with me all over the country. I had a nun in Italy over eighty years old who fasted with me, and there's lots of others I don't even know about. I asked people to fast and pray with me. In the olden days they fasted sixty days in the desert.

BRYANT: So you fasted for forty days. . . .

HENNACY: Forty days—just drank water.

BRYANT: When the time was just about over, didn't you feel strange or giddy?

HENNACY: Well, I felt kind of light-headed. You know how you feel when you are floating through the air—you have feet but you don't use them. I walked along, kinda light, but I did have one trouble, I got cramps in the bottom of my instep. Other than that, I guess I felt wonderful. And, of course, you lose your appetite before you start—I really wasn't hungry at all.

BRYANT: What kind of activity did you engage in?

HENNACY: I would picket three or four hours a day and I rested four hours a day—never had a better time in my life. I never had a time when I could sleep four hours in the day, and I probably never will.

BRYANT: It sounds like the perfect way to beat the present economic system.

HENNACY: Like the farmer who fed the horse sawdust and did very well until he died.

BRYANT: Would you be willing to make a guess that forty days are about as far as you would be willing to go?

HENNACY: Oh no, I would be able to go sixty days if I could go forty, but I'm not going to make any predictions—I'll just wait and see. You see, I don't fast to coerce or embarrass the authorities. I probably do it without knowing it, but I do it to wake up the sleepy pacifists and Catholics who ought to be doing more than just sitting around and talking.

BRYANT: One thing that I would be curious about is what it was like to break that forty-day fast.

HENNACY: Well, I passed the food market every day and they looked so nice that I thought I could just eat a bushel. When the time came, I bought a pint of strawberries and I bought some buttermilk. I put them both in the mixer and I had pink buttermilk. I took a taste of it and it was too sweet. You don't like sweet things—you like sour. So the night I broke my fast I went to the Mormon church in Washington with my wife and I think she drank most of the pink buttermilk.

BRYANT: One thing I've been wondering about is how long it took you to regain the poundage you had lost.

HENNACY: The first two days I gained back fourteen pounds. I ate soup and buttermilk and it just soaked into my pores, I guess. However, in the next two days I lost four of those pounds.

BRYANT: The way you talk and some of your stories lead me to believe that you come right from the grass roots of this country. Just where were you born?

HENNACY: I was born in southern Ohio right next to the West Virginia line. My mother's folks were Quakers. I got baptized a

Baptist when I was a kid, but it didn't take. I heard Billy Sunday and I left the church and was an atheist. Those were good days for the Socialists and I got to be secretary of the Party—the Socialist Party—in Lisbon, Ohio, when I was sixteen. My dad happened to be Democratic mayor. That's the kind of background you got to have if you're going to beat the whole system. I'm only a Catholic five years.

BRYANT: In your early days would you say there was a background of farm life or small-town life, or——

HENNACY: It was farm life until I was eighteen—a little bit of small-town life when I was in high school. I went to a small college—Hiram College up by Cleveland—and then the University of Wisconsin. I was a pacifist and a vegetarian. I didn't believe in killing animals, but I did believe in killing capitalists until I got to be a Christian and a pacifist and an anarchist—those all came at once, the Holy Trinity.

BRYANT: Since we are on the subject of your background, and I know there must be a great many people listening to this program who must wonder how in the world you got this way, let's pursue this further. You've told us about your earliest days; now I think our audience would like to hear just a little about how you found yourself in solitary during World War I.

HENNACY: I refused to register for the Draft in Columbus, Ohio, as secretary of the Socialist Party, and they pinched twenty of us. The others gave in and they were going to shoot me Monday if I didn't go. But I wouldn't go, and if I hadn't made that decision, I guess I'd be a good bourgeois today. But they weren't going to shoot me—they just wanted to scare me. I went to my mother and asked her if she wasn't afraid her son would be shot. She said, No, she was only afraid they'd scare him and make him give in. She's eighty-seven, living yet—a good Quaker. So that's the right spirit. So, I was an atheist and I was a Socialist, but I wasn't a pacifist. I'd fight in a good war, but there wasn't any.

Anyway, when I got down to Atlanta, I led a strike against bad food. I got locked up in solitary. Well, I had nothing to read but the Bible. If I'd had the phone book or a cookbook or the Almanac, I'd have read them. But all I had was the Bible, so I read it. In there it said, "Love your enemy." Well, I loved everybody in the world but the warden. If you didn't love him you ought to kill him—he's a German. That's what the war was about—to kill bad Germans. So I was in there and I had to do one of three things: kill myself, kill the warden or love the warden. It took me six and a half months to love the warden.

BRYANT: How in the world did you finally come to love the warden?

HENNACY: I read the Bible—the Sermon on the Mount. If you loved everybody in the world, then you were a Christian. If you loved everybody but the warden, then you were not a Christian. I thought I was Hennacy fighting the world. I looked there and there was Christ—he was a better rebel than I was. Now, nobody can tell me anything except a guy who is better than me—so Christ is much better than me, I know that. But I had to get locked up in solitary to see it. Before that I was too busy trying to change the world by outward methods. You see, if you want to change the world there are three ways of doing it: first, you get 51 per cent of the ballots . . . after I got out of solitary I was a pacifist and I didn't shoot. I read Tolstoy and I found out that getting 51 per cent of the ballots won't do any good either, so I quit voting. The only thing left was to change myself. Well, solitary changed me—it was the grace of God, I guess. I'd never do it if I didn't have to. I had to. In there I could have got killed. I wrote out to the newspapers about them killing fellows in solitary and skinning them out and beating. I wouldn't tell how I got the information out, so I did time in a couple more jails—that's when I read Tolstoy. So, it was a very good thing. The first hurdle was in Columbus, Ohio, when I didn't "chicken-out"; the second hurdle was there in jail where I didn't give in and I didn't "squeek" on the fellows getting letters out, and leading the strike. I've covered lots of hurdles. This last one of forty days, I guess that's a big one. I wouldn't have thought of doing that a year ago, but I don't know what the next one is going to be. It's always going to be something. God will give you enough to do if you've got guts enough to do it.

BRYANT: Going back to that World War I experience—after that you considered yourself a Christian . . .

HENNACY: Yes, but not very orthodox—I spelt God with a little *g* and two *o*'s, I suppose, but that's pretty good for an atheist.

BRYANT: Wasn't this Christianity accompanied by your leaving Socialism for Anarchism?

HENNACY: Yes, because if you're going to be good, you can't be good—you've got to be all the way. The Sermon on the Mount says that you must love your enemy and turn the other cheek and be without evil, and he without sin casts the first stone. If you've taken any part in prisons and war, then you're casting stones, so the only way to do is quit that. Now if you don't know any better, you don't have to quit; but I found out better and I sure had to do it. It would be what Catholics call a "mortal sin" if I didn't. See?

BRYANT: What about the interval of time between this World War I experience and the time you found yourself moving in the direction of the Catholic church? Actually, you heard about the Catholic Worker movement a long time before you entered the church, didn't you?

HENNACY: I heard about it when I was a social worker in Milwaukee in 1936. A man tried to knife me. My boss wanted me to take him into court, but he'd been to court twice for knifing people, so I wouldn't do it. I said, "You've had him in jail twice and he didn't learn anything, so you better try my way—return good for evil. Not jail." He said, "You ought to get acquainted with those crazy Catholics in New York." He was a Catholic and head of the Legion.

I asked a priest about them and pretty soon I got my first *Catholic Worker* and commenced selling them on the street. I helped found the Catholic Worker in Milwaukee in 1937, but I never got to be a Catholic. Father George Dunne, down here in Santa Clara now—somebody asked him, When is Ammon going to become a Catholic? The Father said, "When it goes under-ground." I was seventeen years around the *Worker* and writing in it eleven years before I got to be a Catholic. It was through the grace of God and Dorothy Day . . . there isn't any sense in a radical being a Catholic—that's the worst church there is. That isn't my fault and it isn't Christ's fault. It got organized and it commenced to press the church, and the church pressed the state and it got corrupt. Well, that's too bad, but it don't need to be.

BRYANT: Do you think the last thing you ever did for which you'd like to be doing penance was being a social worker in Milwau-kee? Is that your last major sin?

HENNACY: I expect that's a pretty bad sin, but I did some good then. I founded the first union of social workers in the United States and drew up the plans when the rules were pretty bad. I can't figure many sins of commission. I probably have a lot of sins of omission and I'll probably suffer for them in Purgatory some time, but I'm trying not to do very many of them. Of course, the Catholic Worker, what we do all the time there in New York by the Bowery, is help these poor people. But even those we help—we could do it more gracefully. Somebody once asked what the Catholic Worker did, and they answered that they help the undeserving poor. And somebody else said, "Well, we comfort the afflicted and afflict the comfortable."

BRYANT: One thing that always seems to bother people in your audiences, that I have noted, is your saying on the one hand that the Catholic church is the worst church there is, which I think you said again just a minute ago, and at the same time saying that you go to Communion every day. What do you tell them to help clear this up—or is there any way to clear that up?

HENNACY: They wonder why I joined the "worst" church. If Dor-othy Day had been a Mormon or a Quaker, I'd have been a Mormon or a Quaker. That's Dorothy Day the founder of the Catholic Worker. I always said that the only person who can tell me what to do and shove me around is somebody bigger than I am: She is! I've known most of the best pacifists and radicals in my time and Dorothy Day has got it all over any of them—twice over! She happened to be a Catholic. I didn't join the church because I read any theology. I was praying one night at our farm, and it came to me, I'm a Catholic. In the morning I said, "Dorothy, I'm a Catholic; what am I supposed to believe?" She pretty near fell over. "I'd believe that Jonah swallowed a whale if that was what I was supposed to believe." She gave me a book called *The Spirit of Catholicism,* and I read it. I already was a Catholic. You see these 2 per cent of corrupt Catholics scared me away from the church. The real teaching of the church is all right. You ought to be a Christian if you follow it. The dictionary says that a Christian is a follower of Christ . . . kind, kindly. It doesn't say anything about all these things that all these churches got in them.

Of course, the Pope says that a Catholic cannot be a conscientious objector in a just war. Well, there isn't any just war at all in my opinion, but in every country every priest, rabbi, Protestant ministers, and even some Quakers say that this is a just war—this one. The other countries got the bad war—we got the good one. And so they all bless it. Well, God doesn't have any country—we're all brothers. St. Peter, when he was arrested for speaking in the street and God got him out and he went back again—they said, you can't talk the name of Christ on the street. And Peter said he would obey God rather than man. The church says that you got to obey the civil authority—you got to obey the law. A bad law is no better than any other bad thing, so you got to go ahead and disobey laws. I obey good laws. You don't live long if you go against the red lights. So I just go ahead and obey the laws—an anarchist is one that doesn't have to have a cop to make him behave. He will behave without a cop.

BRYANT: One of the most interesting things about the whole Catholic Worker movement is the attitude of the Catholic hierarchy toward it. You operate in the Cardinal Spellman territory

—would you mind saying what you think the attitude of the hierarchy is toward you?

HENNACY: If you call up the Chancellory and say, What about Dorothy Day? She has gone to jail for four years now, refusing to take part in air-raid drills. That's not obeying the law, and a scandal for the church. What about it? They're not for us and not against us. If they was for us, money wouldn't come in from the big shots—if they was against us—well, I don't think I'd sleep so well. So that's up to them. It's because we live "poor," and they know they ought'n to be living quite so "rich." They respect us; they wish we weren't so radical, but that seems to go with it.

Cardinal Spellman had a seminar on scabbing and digging graves in the graveyard strike in '49, and we have pictures of him. That ought to be one good entrance into heaven. But he has a lot of patience with us—he never picked at us. We don't despise him—he's our cardinal. He could "shell us out" and he hasn't, so he isn't near so conservative in action as he might be in theory.

BRYANT: So you haven't had a suspicion that you were being threatened by the diocesan authorities?

HENNACY: No. Individual Catholic priests in some places in the country, and bishops won't allow us to speak. But that's all right —it's a big country and we can speak in lots of places. I've spoken in hundreds of churches and seminaries. Deans have asked us to speak. They say, "These kids are going to graduate to be priests and they don't even know if Thomas Aquinas died, so you go ahead and give them this stuff. They won't become anarchists and pacifists, but they will think a little. You see, the tendency is for these Jansenist Irish to talk about low-neck dresses and not talk about any of these low wages here on the coast—especially for the sailors.

BRYANT: We've been talking a good deal about the Catholic Worker in regard to the Catholic church . . .

HENNACY: The Pope has blessed us three times—not because we're radical but in spite of it.

BRYANT: Yes, and not only that, but it is true that all of you there are orthodox people—in no way do you question anything that is fundamental.

HENNACY: No. We go to Mass and Communion daily, not because we are so pious, but because—I do because I started late and I might as well make up for it. I think I get grace to fight this world by going to Mass and Communion—taking the body and blood of our Lord. It isn't symbolic, I wouldn't say actual body and blood for you non-Catholics that are listening. So we're just as orthodox as anyone. Somebody once asked me if I believed in the infallibility of the Pope. I said that I did when he was infallible. And that's just on faith, not morals, but faith in the Father, Son, and the Holy Ghost, Mary ascended . . . those things. But whether Frank was a good man, or Joe McCarthy, or how to vote—the Pope is not my boss on that. Christ is my boss and what he said in the Sermon on the Mount. That's an individual interpretation—sure. I don't want to be a rubber stamp.

BRYANT: Another thing that I believe bothers people is your asking people to join with you in the Catholic Worker movement and at the same time you tell them that this movement had no chance of succeeding, at least as they ordinarily understood the term. This, I notice, really puzzles a good many.

HENNACY: The younger ones, especially.

BRYANT: Yes, especially. They are looking for a movement and they want to know what the movement is for. What is the Catholic Worker movement really for?

HENNACY: We are here in order to show that it's possible to approximate the life of Christ and the early Christians like Christ said in the Sermon on the Mount: Love your enemy, return good for evil, relieve the poor. Somebody asked me when I was in Wall Street, soap-boxing, "What are you first—a Catholic or an anarchist?" I said, "Now, let's see, first, I'm a Catholic; I go to Mass and Communion daily—reverently, I hope. Second, I relieve the poor: that's the hardest thing." Remember, Christ told the rich young man, "Go and sell all you have and relieve the poor." (I've got Presbyterian clothes on me and all kinds of clothes people gave me.)

The third thing is to love your enemy. Now that's pretty hard. Eric Gill said that the early Christians said, "Behold how they love each other," and the modern ones say, "Behold how they hate Communists." But we should love this enemy—whoever it is. Then we should bring that out in the world in some way in which you can work with other people—don't just be a hermit. And the next is to be a worker and not a parasite—that cuts out all Wall Street, you know that.

The next is to be an anarchist. Now if you're going to lead a dedicated life and then going to vote for one millionaire candidate for governor of New York, what difference does it make? All the people who are in authority and in government may return evil for evil in courts and prisons and in war. They deny Christ. Christ says not to do that—to return good for evil. These people are not to be blamed if they don't know any better, but we know better. And we sure got to do it. It would be a mortal sin if we didn't. So just to be a negative anarchist and say that I'm against the government, well that's no good. We feel you got to lead a dedicated life. We think that's the only way.

Speaking parenthetically, there are some things I don't do—I don't smoke, drink, eat meat, or take medicine. So when comes the revolution tomorrow—I'm talking about the political revolution—if I don't have a cup of black coffee or an aspirin or a cigarette, I'm not going to worry. Some people couldn't revolute. I'm not telling other people to quit all this, but you people can go on drinking and smoking as long as you can. But don't get discouraged when you don't get what you want. You can come around and read the *Catholic Worker*; you can be a Buddhist anarchist or a Quaker anarchist, but we invite you to get our paper—twenty-five cents a year. You'll get it all the rest of your life if you'll send us a quarter.

BRYANT: Some of those ideas you mentioned are basic to the Catholic Worker movement, aren't they?

HENNACY: Yes, these last are just mine. There are plenty of people in the movement who don't do as I do. Dorothy and I don't drink because we feel that is the besetting sin of the Bowery. If we'd take one drink, then somebody else would take twenty-one. We don't smoke because we got too many things to do. There are only two vegetarians around there, so that isn't so important. You either eat meat or you don't, and I don't.

BRYANT: This also applies, doesn't it, which some of you have done—you in particular—of telling some of the young men not to register for the draft?

HENNACY: No, the Catholic Worker position, if you can call it that, is to refuse to register for the draft. That's the ultimate position: if you can't do it, well, do the next best. Another thing is that we don't pay taxes for war. I worked for eleven years as a migrant worker in New Mexico, and at the end of each year I said, "This is my name and this is where I live. Try and get it!" Most of the tax men are Catholics and they kind of worry about it. When I get pinched, I can get sixty years in jail for not paying taxes, but they're not going to do it. And if they don't hurry up, I won't live another sixty.

BRYANT: Aren't they doing anything about it now?

HENNACY: No, the last tax man I saw said, Well, I'll put your case at the bottom of the basket. We've had T-men in from Washington. Dorothy Day doesn't pay taxes either, but she doesn't put a return in, but I put a return in. I'm not making enough now, but if I were speaking enough I'd make some. The last man asked me when I made the last money, and I told him Springfield College in Massachusetts for a talk—$25 and expenses. He asked me where I was going to talk next, and I told him I sure didn't know and even if I did know, I wouldn't tell him. On this trip I'll make some money, but I don't know if anybody pays me—I don't ask them. And what I get I always give to the Catholic Worker to feed the poor. We have a bread line and a coffee line we feed every day. In Portland we feed a thousand a day at a Catholic Worker house there.

BRYANT: Wasn't there a time when there were many more Catholic Worker houses across the country than there are now?

HENNACY: We had about thirty-four Catholic Worker houses and several farms—and that was before the war, but if you're just a pacifist between wars, that's like being a vegetarian between meals—it doesn't mean anything. When the war came most of them quit—they couldn't help it. We had a 170,000 circulation and it got down to 30,000; now it's up to 62,000 all over the world. Some people have canceled their subscriptions—some of the churches—in this town, even, because we went to jail on the air-raid drill. That's breaking the law. Well, it sure is, and we intend to keep on breaking it!

BRYANT: What do you think about the need for the opening of more houses?

HENNACY: It would be very good. If we found somebody to run a house and found a place, we'd do it. But that's up to the individual. There is a house in Montreal; one in Washington, D.C.; two in Detroit; Rochester; New York; and Portland, Oregon. There could be more, but we haven't found anybody that would do it. Anybody that's capable of running a Catholic Worker house could earn $1,000 a month in industry coordinating unfit people.

We take people from the bottom of the cliff and help them. Some people say, how come they fall off the cliff? We've always had people falling off the cliff—we've always had war, we've always had poverty—we're bound to: it's God's will. Some people say, Let's put a fence up there and protect them. Make a law—"thou shalt not fall over the cliff." Well, they'd jump over the fence—they're bound to hurt themselves. And because we are down there at the bottom of the cliff helping to pick people up, we have earned the right to talk about a society where people will live without fences, without laws. The Hopi Indians I'm going to visit pretty soon, they've lived there in Arizona for a thousand years—no law, no court, no police—and no cliff, and no fences on the cliffs. The last time I was there the kids don't fall over the cliff. They're told not to. These people are anarchists and pacifists—they don't know what the words mean even, but they went to jail during the wartime. They're good people. But they are getting messed up by the government and the government missionaries—you know that.

BRYANT: I wonder if we can go back now to something I think bothers people and continues to bother them, and that has to do with success and what the standard of success is in the Catholic Worker movement. Let's just take this phase for the moment: I've had people say to me, "Well, what difference is there between the Catholic Worker movement and a lot of other charity movements—except that it's got a lot of peculiar people at the head of it. You run a flophouse, you run a soup kitchen, people come in and perhaps sponge off of you for perhaps many years. The drunk comes there to recuperate and then he goes out and gets drunk again. It's just another brand of flophouse." This is the main sign on the surface of Catholic Worker activity.

HENNACY: The only difference that I can see is that we live there —we eat the same food as they do (except me, I'm a vegetarian and I don't get as much as they do), and we have the bedbugs, and we walk around the vomit, and the bricks come by our ears when they break the windows. They don't break the windows of the saloon where they bought the liquor, they break ours who're trying to help them, see. We live among these people. I don't know any other folks who do that. They live in nice places and come down and help the poor, but they sure get back out of it. They stay only about eight hours a day, but we live there all the time. I'm not bragging about being humble—we don't brag—but we are saying that we know what the world is and we're practical. We solve people and sober up people that nobody else can sober up. Different agencies send us people. They say, We can't take him and you can take anything. I guess we do. It takes a lot of patience and patience is what we got lots of. If we didn't look forward to a new society that will be better than this, I don't think we'd be able to bear it—we'd burn out. We don't get angry about some things that would anger some other people because we are here to take all this sort of stuff. We feel that the I.W.W., and the Socialists, and the anarchists, and the Communists—all these people who once taught an ideal society—they are all done for, they all succumbed to prosperity. And there is nobody left to tell about this corrupt society. We've got to say, This isn't God's society. You don't fight for God and your country. Atom bombs are not going to save us—they're going to kill us. We refuse to pay taxes for them— we picket, we fast, we do all these things. And we wake up a few people.

The young people today want a nice clean movement with a nice ribbon tied around it—all pretty. But we don't say that— we say, There is nothing but blood, sweat, and tears. Can you take it?

BRYANT: But even with blood, sweat, and tears you don't promise them a new world . . .

HENNACY: No, you'll have a better world when you got better people. Now if Christ couldn't do it, I don't think Dorothy Day and I can do it. We're doing at it. All I may ever do, if history is ever written, is maybe wake up one person, but he may get to be the Gandhi of America. That would be wonderful. We got to sow seed. I'm not there with the cash register—I'm not there with a book with dotted lines to say, "You are now Saved. Sign here." I'm a part of the Catholic Worker. Nobody is a member of it. They come and take what they can and then generally leave. And it's hard to take. But Jesus said, "He who hath ears to hear, let him hear. He who hath eyes to see, let him see." So our message goes forth to blind people and to deaf people. They aren't all blind and they aren't all deaf.

Now, if I knew the ten people in this area who would make good Catholic anarchists, I'd go and talk to them and I wouldn't bother the rest of you, but I don't know them. They might be in the bank and they might be in the gutter, so I talk to everybody who will listen. And some of them who won't listen. It's not hopeless—if it was I wouldn't be here, I'd be staying home. I'm not a bit discouraged—not a bit. One on the side of God is a majority, Thoreau said. And they said to him, You're out of step. And he said, I'm listening to a different drummer. We hear different music—not this razz-jazz stuff; we hear something better. If you don't hear it, we can't expect you to follow it. But we are going to play that tune. Maybe you'll hear it. It's not our fault if you don't.

BRYANT: One question people ask me—and perhaps they have asked you, too. They ask, What will happen when Ammon Hennacy is gone from the scene, and what will happen when Dorothy Day is gone from the scene? Is the movement attracting enough young people to keep going?

HENNACY: I doubt it. Most of the church hierarchy that I meet tolerate me because Dorothy Day says that I'm pretty good. I do the things easier that are hard for her to do—fasting and going to jail. And the compassion she has I don't have much of—so we complement each other. I don't know—that's up to God.

If we were to die and somebody come along and said, "We'll take over the Catholic Worker and make a success of it," Dorothy Day would say, "Better let it die than be made into a success in the money way." We refused $100,000 from the Ford Foundation and we've refused other money. We don't want big bits of money. We are poor and we are going to have to leave our place in New York City because the subway is coming in there and we don't know where we'll be six months from now. It's all right. God takes care of his own. I'm sixty-five. I'm not going to get a pension or social security—who is going to take care of me? God's got to. I don't depend on the devil or the state.

BRYANT: There is, I believe, an English Catholic Worker that has taken a somewhat different direction than yours.

HENNACY: The English Catholic Worker would be more like the *Commonweal* or the New Deal here. Pro labor union—against bad wars and for capitalism. And the Australian Catholic Worker is the same way.

BRYANT: Do you think there is a possibility that this might happen here?

HENNACY: I don't know—there is no way of telling. We hope not. As Tolstoy said, "Save me from the Tolstoyans."

BRYANT: As a final question, now, I am wondering what you are going to do next. But before we go into that, I'd like to bring up a question that must be in the minds of some of our listeners— and that's this: Regardless of the number of people you may be able to get on your side, there is a vision of a new kind of society which the members of . . . the people in the Catholic Worker have. You have indicated roughly what it is like, but I wonder if you could give us a summary. I don't think you've mentioned Peter Maurin's idea of the "Green Revolution." Would you mention that?

HENNACY: We visualize a society based on the individual and the family rather than the state where people should own property (we believe in owning property, only the wrong people's got it). We believe people should have just as much land or as large a factory as they can handle without hiring anybody. If they can use machinery—so much the better. I don't like to live in a big hotel with all the comrades. I'd like to have some bees and a cow and be out on a farm by myself. People could live together, and some of them do right now. But most of them have succumbed to prosperity: most of us can take the bad times, but it's hard to take it when times get good. But some of them are living without rent, surplus, and profit.

Let me give you that poem that I put on the cell wall when I was in solitary: called "Surplus Value."

> The merchant calls it profit and winks the other eye,
> The banker calls it interest and heaves a cheerful sigh,
> The landlord calls it rent as he tucks it in his bag,
> But the honest old beggar simply calls it swag.

That's our system.

We compromise a little—maybe about 5 per cent. We use the Post Office—we can't afford our own. I'll pay about $30 to the government for riding on these buses. If I had my own bus, the tax man would take it from me, so what can I do?

So, we visualize a society decentralized like Frank Lloyd Wright was always talking about—a society of small units, co-ordinated and federated. Without war, without jails and prisons, and without fighting. We feel that there will be a whole lot of evil removed when the profit evil is removed. But that's got to be done by the individual. We've been called Communist lots of time. But in Russia and the Iron Curtain countries, the enemy of the free worker is the bureaucrat and the Communist. In this country the enemy of the free worker is the bureaucrat and the capitalist. So we unite with all the radicals against any-one who believes in war and exploitation.

When are we ever going to have this new world? Truth is forever on the scaffold, error forever on the throne till the end of time. Well, I'm not taking it. I say, let's get that crowbar underneath and pry a little bit. I'm not going to kid my-self—and I'm doing fine—no ulcers, and do what I can hap-pily. This doesn't wear me out; I feel better than I did when I was sixteen. The odds are greater against me, but it doesn't hurt me, and I have faith.

BRYANT: So you are going right ahead with plans for the immedi-ate future? What are you going to do now?

HENNACY: I'm going up to Portland, where we have the Catholic Worker house, and then to Seattle and Spokane, and then to see some good Mormons in Salt Lake. Then I go down with the Hopis. Then on to Phoenix where the mayor will have me on the air. He usually does. He is not a radical, but he likes me because I'm a good fighter. And then on to Tucson and Santa Fe where my newly married daughter is. Neither she nor her sister is Catholic, nor pacifist, nor anarchist. But they are proud of me because I take this stand. I didn't make them be anything. They will be what they want.

Then I'll go up to Denver and Boulder and Cheyenne. In Cheyenne on the 7th of June. . . . A young Catholic Worker with six children had been reading the *Catholic Worker* for six years. She said to herself, "What would Ammon Hennacy be doing about this dedication of the missile base? He'd be picketing it, but he can't do it for he's fasting down in Washington, so I guess I gotta do it."

So the woman and her six children got in the car. They said their Hail Mary's and they got down there and she picketed the missiles. Now, that's wonderful. Maybe she isn't an anarchist or a pacifist, but she sure acts in the tradition of one. And if she does nothing else, that will be enough. And I'm going down there to see her.

BRYANT: Well, thanks very much. Come back and see us again.

2

Documentary

The House Un-American
Activities Committee
in San Francisco

On Friday, May 13, 1960, KPFA staff members recorded the hearings conducted by a subcommittee of the House Committee on Un-American Activities, inside San Francisco's City Hall, and the riot which took place that day outside the hearing room. Tapes were rushed back to the station and, with the supervision and narration of Elsa Knight Thompson, KPFA's Director of Public Affairs, were broadcast that same day. On June 11, 1960, the first of two documentaries of these hearings was broadcast. The following is a condensation of the two programs: "Black Friday" and "The House Un-American Activities Committee in San Francisco."

(*There is a confusion of voices, followed by crowd shouting, which becomes the rhythmical chant, "Open the door, open the door, open the door, . . ."*)

ANNOUNCER: We present now the first of two documentary programs produced in KPFA's studios on the House Un-American Activities Subcommittee, which met in San Francisco in the supervisor's chambers at the City Hall on May 12th, 13th, and 14th, 1960.

NARRATOR: The impact of the events surrounding these hearings have largely overshadowed the hearings themselves. The story of a token picket line outside City Hall and a group of students seeking admittance on Thursday to a picket line of a thousand and an estimated crowd of four thousand people by Saturday is a story in itself. It is against the background of these events that the hours of testimony, friendly and unfriendly, was heard. Two questions arise out of any consideration of what took place during these three days—questions which it is the right, if not the duty, of every citizen to ask: What are the purposes of this committee? Did the San Francisco hearings further those purposes? Here is Chairman Edwin Willis' statement of them:

WILLIS: One: the extent, character, and objects of Communist infiltration and Communist Party activities in northern California for the legislative purpose of obtaining additional information for use by the committee in maintaining surveillance over the administration and operation of the Internal Security Act, the Communist Control Act, and other security legislation. Two: the past form, structure, organization, activities of the Communist Party and members of the Communist Party, whether in California or elsewhere, for the purpose of aiding the committee to interpret the significance of the present form, structure, organization, and activities of the Communist Party for the legislative purpose of obtaining information for use by the committee in consideration of proposed amendments to the security laws relating to the term "member of the Communist Party," possible use and legislation of the term "under Communist Party discipline," and for use by the committee in consideration of a proposed amendment to section IV of the Communist Control Act of 1954 prescribing penalties for knowingly and willfully becoming or remaining a member of the Communist Party with the knowledge of the purposes and objectives thereof. Three: the entry into and dissemination within the United States of foreign Communist Party propaganda, the legislative purpose being to determine the advisability of amendments to the Foreign Agents Registration Act, designed to counteract Communist devices now used in violation—in avoiding the prohibitions of the law. Four: techniques, strategies, tactics, and devices used by the members of the Communist Party for the purpose of evading the impact of present security laws, the legislative purpose being to reveal factual information to the committee which may require remedial legislation in the interest of national defense and internal security. Five: any other matter within the jurisdiction of the committee which it, or any subcommittee thereof, may designate.

NARRATOR: Three of the witnesses who testified on behalf of the committee were chief investigator William Wheeler; Barbara Hartle, a former Communist Party official from the state of Washington; and Karl Prussian, formerly a member of the Communist Party, and more recently an undercover agent for the FBI. These typical excerpts from many hours of testimony elicited from them by committee counsel Richard Ahrens, throw further light on the task the committee is endeavoring to accomplish.

AHRENS: Did you in the course of the recent past, from confidential sources of unimpeachable integrity, procure certain documents? Please answer the question.

WHEELER: Yes, sir.

A: Do these documents relate to the proceedings of the seventeenth National Convention of that conspiratorial organization on American soil which masquerades behind the façade of the Communist Party?

W: I did, sir.

A: Did you in addition procure, as investigator of this committee, from confidential sources of unimpeachable integrity and reliability, the list of the delegates to the national convention of the Communist Party, who were delegates from the state of California?

W: Ahh, delegates from the Communist Party, northern district of California?

A: That's what I meant to say—I beg your pardon. With that correction, did you likewise procure that information?

w: I did, sir.

A: Was the source of your procurement of this information an intelligent source of unimpeachable reliability and integrity?

w: I consider it as such, sir, yes sir.

A: Is it a source concerning which we cannot make a revelation on a public record because of security reasons?

w: Yes, sir. The source should not be identified in public session.

A: Are you satisfied on the basis of *your* integrity, upon your investigating techniques that the documents which you have procured from this source are *bona fide* in every respect?

w: Yes, sir.

* * *

AHRENS: Now before we proceed further in the specifics, I should like to ask you: were you arrested as a hard-core member, a one-time hard-core member of the Communist Party under the Smith Act?

HARTLE: Yes.

A: Were you actually sentenced under the Smith Act as a hard-core conspirator of the Party itself?

H: Yes.

A: You have, have you not, broke—irrevocably, finally from this conspiratorial force?

H: That I certainly have.

A: You have found the way back to God and patriotism, is that correct?

(*Laughter from audience.*)

* * *

AHRENS: Mr. Prussian, earlier in these hearings I was interrogating a lady, Mrs. Barbara Hartle, who had been in the conspiracy and who broke with the conspiracy, and in the course of the interrogation I observed that in finding her way out of the conspiracy, back as an anti-Communist, she had found her way back to God; and I heard snickering by these young people here. (*Voices in background.*) Is the Communist Party—within the framework of the Communist operation—is there room for concepts of God and spiritual values as we are taught them at our mother's knee?

PRUSSIAN: The Communist Party lowers man to that of a beast in the field. As far as the Communists are concerned, man is material, not spiritual; he has no soul, he has no spirit, there is no God. This is elementary and fundamental to every Communist. One cannot live a peaceable life under Communism and believe in God at the same time. Belief in God tears to shreds the entire Communist conspiracy.

A: Would you tell us whether or not, in the process by which you disassociated yourself from the conspiracy, you were able to find any strength, any spiritual faith, and a re-emphasis in your own life in concepts of a Divine Being?

P: I learned to believe that God is Truth, that man is created in His image and likeness, and therefore man must reflect the truth of God. I had a further association with a Dr. Bailey of the Baptist church; he became a very dear friend of mine—this was all during the period when I was in the Communist Party—and through these associations, and through a study of the Bible and participating in church activities, I regained my faith in God. I am very happy for that, because I'm able to sit here, I believe because of that, and testify before this Committee.

A: How does the menace and strength and force of the Communist conspiracy on American soil compare now within say—with the past ten years, fifteen years?

P: It is a greater menace now.

A: Were you taught anything in the training school which led you to believe, as a trainee of the Communists, one who was being disciplined in the conspiracy, that the actual objectives, the actual motivation, the actual program of the Communist Party was not one of humanity but was one of total enslavement?

P: Well, that is very definitely true. The Communist Party picks no bones about it. If any member of the Communist Party were honest—and they are not—they would tell you that the Communist Party believes in overthrowing the government by force and violence after the prerequisites of the revolution have been attained, and the manner in which they attain these prerequisites of the revolution is by infiltration of social, economic, and political organizations, and in the infiltration of these organizations it is their job to arouse class hatred, to gain leadership within these organizations, and to accelerate the class struggle and teach hatred of the working class against the people who run our industry.

A: Tell us a word about Communist Party discipline.

P: When a person first joins the Communist Party and reads their literature, their pamphlets, attends meetings and listens to lectures and goes to their specialized and general schools and when he begins to participate in violent activities and peaceful activities in the interest of the forthcoming revolution, he finds himself very shortly in the grip of Communist discipline, from which it is difficult to dislodge oneself. The Communist Party controls a member of the Communist Party throughout his life, and right to death he has complete control of a Communist Party member.

❋   ❋   ❋

AHRENS: Are there Communists, under Communist discipline, doing the work of the Communist conspiracy, consciously doing it, who do not have formal membership in the sense that you and I might have a membership in a church or in a club?

HARTLE: Yes, there is a large group of, ah, Communist followers or associates who do not have and maintain formal membership —payment of dues or attendance at the various regular meetings, or even carrying out all of the regular discipline that pertains to all the activities—but they are persons who do follow the discipline of the Communist Party, ah, insofar as their activities are concerned and their field of work is concerned.

A: I've been engaged in this work with congressional committees, developing information on the Communist operation, for fourteen years. I'm constantly amazed—constantly amazed—at the extent to which a relatively few trained, hard-core conspirators, masquerading behind a façade of humanitarianism, can suck in and use and condition non-Communists, and they can do so in great numbers, as we think is now happening right here on the soil on which we are now sitting at the present time. Were you taught the techniques which we observed in this committee frequently, in which one or two comrades can move into a mass organization, and take over that organization and direct it and control it—were you taught those techniques—techniques of mass psychology, and the like?

H: There—there are numerous examples of that. This is the general strategy of the Communist Party, for a few to lead many.

A: We subpoena a Communist, a hard-core, identified conspirator before us to interrogate him; the hue and cry goes up that we are undertaking to suppress his *political* beliefs, and *political* opinions, that we are involved in thought-control and the like. Based upon your background and experience, is a Communist a person who is an adherent (*cries of protest from background*) to a political philosophy as such, or is he a part of a world conspiratorial apparatus?

H: He is a part of a world conspiratorial apparatus. (*Noise from background.*)

A: Is the Communist Party a political party?

H: The Communist Party isn't, never has been, and never will be a political party.

A: What *is* the Communist Party?

H: The Communist Party is a conspiracy to which they intend ultimately, after they have achieved the prerequisites of the revolution, to overthrow our free-enterprise system and establish a dictatorship of the proletariat by force and violence.

A: Is the Communist Party, as a formal entity, the sole and exclusive operation of the international Communist conspiracy on American soil?

H: It so is.

*   *   *

AHRENS: These comrades who have been working here with these youngsters, these young people who have been picketing here and, ah, causing the commotion and the like—do the comrades make it plain to these youngsters that they are comrades, that they are part of a conspiratorial force, that are using these youngsters for their ultimate objectives?

PRUSSIAN: No, they do not. I recall, for example, when I went to Wayne University—I'm just reading this out, I think it's a little off the question, but I think it's pertinent—that a lot of my convictions in joining the Communist Party I received at the university. In the study, for example, of psychology, we were taught human behaviorism, and a materialistic conception of psychology.

* * *

NARRATOR: Among the documents produced by investigator Wheeler was a copy of a letter stated to have been written by one of the people under subpoena before the committee regarding the expulsion from the Communist Party of another witness also under subpoena.

WHEELER: Ah, in November, 1959, the section committee of the A.F. of L. section prepared a document which was presented to the national convention, C.P.U.S.A. in New York City, in which they outlined the difficulties they were having with the leadership in northern California. This document appealed to the National Committee, C.P.U.S.A. to re-establish the A.F. of L. section, to come to San Francisco and investigate the expulsion of Verne Baun and the disbanding of the section. Nothing was done concerning this at all. The section is still out of the Communist Party and Mr. Baun is still expelled, as far as we know, as of this date. The third segment is a report made by the section organizer of the A.F. of L. section for the year 1958. He's been—er, he is known—er, his name is Mr. Leibel Bergman. L-E-I-B-E-L B-E-R-G-M-A-N.

NARRATOR: This is a part of Leibel Bergman's interrogation regarding this letter.

* * *

AHRENS: Do you know a person by the name of Verne Baun, B-A-U-N?

BERGMAN: How does that question relate to this investigation?

A: Very simply, sir—that Verne Baun is the person who, according to your report, was expelled as one of the leaders of the Communist conspiratorial force within the AFL-CIO, and in your report you deplore, and complain to the National Committee respecting the unfair trial practices engaged in by the conspiracy in its expulsion of Baun. And you complained that no person from the section was even permitted to be present—he didn't have the right of counsel, as you have here today. He did not have, ah, information respecting the nature of the charges. No one of the section membership would be allowed to observe him, and you complain as to the outrages of this conspiratorial force, its own violation of its own procedures for an expulsion. Therefore, we should like to ask you if you know Mr. Baun, and, if so, if you could tell us further about him and about any Communist Party activities in which to your certain knowledge he was engaged in. All for the legislative purpose of acquiring information which this committee can use in appraising the factual situation in which we find the internal security laws of this country being evaded wholesale by the conspiracy, being virtually ineffective at this very hour against a conspiracy that threatens freedom everywhere. Now, Mr. Chairman, any explanation or—I respectfully suggest that the record reflect——

CHAIRMAN: I order and direct you to answer that question.

B: After that explanation I still fail to see the pertinency. I want to remind the committee that I'm here against my will; I do not sympathize with this committee——

A: We understand that. You said that before and we——

B: . . . and, and that consequently——

CHAIR.: I'm not going to suggest any particular constitutional amendments that he should invoke, ah, in his own behalf if he's entitled to them.

B: Therefore, Mr. Chairman, I——

CHAIR.: He's entitled to, to, to the constitutional protection of (*word unintelligible*), courts . . . we accord those rights.

B: Therefore, Mr.——

CHAIR.: I'm not gonna remind you ah, ah, ah, every time, just for purposes of delay. Just proceed——

A: I intend, Mr. Chairman, to proceed to another subject.

CHAIR.: . . . he will not, he will not be warned any more.

A: Did you, in 1958,——

B: Well, then, under those circumstances——

A: Did you, in 1958, make a report of, to the, respecting the A.F. of L. section and the ideological crisis section organizers report to the comrades? Please answer that question—whether or not you made such a report in 1958.

B: Going back to the previous question, do I understand that the committee has directed me to answer that question more explicitly than I have stated?

CHAIR.: No, I made no such request. Proceed with this answer.

A: The question is outstanding on this record, Mr. Chairman, and the record is perfectly clear. Is, did you in 1958, make a report to the comrades of the Communist Party respecting the A.F. of L. section of the Communist Party?

B: Going back to that other question, I notice the, the glee with which the investigator wants to slide from one question to another in the, in the hope that I would over—, overlook, that I had failed to avail myself of every constitutional safeguard I had. Consequently, with respect to that question, and to this question, I state the following—the previous question and this one—that under the first amendment of the Constitution, under the sixth amendment of the Constitution, under the fourteenth amendment of the Constitution, under the fifth amendment of the Constitution, and under the whole Constitution, I refuse to answer either one of those two questions.

A: Proceed, now.

*   *   *

NARRATOR: Mr. Baun is the person stated to have been expelled.

*   *   *

BAUN: I would suggest that——

AHRENS: Do you have a recollection, sir, of a——

B: In view of the constitutional provision, I would suggest that the Constitution provides that anybody is supposed to be provided with counsel—proper counsel, I might say——

A: Ah, proceed, Mr.——

B: . . . and that that includes the right of the counsel to speak up in behalf of his client. This committee does not, and has never done this.

A: Do you have recollection of a proceeding in which you were involved, in which you were denied counsel *in toto*?

(*Silence.*)

B: Yes, sir, right here.

A: You have recollection of another proceeding, in which counsel wasn't even permitted within the room—in which you were involved?

(*Pause.*)

B: I'm afraid I don't understand your question, nor do I see the significance of it.

A: We'll be glad to explain the significance of it. There has been on this record identified a report to the National Committee of the Communist Party made by a comrade, which, in that report, is complaining about the expulsion of another comrade, a second comrade who was expelled—according to the report, was denied the privilege of counsel; he was denied the opportunity to know the nature of his charges; he was denied the opportunity to offer proof of his alleged innocence; he was denied even the company of fellow comrades; he was denied any semblance of fair play; and this one comrade is complaining to the National Convention of the Communist Party about this particular proceeding. Now, since you are here before us and can't quite understand the pertinence of this line of inquiry, I'll say to you that this committee is trying to develop information respecting the techniques, mode of operation, of this conspiratorial force which masquerades behind a façade of do-goodism, of humanitarianism, which is sweeping the world, which has destroyed more lives on this planet than any other force since the dawn of time. Now, sir, this committee expects to take back to

Washington with us, by direction or by indirection, considerable information which will be of value to this committee, so we know, in the discharge of this duty which this committee has, to evolve legislative devices to attempt to cope with this conspiratorial force on American soil. With that explanation, sir, I now ask you to respond to the principal question.

B: After that long speech I've forgotten what the question was.

                ❈   ❈   ❈

NARRATOR: Here are brief snatches of conversation which took place on Thursday with members of the audience, all friends of the committee.

ANON. NO. 1: There is one thing I would like to say, and that is that the American public, if the American public will watch it, in this investigation, they are being given these Communists, or Communist-pinkos, have to give their name and address, and that stamps them in the community and it might be an interesting thing to note, that if war ever comes out, ever comes forward, which we hope will never come, different war veteran organizations, knowing these names, can strike the first blow at these people and finish them off before they can do any harm.

ANON. NO. 2: I agree very much with everything he has to say because I'm a grandmother—I have a granddaughter twenty-two years old that's in college—and I know the things she's told us about it, it's over at Cal, and everything that's going on now, and God bless this committee. I hope—too bad we don't have more of 'em.

QUESTION: Do you want to give us an opinion on the proceedings here this morning?

ANON. NO. 3: (*Member of the audience*) Well, I would just say that those poor youngsters are brainwashed. They're actually brainwashed, and I feel sorry for them. And they're—some of them—are nice-looking youngsters, and they look as though if they had a little attention, and some baths, and their hair combed, and some parental discipline, they might become good citizens.

QUESTION: Rev. George Moore, Pastor of the First Baptist Church of Walnut Creek, you were here during the proceedings this morning. I'd like you to give us your opinion of the proceedings this morning.

REV. MR. MOORE: I thought that the counsel did very well. They uncovered much that should be uncovered; we're looking forward to their uncovering more. That this matter of Communism must be exposed, and only those who have reason to hide, have reason to fear.

QUESTION: And what do you think of the students who were in here this morning—I should say, the young people——

REV. MR. MOORE: They appear to me to be a well-disciplined corps. They seem to be Communist-inspired. I can't be dogmatic about that, but they certainly give every evidence, every reason to believe, that they have Communist inspiration.

QUESTION: Do you have any particular reasons for this opinion, other than the fact that they seem to be——

REV. MR. MOORE: They work as a unit, and one only needs to look at them and you can see the difference between those who are pro and those con.

QUESTION: I see, well, thank you very much.

REV. MR. MOORE: You're very welcome.

❖ ❖ ❖

NARRATOR: Fred Haines, of the KPFA staff, was at the City Hall all day today, armed with a portable recorder. He has some extremely interesting material to bring to you, but first he wants to explain to you the background of the recordings that you are about to hear.

FRED HAINES: About two hundred students had sought entrance to the chambers in the morning and, not being admitted, waited in the small rotunda outside the doors, where they chanted, "Mr. Willis, we're still here!" and sang, "Abolish the committee, they shall be removed," to the tune of an old spiritual made famous as a "Wobbly" song. Besides their opposition to the committee and its tactics, they had a more specific grievance: although the hearings were supposedly open, almost all the spectators were admitted on presentation of invitation cards signed by William Wheeler, the committee investigator, and given out to conservative groups, or so-called "friends of the committee." After the "white cards" had been admitted, the remaining fifteen or twenty seats were opened to the public. At the close of the morning session, Sheriff Matthew Carbury of San Francisco County spoke with the students.

SHERIFF: This young lady had a question earlier, let's——

SPOKESMAN FOR DEMONSTRATORS: (*Interrupting the sheriff.*) . . . by hands, please.

VOICE: Quiet.

GIRL: If you don't want us out here—Are the white cards still going to be let in first?

SHERIFF: My dear young lady, I explained yesterday and today as far as white cards, I knew nothing, did not know anything about it; as far as I am concerned it's the people who are here who will be admitted by the committee.

SPOKESMAN: We will cooperate, and if they cooperate with us at two—and let us in—on equal come basis—then at two o'clock, you'll hear from us again, at two o'clock. Sheriff, is that right? We shall cooperate with you. Until two o'clock. And if you keep your promise, and let everybody go into that hall, on a first come, fire serve (*he is constantly interrupted by voices in the background*), let me finish, first come, first serve basis, we'll cooperate. But if we're kept out of here, if we're kept out of here—I—I——

SHERIFF: I have nothing to do with admissions. I told you that.

SPOKESMAN: I know that. I'm sorry. If, at that time, we find out that all law enforcement agencies, including the committee which says it is a law enforcement agency, will allow people to go into that hall on a free and democratic basis—that is first come, and first serve, *we* will cooperate with the law enforcement agencies. However, I would suggest to the group——

SHERIFF: I don't think it's necessary to go beyond that——

SPOKESMAN: However, I would suggest to the group——

SHERIFF: I promise you full cooperation.

SPOKESMAN: . . . if the law enforcement agencies, either true, or not so true, (*laughter*) do not cooperate with us, that we do organize, that we do use our, our free assembly, our right to petition. We do it orderly, but we do it loudly. Are you with me? (*He is acclaimed by the group.*)

FRED HAINES: That was the discussion with the sheriff which made many students suppose they would be permitted to enter the hearing after lunch—and to wait quietly through the noon hour. Others, more cynical, somehow procured white cards for their *own* use. Shortly after one o'clock, the police formed a separate line of "friends of the committee" and proceeded to pass *them* into the chambers. The students, lined up four or five abreast behind the center section of the barricade, grew angry and surged against the barricade, but responded to the cries of their leaders to wait and see what the police would do. Police officers laid hands on the students who had gotten into the "friends of the committee" group, but let them go, confused when the students produced white cards. They did eject Doug Wachter, however, in spite of his white card and the fact that he had been a witness and that his father was testifying that afternoon. The police admitted fifteen or twenty students, then closed the doors to the rest. The students conferred, and decided, since they had not been admitted "first come, first served" as the sheriff had intimated, to resume their protest by singing and chanting. I was able to observe the following events only because I was not in the press box inside the chambers—other members of the press were locked in during the first moments of the disturbance. As the students resumed their singing, officers of the San Francisco motorcycle squad, in helmets and leather jackets, appeared behind the barricade with two fire hoses. Here is how one student describes what followed.

DEMONSTRATOR: People started yelling to sit down because this was a threat.

ANOTHER VOICE: He said: "How would you like some of this?"

DEMONSTRATOR: Oh yeah, so this guy says "how," so the cop says: "How would you like this?" pointing the hose at us, and . . .

OTHER VOICE: Some of them moved away, and others sat down.

DEMONSTRATOR: And then—and then there was a call to sit down to show that we weren't being violent. And everyone sat down. And then the cop . . .

OTHER VOICE: Is this how it was put, he said, "Let's show we're not violent"?

DEMONSTRATOR: Well, I don't think that was it. It was a call to "sit down."

ANOTHER VOICE: It was a call to sit down with their hands in their pockets.

DEMONSTRATOR: And everyone sat down—more or less—except a few people standing up around. And then, the cops just turned on the hose and started lashing out, and they, a few people, moved away, but most people stood their ground, and then some people stood up with their backs to the hose, and sort of shielded the rest from the water. And we just stood our ground. And, then there were more hoses brought in, about two or three more and the—but that didn't do any good so eventually they shut off the hoses and without any warning at all the cops just charged and pushed people all around. One guy had his wrists——

OTHER VOICE: (*Breaking in upon the demonstrator.*) . . . they, they, the people stood up, and blocked the water.

DEMONSTRATOR: Yeah.

(*Crowd background noises.*)

FRED HAINES: This is how it started—the police were picking up the students bodily, many of them were sitting with their arms folded or in their pockets—the technique of passive resistance. The police charged them in a cordon and were driving them back out of the area before the doors, down onto an upper landing between a very long stair flight that led down to the main floor. Several students were injured in this. The police would pick them up and throw them across the wet floor—one was very badly hurt—one of the witnesses who testified before the hearings went to the students and got him over to the side where the fire hoses were not playing so strongly, and then he went out into the middle of the fray and began protesting too, and his wife followed and she was on the side—the police turned fire hoses on them as well, striking them in the face. The students again all sat down on the landing and linked arms in long chains of seven or eight, refusing to be moved—they held their posters up and they sang and they raised their right hands in the V for Victory signal. At first just one or two, then six, seven, or eight, and they sang the "Star Spangled Banner."

(*Crowd is heard singing.*)

FRED HAINES: As you hear now, in the background, they are singing the "Star Spangled Banner" at the top of their voices. Many of those who were wounded or injured——

(*Singing finished, there is applause and cheering.*)

The cheers are because the police are leaving. They are filing out, and they begin the chant again.

(*Students are heard chanting.*)

Students were being thrown, rather brutally across the floor, and were unable to keep their balance in the flood of water on the marble flooring here and seemed to be very hurt, but I see none of them now. Perhaps they've all, they're all better; they've all recuperated. Police now are clearing the way through the center of the students.

(*The crowd roar grows in intensity, mingled with boos.*)

FRED HAINES: Police are hauling out a bearded student. A woman —a woman is protesting, and they're dragging her out, too. The police who left the upper floor here have suddenly reappeared on the lower floor, and they seem prepared to—to start hauling the students down the stairs from behind, either one by one or in pairs. The major part of the students are now kneeling, sitting on the upper stairwell. The police are on both sides of them. The police are——

(*The crowd noise increases, a great roar.*)

FRED HAINES: The kids are sitting down again, with their hands in their pockets, or with their arms crossed. The police are taking them by the arms and hauling them bodily down the long stairway to the main floor.

(*Above the roar are heard the screams of a girl.*)

FRED HAINES: A girl is screaming and refusing to be taken. The principle here is apparently passive resistance. None of the students seems to be striking back. The students are now being taken out one by one, and the students have started again, somewhat weakly, their chant of "We shall not be moved."

(*The voices are heard clearly, "We shall not, we shall not be moved."*)

FRED HAINES: The police have grabbed a Negro by the ankle and are dragging him down the stairs on his—(*his voice betrays fascinated disbelief*)—on his *back*, by the ankle.

(*The singing and crowd roar continues.*)

FRED HAINES: People in the rotunda in the audience are now seen to be clapping. Apparently they are on the side of the police. Girls are being thrown down. The students are giving each other advice, "Let them drag you down, let them drag you down." They have their arms linked together so they can't be moved separately. They must be taken down in pairs. Again the technique of the police seems to be to grab them by the ankles and to hold them down on their backs, down the stairway of some fifty or sixty stairs. One policeman is presently dragging three girls all at once together.

GIRL: No! Get your hands off me.

POLICE: . . . what I tell you. Come here, come here. Get out.

GIRL: No! No! NO! NO! NO!

(*Crowd melee, occasional individual protesting voices and shouts rising above the general roar.*)

FRED HAINES: A girl student has advocated that they all get up and leave, and most of them have. There are about fourteen or fifteen left, and they have gotten up and moved now for the most part. Doug Wachter, the boy that was subpoenaed yesterday, has just gotten up and moved out. The police are helping one girl down, who looks somewhat dazed. They let her walk down.

(*There is still considerable background uproar with distant shouting.*)

FRED HAINES: At the present moment, all students have been re-moved—have been removed from the upper landing. A few of the boys and girls are going down the stairs. One or two are still being dragged. The police are advising those who wish to walk down to hold onto the handrail because the steps are running with water and very slippery. The, the crowd, on the main floor seems to have grown some. They're not only removing the students from the stairway, but from the upper landing. From the stairway they are hauling them all the way out of the building. I see a policeman rassling with a girl right now. Another girl is fighting back. There goes the principle of passive resistance. Ahh. The first girl seems to have been kicked. Other people coming to their defense are also being thrown out.

VOICE FROM THE CROWD, NEARBY: What was that, what resistance, the leader of passive resistance?

FRED HAINES: There are still about half a dozen students sitting on the main floor. There are at present one, two, three, four, five, six, seven, eight, nine, ten, eleven, twelve, thirteen—thirteen po-licemen surrounding them. They are trying to break them apart. They link their arms together so they cannot be moved separately, but must be moved as a group, or else broken apart to move.

❂   ❂   ❂

NARRATOR: The recording which follows was made *inside* the chamber as the committee took its noon break Friday. The hearing was about to reconvene: The audience was already seated, and outside on the wide marble stairs there was a crowd, mainly students, of around one hundred fifty people. As you listen, you will hear the news that the police have turned the fire hoses into this crowd.

DALE MINOR: (*KPFA reporter.*) There's a good deal of commo-tion outside the doors—the—chambers right now. I can't tell what is going on—we'll have to learn in a few moments. They seem to be forcing their way in— No, those are newsmen trying to force their way out.

(*The noise of the crowd is louder, at times drowning out words.*

A door slams. Above the crowd roar a man, barely audible, inquires, "Anybody hurt?")

M: The motorcycle boys have arrived on the scene and seem to be—ejecting once again. All this is going on *out*side the doors of the council chamber and I'm just about getting trampled by curious pressmen.

(Above the hubbub and the nearer but indistinguishable individual voices, the sound of a chant begins and increases.)

CHANT: We shall not be moved, we shall not be moved, we shall not be moved . . .

M: I can't really see a great deal from this point, other than white crash helmets and blue officers' caps—the—demonstrators are, for the most part, off to the side of my field of vision.

(The chanting ceases and above the hubbub are punctuations of individual shouts. The sound of the crowd is intense with a note of dismay, disapproval.)

M: A full-scale riot seems to be underway outside the doors—fire hoses and everything.

EXCITED MAN: *(Shouting in distance.)* Do you know what they're doin'? They're beat'n 'em up and turn'n the hoses on 'em. *(The crowd noise changes to dismay and boos.)*

MAN: *(Again.)* Bunch of filthy Fascists, that's all. Bunch of filthy Fascists—that's all they are.

(General crowd confusion with occasional individual voices and exclamations.)

ERWIN GOLDSMITH: *(Recording engineer.)* Boy, what a mess out there. What a disgusting place.

M: And here, having just come through the thing is—Erwin Goldsmith. Erwin, come here and tell us something about what's happening outside. You just walked through it, so, what's going on?

G: Well, the police are spraying—with water hoses and the whole City Hall looks like a big pigsty, right now. They're sweeping them, literally sweeping them, down the stairs.

(The crowd noise is quieter, and near voices are heard discussing the scene.)

VOICES: They ought to turn the hoses on *them!*—How are things going here?—They had to use violence.

(*The crowd roar continues, with the sound of "God Bless America" distinguishable above the tumult.*)

G: The students are sitting. They are being sprayed by water hoses at point-blank range, and they are just sitting there, singing, "We shall not be moved."

M: The students aren't moving at all?

G: No, they're not moving. They're sitting at the top of the stairs, and the police are spraying them—about six to ten officers holding the hoses and they're spraying them at point-blank range.

M: Would you like to say something, sir?

MAN: Oh, I'm from the *Daily Californian.*

M: And what is your name?

MAN: I'm Bob Morritson. Personally—I saw, ah—I saw about—about six policemen beat a student to the ground, and the guy looked like he weighed about 120 pounds. And these six policemen, wearing these helmets, beat him to the ground. The last I saw him he was lying up against a pillar, and these policemen were propping him up, and he, he looked—he looked—just, just completely beaten. Again, the policemen were spraying the students with hoses, and one girl was trying to get in and she ran into a mess of—about another half a dozen cops—they shoved her back out and, well—I didn't see what was going on right now. And then another guy tried to turn off the hose. And one man, without a uniform—I don't know who he was—he was pretty big—and another couple or three cops, they beat him down, and I don't know what happened to him.

M: I see. Well, they are still evidently sitting out there, under——

MAN: Ah, apparently. I don't know. Then they started singing, "God Bless America," while the police were——(*His voice is drowned out by a swell in the crowd's roar. A nearer voice says repeatedly—*)

VOICE: Outside ladies, outside, outside, outside, sir. (*Loud crowd noises.*)

M: . . . Some of the people ejected from the press box—who evidently did not have the identification required by the checking officers. (*Crowd noise continues in background.*)

M: And it still seems to be continuing. They—are still—at last accounts—sitting outside—the chamber doors, on the steps—singing—(*Singing heard faintly.*)

M: Erwin Goldsmith has just returned from outside the chamber doors. Erwin, what's the situation now?

G: It looks like a swimming pool out there. The students are still singing, "We shall not be moved"—looks like the city of San Francisco turned the whole Hetch-Hetchy water supply on them. City Hall literally was swimming. And they were just sitting there, trying to keep from being swept down the stairs by the flood.

M: Are they still—turning the hoses on them?

G: No, the hoses finally stopped. There are almost as many policemen up there as there are demonstrators. And—ah—of course it takes a number of policemen just to hold the hoses.

M: Do you know if anyone was injured?

G: I saw blood. Yes, it might not have been very serious, but there was one man screaming for an ambulance, who had been dragged away by the police. And there was blood mixed with water, on the floor of the City Hall.

✻   ✻   ✻

NARRATOR: Haltingly, and with many witnesses absent, the hearings got underway again.

DALE MINOR: Mr. Ahrens, counsel for the committee, has just entered the chambers, and Representative Willis has entered behind him. Evidently proceedings will get underway very soon. It looks as though they're going to get underway with the crowd outside as a background in spite of all the S.F. police and the Sheriff's Department officers can do about it.

(*Noise around microphone:* "Yeah, that's right. That'll be the wind-up.")

AHRENS: Mr. Archie Brown, please come forward, remain standing while the chairman administers an oath.

VOICE: No, counsel, if you care to just, please, kindly come forward here, please, sir.

BROWN'S COUNSEL: Again we apparently have a problem. I communicated with Mr. Brown, as a matter of fact, I had lunch with Mr. Brown, and ah, he, ah, I told him what the committee told me, and he said, "I'll be there; I always respect an order of Congress."—that was his reply—but when he came back here, I think he was met by a fire hose, and he was refused admission here, and I haven't seen him since.

CHAIRMAN: Ah, if you will there, will you kindly request the officers there to announce in the hall he's being paged. Counsel, would you kindly accommodate the committee by asking Mr. Brown, notifying Mr. Brown, that he has again been called for appearance here. If you have lunch with him tomorrow, we'll take him tomorrow afternoon, or if you see him or are in contact with him——

B's COUNSEL: Well, may I——

CHAIR.: It is the position of the committee that he is under a continuing subpoena and he has not been formally excused from his attendance at these sessions. So, if you'll do that the—there'll be accommodation here.

B's COUNSEL: And pursuant to that, may I address the chair? He has tried twice to my knowledge to get into this room, and each time he's been refused the right to get into the room. Now, if the subpoena means something, it at least should amount to as much as these little white cards. (*Laughter.*)

CHAIR.: Well, if you see him, next time you ask him——

B's COUNSEL: Now—I'm going to tell the committee this: that unless they let him in that door, the next time he comes there with me, I'm gonna tell him then to go home, if he wishes to.

CHAIR.: Well, if you anticipate any particular time he might be here, just let us know; we'll be certain he is admitted to the hearing.

B's COUNSEL: What time, what time do you want him here tomorrow?

CHAIR.: We'll take him any time he shows up. (*Noise.*)

*   *   *

NARRATOR: Despite dramatic and frequent interruption, however, hour after hour interrogation took place for three days, and witness after witness invoked the rights afforded by the Constitution of the United States. What follows are highlights selected from representative testimony by a number of witnesses.

AHRENS: There's what's called an immunity statute, properly known as immunity statute, pursuant to which this committee can set in motion legal proceedings which, if consummated, have an ultimate result of granting an immunity to a witness—immunity from any criminal prosecution for certain factual material which he might reveal in testimony. It is the judgment of this committee that you, sir, having been a leader in—so we are advised—unimpeachable sources—having been a leader in the dissident group within the Communist Party—have information which would be of extreme value to your government via this committee. In its attempts to legislate on Communist activities, attempting to protect this country, under whose flag you and I both have protection, against the workings of the Communist conspiracy. It's our information, sir, that at one time you were—until 1957, at least—very active as a regional representative in the Communist Party itself, and that under leadership of yourself and others, a dissident group has been developed within the Communist operation. We say quite frankly we know very little about it—except that we think there is very significant information here that ought to be available to this committee. Now, with that explanation I ask you this question in all sincerity: If this Committee on Un-American Activities should initiate the proceedings to grant you a complete immunity from criminal prosecution based on any information, direct or collateral, which you can give this committee in the course of testimony, to serve your government, and if those proceedings are consummated so that you are granted such immunity, would you accept that immunity, and would you then testify fully and freely respecting all items of information on which we might interrogate you within the purview of this committee's jurisdiction?

FIRST WITNESS: At the consultation of my attorney, I would suggest that you consult with him after you make up your decision, and, ah, there's no use discussing.

A: Well, you see the policy we have, we would not want to initiate such proceedings, carry through to an ultimate conclusion, if possible, an immunity for yourself, unless we had some indication from yourself: of course, I'm not personally in a position to make any commitments for the committee; the committee is autonomous. I only work for the committee. We could not make any commitments unless we had some indication from yourself that if you were granted a complete immunity from penal prosecution for any information which you might supply to this committee, directly or indirectly, you would accept the immunity, and you would testify fully and freely on all items of information which you might be interrogated within the jurisdiction of the committee.

CHAIRMAN: And you understand, of course, that that interrogation could not be done today or, ah, anything of the sort; proceedings would have to be initiated, so, ah, that would leave you time for, to think about it.

W: I am here under subpoena—I would never have voluntarily appeared before such a committee as this——

A: Would you speak a little more loudly?

W: (*With irritation.*) I said, I am here before this committee——

A: Yes.

W: . . . under subpoena, and I would never have appeared here or anywhere else unless I were under subpoena. I think that answers your question.

A: It does answer our question; Mr. Chairman, I respectfully suggest that we conclude the staff interrogation of this witness.

CHAIR.: The witness is excused.

❖   ❖   ❖

NEW WITNESS: By the way, if the television men want some news they can put those lights on.

AHRENS: Do I understand, do you want the lights *on?*

w: I want the lights *on,* precisely, I want the fullest glare of publicity on this committee's activity.

A: Where and when were you born, please, sir?

w: I was born in New York City on June 4, 1917.

A: Are you now, or have you ever been, a member of the Communist Party?

w: Sir, I am forty-two years of age, and have never had to face a jury as defendant, or grand jury as witness, in my life. My research and writing have been so public that two committees similar to this one, the Senate Internal Security Subcommittee and the McCarthy Committee, subpoenaed me as far back as eight and seven years ago, respectively, for having written a book titled *The Soviet Far East and Central Asia.* No indictment resulted from those hearings, either, or from my continued public speaking or writing since that date. Clearly, therefore, I have engaged—I have committed *no* crime—under the laws of this country, and am not engaged in subversion. Consequently, I refuse to testify on the grounds that as a radio and TV public affairs broadcaster active in those capacities today, the subpoena issued to me interferes with the rights of my stations to schedule informational programs on their merits, and is thus a direct violation of the First Amendment guarantee of freedom of speech, and of the people's right to hear. Further, as a scholar with a twenty-year record of research and public writing and lecturing in my chosen field, the study of the Soviet Union, a field admitted by all to be one in which this country is in vital need of knowledge, I refuse to testify on the grounds that the subpoena is a violation of freedom of inquiry—which can only be expressed through the free speech and free press guarantee in the First Amendment—to the academic community as to all others. Lastly, I certainly shall *not* answer questions representing allegations against me made by persons not present and not identified, whom I cannot confront and whom my lawyer cannot cross-examine as to their truthfulness. To rest my case solely on the First Amendment would, as thirty-six cases now in the courts show, condemn me to years of court action at enormous cost. It would cost me my home and impoverish my family for a very long time to come, which is of course what this committee desires. Therefore, I also refuse to testify under my right not to be a witness against myself, a right originated to protect the innocent. The guilty can be convicted by the testimony of others if there is any real evidence to present.

A: Do you honestly apprehend, sir, that if you told this committee truthfully while you're under oath whether or not you are now this instant, or ever have been, a member of the Communist Party, you would be supplying information which might be used against you in a criminal proceeding?

W: Honorable beaters of children and sadists, uniformed and in plain clothes, distinguished Dixiecrat wearing the clothing of a gentleman, eminent Republican who opposes an accommodation with the one country with whom we must live at peace in order for us all and our children to survive. . . . My boy of fifteen left this room a few minutes ago in sound health and not jailed, solely because I asked him to be in here to learn something about the procedures of the United States government and one of its committees. Had he been outside, where the son of a friend of mine had his head split by these goons operating under your orders, my boy today might have paid the penalty of permanent injury or a police record for desiring to come here and hear how this committee operates. If you *think* that I am going to *cooperate* with this collection of (*pause*) *Judases,* of men who sit there in violation of the United States Constitution —if you think I'll cooperate with you in any way, *you are insane.*

✻　✻　✻

AHRENS: Did you live in Denver, Colorado, prior to the time that you moved to California?

NEW WITNESS: Mr. Chairman, before I answer that question I would like to state to the committee that I am ready and willing to answer questions pertaining to my life and activities regarding *myself* personally.

A: I was just asking you if you lived in Denver, Colorado, before you moved out here. . . .

CHAIR.: Ah, you are ordered to . . .

W: . . . myself, personally, on condition that no questions will be asked me regarding any persons or associations.

A: Well, do you answer the question: is that your answer? If it is, proceed. (*Gavel rapping in background.*)

W: I repeat my offer, that I will answer any of these questions, ah, pertaining to my life and activities, regarding *myself* personally, on condition——

CHAIR.: Ah, I have ordered you to answer the question, you haven't answered it. Now, counsel, proceed with the next question.

A: Next question is, the first question, which he didn't answer and which we got off of, namely, how long have you lived in these parts—in California?

W: I take it from what you say that you are rejecting my request, ah, ah, my offer to talk about myself.

A: Kindly answer the question—we, ah, you can talk about how long you've lived here—that'll be a start in that direction. How long have you lived here in California?

W: Well, since you refuse me the privilege of answering only questions pertaining to myself, and I will in no circumstances be an informer, you now force me to stand on my constitutional right of not being compelled to testify as a witness against myself.

❋   ❋   ❋

CHAIRMAN: What is the outstanding question?

AHRENS: The outstanding principal question, sir, is where did you live prior to the time that you moved to California?

CHAIR.: I direct you . . .

A: . . . two years ago.

CHAIR.: I direct you to answer that question.

NEW WITNESS: I decline to answer that statement upon constitutional grounds.

CHAIR.: Proceed with the next question.

A: The next question is——

W: He's not giving me a chance to state my grounds.

CHAIR.: Proceed with the next question.

W: Ah, may I say that I was subpoenaed last year, my name was smeared in the headlines of all the local newspapers——

CHAIR.: (*Gavel.*) *Next* question.

W: I have been harassed for one year, and this is now my opportunity to speak, and I would like to have it.

CHAIR.: I respectfully suggest that if this witness is in truth and in fact attempting to answer on constitutional grounds, she be permitted to do so but if on the other hand she is going to give another Communist Party speech (*murmurs from the audience*), I think it is quite proper she be denied the opportunity to use this committee as the forum.

W: These are my constitutional grounds, Mr. Chairman, and I wish to state them in my own words.

CHAIR.: All right. State your constitutional grounds.

W: I repeat, last year one hundred and ten California teachers——

CHAIR.: (*Gavel.*) That is——

W: . . . were subpoenaed by this committee.

CHAIR.: That is not, ah, constitutional grounds.

W: I am not a lawyer. I wish to state these grounds in the best way that I can——

CHAIR.: You . . . you——

W: . . . and I demand the right to do so.

CHAIR.: You are not a lawyer, but your lawyer has been advising you constantly during this haggling.

W: Yes, but this statement was prepared by me, and I wish to be allowed to read it.

CHAIR.: How long is that statement?

W: It's handwritten, two pages.

CHAIR.: Go on, read it.

w: Last year, one hundred and ten California teachers were sub-poenaed by this committee. In northern California, forty teachers had their names smeared on the front pages of numerous local newspapers. This was done just before the end of the school semester, and prior to summer vacation. One hundred and ten California schoolteachers, tired from their year's work, had no vacations, no opportunity to rest, because the committee postponed the June 17th hearings and scheduled them for early September. Thus harassment and continued press publicity followed the teachers all through the summer. The committee then postponed its hearings until October 14. No explanations were given for these postponements. Widespread public protest, coming from church groups, ministers, professors, teachers' organizations, labor unions, newspapers and individuals, finally caused this committee to cancel the hearings entirely. If you are interested, Mr. Chairman, in seeing documentation of these protests, may I refer you to a document of unimpeachable integrity—the speech before the House of Representatives of Hon. James Roosevelt, dated Monday, April 25, 1960, in which he calls upon the House of Representatives to abolish this Committee on Un-American Activities. This story could and should have ended here. But no, this committee had not finished its dirty work; it sent its files on the teachers to the State Superintendent of Instruction, and then, not certain that these would be used against the teachers, ran around the state and deposited these files with local district attorneys, who then dumped them into the laps of the school boards, whether requested by them or not. This year the committee returned. The school boards were informed as long as three weeks before subpoenas were served that their employees were in danger. Many school boards, intimidated by the representatives of this committee, informed their teachers they would not be rehired, there are at least six such cases in this area alone. Many teachers subpoenaed last year have now been resubpoenaed. Community protests are again pouring in. The academic community is aroused by this repeated threat to freedom of thought and inquiry. This committee has no right to inquire into this area. The committee has no right to question me as to my thoughts, associations, and activities.

* * *

w: Now, if I may address myself to the other question, that your *belligerence*, Mr. Ahrens——

CHAIR.: Well, now . . .

A: The question—Now listen, Counsel, you're not going to attack me any further.

w: Well, you've been attacking people all day, Mr. Ahrens——

A: No, I have not, Counsel, and you know it. . . .

w: Can't you take it? You can only—— (*Gavel.*)

A: I take it every day here, and I take it by people who make you look like a cream puff. (*Gavel.*)

CHAIR.: Now, is there an outstanding question?

A: Yes, the outstanding question, sir, is: Are you now, or have you ever been, a member of the Communist Party?

w: Now, I submit—I'm answering this in my own way, and *no*-body is going to put words in my mouth—that goes for Mr. Ahrens, and that goes for the members of the committee. Now, I'll answer the question if you'll allow me to do so. Won't you please permit me to answer it? All right, now—I know, and you know, that that question is not asked in good faith, and I'll tell you why, and this is part of my legal objection. It wasn't very long ago that your committee came out with a publication—I have it right here—it's called "Communist Legal Subversion— the Role of the Communist Lawyer." Now, on page thirty of this publication there appears what purports to be an official biography of someone by the name of Bertram Edises of California. It goes into great detail; it purports to indicate that Mr. Bertram Edises was identified as a member of the Communist Party, etc. etc., that he has served as a member of the legal staff of the East Bay Civil Rights Congress since its inception, that the Civil Rights Congress retained Edises to represent certain defendants in both state and federal courts; it goes on to say that the activities of Bertram Edises on behalf of the Communist Party have not been confined to the Civil Rights Congress, and so on, and so on—a remarkably detailed purported biography. Now, it so happens that, although I have been subpoenaed four times, this is the first time that I have ever testified before this organization—before the Un-American Committee. And therefore, I can only conclude that you got this information, which you published at government expense, and, ah, which you didn't set forth in any doubtful form at all, it's all set forth as gospel fact, it is findings of fact, and I can only conclude that you got the information from your so-called "reliable, unimpeachable sources" that you have been bragging about——

CHAIR.: No——

W: Now, just a minute——

A: You skipped something as you were reading this report, Mr. Edises——

W: Oh, you know, you know the facts, Mr. Ahrens? Then why do you ask me that question?—when you already claim to know the information?

A: Mr.——

W: Why do you do it?

A: Mr. Chairman——

W: You can only have *one* purpose, and that is to try to embarrass me, to humiliate me, to pillory—me. And that is the whole function of your organization, Mr. Ahrens; that's all you do. You go through the motions; you come into a big courtroom, you've got an American flag in front of you——

A: Mr. Chairman, I respectfully suggest this witness——

W: . . . and yet you——

A: . . . be directed to answer the outstanding principal question.

W: You're just a mock court.

A: We have been baited—by experts and you fall far short of——

W: You're just a kangaroo court, that's all——

CHAIR.: You have been directed to answer the question; will you come to the point?

w: I decline to answer this question on the ground that it is un-mistakably clear, unmistakably clear—Mr. Scherer, will you please pay attention—?

SCHERER: I move . . . (*laughter*) . . . Now, Mr. Chairman, Mr. Chairman, I move the witness be escorted from the courtroom; he is utterly in contempt of this committee. I'm ashamed he's a member of the bar.

w: I insist on being permitted to answer your questions.

COUNSEL: Mr. Chairman, is my client excused as a witness?

VOICE: Wait, Counsel, wait.

COUNSEL: Is my client excused?

VOICE: Wait.

COUNSEL: If he is——

CHAIR.: Well, now wait a minute, wait a minute.

COUNSEL: All right.

CHAIR.: I would like as chairman of this committee, ah, I would ask my colleague to defer his motion just for two minutes to give this gentleman an opportunity to answer the question.

w: Thank you.

CHAIR.: If not, I will—unless you come to the point and answer the question if motion is proper, I will have to carry it out.

w: Very well.

CHAIR.: Won't you please state your constitutional grounds.

w: I got a little bit excited there. I'm sorry.

SCHERER: This is all a show, typical Communism line.

w: Mr. Scherer, if you are going to abuse me, I'll just get up and leave.

CHAIR.: All right.

w: If you will treat me and other witnesses with courtesy, I'll give you courteous answers, but if you browbeat me I'm not going to give you courteous answers.

A: Mr. Chairman, I respectfully suggest that the witness now be ordered and directed to answer the question.

CHAIR.: I direct you to answer the question. You know the rules. Namely, are you now a member of the Communist Party?

w: Now, I am not going to answer that question, and I want to tell you why. Am I mistaken, Mr. Ahrens, in my assumption that you had the honor of having something to do with the drafting of the so-called Communist Control Act in 1954?

A: Mr. Chairman, I respectfully suggest that the witness again be ordered and directed to answer the question.

SCHERER: Just a minute, just a minute, Mr. Chairman, I move that this witness be dismissed, that he be ejected from this room for complete and utter contempt of a committee of Congress. As I said before, I am ashamed that he is a member of the bar.

CHAIR.: You still have half a minute left—I said two, so you have half a minute to answer it on constitutional grounds.

W: In the Communist Control Act of 1954 there is a definition of a Communist—Mr. Willis, may—would you please listen?

VOICE: I renew my motion.

CHAIR.: All right, I so order. Will you escort the gentleman out?

COUNSEL: Do I understand that he is now excused from this subpoena? I want to get a straight legal record, Mr. Chairman. I think we are entitled to it. Is he excused from the subpoena, Mr. Chairman? May I inquire on the record?

DALE MINOR: Mr. Edises is now being escorted out of the hearing chambers.

CHAIR.: Yes, he is excused.

COUNSEL: He is excused. Thank you very much.

*　　*　　*

NARRATOR: The repercussions, legal and nonlegal, of the San Francisco hearings of the House Subcommittee on Un-American Activities have been widely felt. And the questions with which we began continue to be asked. What are the purposes of this committee? Were those purposes served by the San Francisco hearings?

3

Trees and Mountains
Interview with Ella Young

Ella Young's conversation with Wallace Hamilton, Public Affairs Director of KPFA, was perhaps one of the most often requested broadcasts in the early years of Pacifica. Poet and author, Ella Young came to the United States from her native Ireland to lecture at the University of California on Celtic mythology and Gaelic literature. In Dublin she had been involved in the Abbey Theatre, and in the Irish cause. Friend of William Butler Yeats, Maud Gonne, AE (George William Russell), and others in Ireland, Ella Young continued to be close to such poets and artists in America as Elinor Wylie, William Rose Benét, Van Wyck Brooks, and Robinson Jeffers.

Describing America in her book, Flowering Dusk, *Ella Young had written, "This country is a lioness, a tawny, alert, passionate, austere, beautiful, splendid—perhaps terrible—thing." This is how she described her relation to "Trees and Mountains."*

ELLA YOUNG: Do you know Robinson Jeffers' "The Tower Beyond Tragedy"? You ought to. If you are making yourself acquainted with it, turn to the great speech of Orestes: he has wandered out, half mad, and when he comes in there is a magnificent speech where he says that now he cares nothing for the kingdom because he has touched something greater; he has reached to a comradeship with the earth. Robinson Jeffers, who has himself reached to a comradeship with the earth, has put down in English words a most magnificent description of the great ecstasy of the union with the earth.

An English writer—Richard Jefferies—wrote a story some time ago. The entire story is taken up with an account of how he lay on an English mountain. Suddenly he felt the beating of the heart of the mountain and he understood that he was part of it and in touch with it.

The Indians in this country knew about that, long ago. All the Pueblo Indians are protected by a Mesa—a sacred mountain. They also have a sacred lake because of its being the emblem of the goddess. Then, they worship the sun. The sun is born of the dawn goddess—the earth—and the Great Maker of the earth. By dint of this fellowship, the Indians can get weather any time that they like it. They can also get crops that are not eaten up by pests. They can sit in houses with windows without any glass and not a single fly comes in. In all the houses in which whites live there are all kinds of flytraps and fly screens, millions of dead flies fall in heaps every day but still the flies are there.

I have seen in flats of the Santo Domingo Indians, pieces of cord stretched about with meat drying and not a single fly on any of the deer meat. These are some of the things that accrue to you if you make a fellowship with nature. On the other hand, you can never talk about the conquest of nature. You can never go out and drag a wildflower up by the roots, and you can never throw cigarettes about and you can never smash up things. If you do, nature doesn't help us when we get stranded someplace.

I've known people in the Vedic Islands to walk through a rainstorm and come out without a single drop of water on them. The Chinese also said that their saints could do the same thing. Saint, in their world, meant someone who had made contact with the nature gods. Saint in the Christian world also means someone who has made contact with the Ages and with God—

this corresponds to the nature gods. Christian gods could also walk through rain if they wanted to—or walk through fire.

HAMILTON: What do you think the particular spirits are that inhabit a mountain?

ELLA YOUNG: To begin with, the mountain is alive. And to go back further than that, the earth is alive. The earth is a great living thing and is greater than we are. The earth has many things that we haven't, but we haven't got anything that the earth hasn't got. If you will go out into the desert, you will see how nature has designed trees that follow the curve of the hills, and she has planted them exactly where you, if you were a landscape gardener, would have planted them.

Then let us see how nature has fashioned sculpture: look at her shells. Look at the way she has carved the mountains.

HAMILTON: Would you say that a mountain that has a spirit in it can help? Perhaps as it helps the Indians?

ELLA YOUNG: Oh yes. You can make contact with the earth.

HAMILTON: How do you do that?

ELLA YOUNG: The only magic is through love. To begin with you'd have to get away from the idea that we can talk with the earth. One of the great virtues in occultism is humility. All the temples that have been made for initiations have very low, narrow passages to symbolize the fact that you are to throw away your human arrogance and pride—your human greed. You must approach, not to conquer but to be taught, to be helped.

HAMILTON: Do you think you can be taught by a mountain?

ELLA YOUNG: I think there are many white people who want to approach mountains in that way—the way the Indians do. And they are approaching them. The thing that you can most easily get from a mountain would be a response, but that would depend on how sensitive you are, so you would feel the response of the mountain if the mountain sent you one.

I think the very thing to begin with would be a tree: if there is some tree that you love particularly, you could get into the habit of saying a greeting to it every time you pass. Don't do it with the idea that you want to get a response—just do it with the idea that you love the tree. Some day you will get that response. I remember once that I passed a tree and I forgot to send a greeting and the tree said to me, "Why are you going past without a greeting?"

HAMILTON: What would you say to a tree in the morning? Would you bid it a good morning?

ELLA YOUNG: You could say that mentally. You could also say a lot of complimentary things. In fact, if I could make a poem, I'd come and say it to that tree.

You see, I can talk to some of the big cats, and one time I wanted to make the acquaintance of an ocelot. The ocelot was in the Dublin Zoo, and people almost never saw the ocelot because he had a house high up in his cage and he kept himself inside that house. In the Dublin Zoo that place would be very empty if you went on a day that you paid. So I paid because I wanted to see the ocelot. I went close to the cage and I began, "Glorious One, Magnificent One, Magnificent Golden Eyed Lord of the Forest, Divine One, show yourself." I was saying this mentally. After awhile the ocelot put his head out. "Who is calling me?" he said. Then he saw me. "Just one of those humans," he remarked. And he retreated. I began again. This time I made a little poem for him and he came out again. Then he knew. He said, "I'd like to sniff your fingers." I told him to come on and I held out my fingers. He came down to the bars to sniff my fingers. After that the ocelot began to purr. Then he leaned up against the bars so I could stroke him. After that, every time I came there, he came down. As soon as I left, he went up to his house again.

One time I had said goodbye to him and he had gone up into his house, then I remembered there were some little birds I wanted to talk to. I was talking to them when the ocelot came out and said, "Are you going to stay? If you are going to stay I'll come down." I said (mentally, of course), "No, I'm not going to stay." And the ocelot went back.

It might be easier to talk to animals, but you can talk to trees and the mountains; you can talk to the earth. You must make a

sort of a roadway to them, and you make it by sending out love.
If you have sufficient love, you can get a response very easily. It
is very easy to get a response from a tree.

HAMILTON: What happens when you try to prune a tree?

ELLA YOUNG: You must tell the tree that you are trying to help it.
And you shouldn't go in and slash and break a tree. Say a little
Round to it and help it. In old England when the fruits were
beginning in the orchards, they went out and sang songs to the
trees and they poured out libations of ale to them. That kind of
friendship with nature is very old—it was one of the first religions.

HAMILTON: What sort of things does a tree talk back to you after
you open that line of communication?

ELLA YOUNG: That tree I was telling you about says words to me,
but some trees—the Redwoods particularly—send out a lovely
feeling. And then while you were looking at the Redwood tree
(and you had friends among the earth spirits), sunlight would
come and perhaps some golden leaves would fall. But you see,
you must be quite content that you love the thing without asking for anything because then you fall into the trap of asking
for phenomena. You just have to be content to know that you
love that tree, and you know it is alive and you want to come
closer to it.

HAMILTON: Are there some trees you can't love—who have perverse spirits?

ELLA YOUNG: If you can't love them, then you let them alone. You
always begin with the things you can love. Unfortunately we
are told that you have to love all humanity. Nobody loves all
humanity. He doesn't love his neighbor when that neighbor is
putting on some kind of a program that he hates. I don't think
he is obliged to love his neighbor. But the Great Brotherhood—
the one brotherhood that you could have—is with the animals,
the angels, the stones, the trees, all the good human beings, the
things that you could love. If you don't like toads, then you
needn't worry about making friends with toads.

HAMILTON: It would seem rather difficult to establish a personal relationship with a mountain.

ELLA YOUNG: Oh yes, you can, but it takes quite a long while. A mountain like Shasta might be easier. I spent a whole year greeting a mountain five or six times a day before it gave any response at all. But if a mountain does give a response, you could ask it for the sort of thing a mountain might give you. If, for instance, you had only one day to visit that mountain, you could ask the mountain to give you fine weather. That would give you an opportunity to come closer to the mountain.

HAMILTON: And when you have come closer to the mountain, what does the mountain say to you?

ELLA YOUNG: The fact of the matter is that you don't go to the mountain for something it can say to you. What the mountain gives to you is something beyond intellect. You know we have the ordinary consciousness, the subconsciousness, and the transcendent consciousness—that is where the mountain touches you. If you can really make contact with the mountain, then suddenly everything changes, you could see colors and that sort of thing. What you would get would be a sense of oneness with the mountain. And a sense that you and the mountain are both divinities.

HAMILTON: Does it require that you climb the mountain?

ELLA YOUNG: No, all you need is to think of the mountain. You could do a lot of greeting to a special mountain without being there at all, because both time and space are irrelevant to thought.

HAMILTON: Are there some mountains that are particularly important? Are there some that are inhabited by spirits that are healthy—happy? Are there others whose spirits are perhaps evil?

ELLA YOUNG: No, I don't think there are any mountains that are evil. The only parts of the earth that are evil are the parts where human beings have desecrated it. There are no evil spirits in the world—I have never come in touch with any.

HAMILTON: A mountain like Lassen—I'm wondering about Lassen.

ELLA YOUNG: Yes, I know Lassen. I made contact chiefly with a beautiful forest and trees that are at Lassen. I was sort of camping out in a sleeping bag in Lassen. I'm very fond of Lassen, but I never make a special contact with Lassen; I have more with Shasta and particularly with Mount Taylor. When I was passing that, coming into California, that mountain reached out and gave me a greeting. A wonderful mountain!

HAMILTON: How about Mount Tamalpais?

ELLA YOUNG: Yes, one can easily make contact with Tamalpais. Mount Diablo is another. Between the two is a path. When I was there I used to hear the fairy music. There is a great and marvelous music that many Americans hear and that many Irish hear. It is orchestral. The fairy music is very beautiful music, but it varies so much that I cannot attempt to give any kind of description, but it can be heard in America and I heard some of it when I was staying at Sausalito. It is some orchestral music like nothing you've ever heard before in your life. There are far more instruments in it than in an ordinary orchestra. There are violins and there are great bells. There are great voices in it. It has a tremendous kind of litany in it; it has a kind of a beat in it. Sometimes there is a little song that sounds sort of like it was played on a flute. And if you are in a magical place and are receptive to it, it is simply everywhere.

HAMILTON: Are there magic places around here?

ELLA YOUNG: There are magic places everywhere. Every now and then there is a psychic fountain coming up—a psychic fountain of energy and that is a magic place. The old Druids were capable of recognizing those places and they very often put their temples on those places because of what came out of the earth. I have found some of those places in Ireland. In California there are so many houses being built that I wouldn't be surprised if they have covered all the places up and the fountains have gone away. But I think Tamalpais still has it.

I found a curious thing—the part of Ireland that I think the most magical is the Giant's Causeway. I used to go there and that always gave me a very personal greeting. On one occasion I went there and found the whole place spread out with people; they were from England and were the kind who would generally go to Coney Island. They weren't doing anything particularly—just singing and dancing around. I was furious. I just felt that if I had sufficient power I'd wither them all up. When I got a bit away from the Causeway, the Causeway said to me, "But I wanted them to come." Then I was sure I saw that these people could have done something that would have amused them a bit more and would have cost them a lot less. There was something stirring in them that made them want to come to this Causeway—for it was a very, very sacred place. And that sacred place wanted them. That sacred place wants anyone who wants to make friends with it and it is very gracious. Maybe it sees more in those people than I did.

HAMILTON: How about Stonehenge?

ELLA YOUNG: No, I've never been there, but that must be a very sacred place. You know that some of the stones there were brought from a very great distance—nobody knows how they got there. Another sacred place in Britain is Avalon. That has a zodiac carved out of the earth. You'd have to be up in an airplane to see it, but it is there.

Then there was the House of Angus—that was a temple of initiation and was built on a great flare. Always when we went to it, you could feel this fountain coming up. People who were not very psychic would say, "Why, the sun has come out!" And they would feel so happy.

When you go into the Doon of Angus—and you can see that it is the house of a god and it is connected with Mannanon—you go through a narrow passage and then you come into the great central room which is built of great blocks of stone and goes up to a point. In this room there is one great standing stone. When they moved it, they found a great basin of stone underneath it. Then there are three little side chapels. In the old days this is the place where the ancient Druids offered up their human sacrifices. Those of us in Ireland who went on pilgrimages there regarded it as a temple. All the old temples were only temples of initiation. They were places where someone who was to get the "great initiation" went to meditate and prepare for that initiation.

One day I went there by myself and I bribed the custodian to stay away with the candles, and to lock the place. I sat down just inside and there was a kind of dusk because there is no place to let in the light. I sat down and I was meditating; it must have been the right time of the year for suddenly light began to come in like water—it flowed in like waves and concentrated itself on the great monolith which turned into a shaft of light. The whole place always gave me the happiest feeling. But that's all gone now. . . .

I was talking to the Jefferies'—they loved to go to Ireland. And I asked them if they had been to the Doon of Angus. They said, yes they had, and I asked them hadn't they felt that marvelous fountain. And they said, no, they hadn't felt it. A very strange thing happened to them when they were there—the custodians said that five or six days before they were there, they heard a tremendous sound just as if the place fell to pieces in the night. They were afraid to go out. But in the morning they went out and they expected to see that a great part of it had fallen—but nothing had fallen—only the divinity had gone.

HAMILTON: Would you say there are some places in California, if they had been lived in as long as Ireland, could also be called holy places?

ELLA YOUNG: It isn't the fact of being lived in—it's the fact that the nature spirits are there. California is the most magical country that I've ever seen, outside of Ireland. This is the most tremendous thing: the desert is living, the lakes are living, the mountains are living. Great archangels you would call them if you saw them.

HAMILTON: How about Yosemite?

ELLA YOUNG: Well, of course, I never got in touch with anything there except the trees. If you want to get in touch with anything there, you'd have to be by yourself and for a considerable time. You could condition yourself in advance if you knew you were going to a place by sending greetings morning and evening—all the time sending greetings. Distance doesn't make any difference. Greetings can reach you from the other end of the world. When you go to the mountain you could say that you just had so many days, and then you could just be content with whatever you could get from the mountain. Sleep as close as you can to the mountain, in a sleeping bag—and just let yourself relax. The tenser you are the less you will get for a message from the mountain. Just lie down and see what happens.

4
___

For Independence
Day, 1962
by William O. Douglas

*What follows is edited from a talk given by Justice Douglas at the
University of Judaism, Los Angeles, July 1, 1962, and broadcast
by Pacifica stations.*

We of the West—powerful in ideas as well as in armed forces—
are somewhat crippled. Our strength is sapped not by subversion
but by fears and prejudices. These include the racial problem, the
growing insecurity of our people, the trend to conformity, and to
conservatism, the domination by the Pentagon and the CIA, and
the decline of the great debate. As a result we walk mostly alone.

There is a long history behind this decline in American prestige that started after World War II ended.

The Civil War was preceded by a profound debate about a
matter with which the underdeveloped nations are well acquainted. Our debate concerned the meaning of the Declaration
of Independence and its ringing words, "We hold these truths to
be self-evident, that all men are created equal, that they are en-
dowed by their creator with certain inalienable rights, that among
these are life, liberty, and the pursuit of happiness."

It took the Civil War and three constitutional amendments to seal the idea of equality into our constitutional fabric. In spite of these amendments, racial discrimination fastened itself onto our communities, north as well as south. Americans of African and even of Mexican ancestry were segregated into separate schools. Restrictive covenants became a way of life; and in spite of federal financing of housing that has extended into the billions, those covenants are firmly rooted in most communities. Colored people are still excluded from juries and from voting lists.

Racial discrimination appeared even in governmental employment. State laws emerged, aimed at the practice; and the Forties and Fifties saw progress. Yet Americans do not today speak in one voice. Racial discrimination is still a force for disunity. Many trade unions—either by reason of a constitutional provision in a charter or by reason of habit and practice—still bar Negroes. The teachings of the Declaration of Independence are not always remembered.

The racial problem is only one of several that saps our strength. Automation promises to make the machine more dominant over man than ever before. With that domination comes insecurity at the prospect of unemployment. Idleness, even when the idle people are paid, is a corrosive influence. There is therapy in work; it creates joy and a sense of fulfillment. A nation of idle people is a weak nation though everyone receives a handsome pension.

This problem of the domination of the machine over man is not a new one. The mood of the fifty years preceding 1861 is often referred to wistfully as the romantic age. Yet there were then shaping up voices of discontent who were to be heard for a century. A working men's meeting of September 26, 1829 (as related by Mark and Schwaab in *The Faith of Our Fathers*) complained that there was as yet "no system of education . . . for the poor," that monopolies strengthened "the aristocracy" and reduced "the power of the farmer, mechanic and labourer," that "half of society are the slaves of etiquette and the other of excessive labour," and that the "producers of wealth are poor and dependent, whilst the consumers are rich and powerful."

The gilded age that followed the Civil War proved that those complaints were based on fact. That gilded age was a *laissez-faire* period, when individualism was rampant and human rights were made secondary to property rights. During the thirty-odd years of the last century and the first decades of the present one, no almanac of liberty would record many victories of human rights over the machine. The legal dimensions of the problem have greatly changed but the central issue remains. Who will own the machines that supplant men? How will men find "work" that is so vital to human welfare?

The Civil Service that was to save government from the "spoils" system has produced vast bureaucracies that are heavy-footed and under watchful eyes. The loyalty-security programs governing employees now reach into the private sector. All who do business with the government need security clearance. The engineer who has given his best years to reach a $15,000 salary loses everything if he is branded a poor security risk—his professional standing and his livelihood as well.

Big corporations, like big government and big unions, breed noncontroversial men and women. At the managerial, engineering, or administrative level there may be debate and controversy. But on the larger public issues of the day, the voices of employees are largely mute. The commercialism of television and radio has made like change. Sponsors do not want their products identified with controversial programs nor with controversial commentators. There has been such a deadening effect of radio and television on the American mind that we may have reached a point where men and women who will sponsor unorthodox points of view must be subsidized by foundations.

The dialogue that has characterized the free society has not disappeared from the American scene, though it has declined.

We are passing through momentous times where no debate takes place even on crucial issues. Why has silence overtaken us? Why has the pattern of no discussion reached into atomic testing, disarmament, Berlin, and other issues that involve the problems of survival or extinction? Is foreign policy—the key to life and death for all forms of life in this nuclear age—beyond the bounds of debate? If so, how can we, the people, ever free ourselves from military domination and assert our sovereign civilian prerogative over all affairs of state—over war as well as over peace?

A survey of newspapers from coast to coast shows the low estate of dialogue on domestic as well as foreign issues. Money-makers have taken over the press. They want readers and advertisers; and so they cater to the low common denominator in the populace. To that fact must be added the further one that the owners are largely conservative. The result is a press which with few exceptions gives no true account of forces at work in the world. Those who live in the average American town have no chance of getting an accurate measure of the world problem. Ignorance alone is tragedy enough. Further tragedy lies in the fact that the people of the United States—the ones who could, if awakened, take up the challenge of the cold war and win it—are largely immobilized. Fears of Communism are subtly transformed into fears of the unorthodox.

The affluent society is also responsible. Those who live in ease are not the ones to go in search of the Holy Grail. Yet more recruits are needed today for our modern crusades than ever before. Enterprise that is wholly or largely dependent on government contracts is not "free" in the historic sense of the word. Competition that developed resourcefulness and ingenuity, competition that released energies from thousands of little springs the country over has disappeared from large areas of our society. There is competition for government contracts. But spoonfed business does not have the daring and ingenuity of free enterprise.

The growth of bigness has had crippling effects. A nation of independent businessmen has become a nation of clerks. Those who owned and ran the lumber mill had a community function to perform, as well as a business function. They were alive to community needs and they contributed to the solution of community problems. When that lumber company was swallowed up by a giant, control over it was transferred to an office in a skyscraper in New York City. The town that was dependent on the lumber mill became only a statistic, not a congregation of people. In the total-ity of the corporate empire it might be better to close the mill. People will parade and protest; but the men in the faraway sky-scraper do not hear them.

Big business, big government, big unions—each has helped erase some of the qualities of individuality from Americans. As the individual has become more and more submerged, his voice is more indistinct.

The Pentagon that gets roughly forty-five billion a year also makes for conformity. Through a thousand influences that reach us since World War II, we are conditioned to the idea that the Pentagon has the answer to Communism; and for far too many years we have rested secure in that belief. Containment of Com-munism by military programs became a new Maginot Line. Each of us became a military expert of a kind. What islands should we surrender? Should not the East Berlin wall be demolished? While the Marshall Plan worked well in Europe, it was not suited to the underdeveloped areas. We overlooked the fact that our foreign aid program was used not to re-establish viable democratic socie-ties but to shore up old feudal regimes. Dollars and guns were our security.

People who see a world packed with Communists or who will make no pacts with them are more and more ready to accept the security of military solutions.

The danger of the impact of this psychology on us was sum-marized by Eisenhower in his farewell address to the nation.

> In the councils of Government, we must guard against the acquisition of unwarranted influence, whether sought or unsought, by the military-industrial complex. The potential for the disastrous rise of misplaced power exists and will per-sist.
>
> We must never let the weight of this combination en-danger our liberties or democratic processes. We should take nothing for granted. Only an alert and knowledgeable citi-zenry can compel the proper meshing of the huge industrial and military machinery of defense with our peaceful meth-

ods and goals, so that security and liberty may prosper together.

The tie-in between our military and our industry is no casual thing. In a few communities three out of four or even five out of six families are dependent directly or indirectly on Pentagon *largesse*. What would happen in city after city if real disarmament was announced tomorrow? Transferring our economy from a military to a consumer regime would present difficulties comparable to taking a human being off drugs. Would the military stand idly by and watch their bureaucracy and their power wither?

The influence of the Pentagon abroad is destructive of the democratic ideal. It has almost always been identified with kings or feudal overlords whose pretenses of reform have been hollow.

Thanks largely to the Pentagon, Thailand has lost all the momentum of her 1932 revolution and has reverted back to the kind of dictatorship she knew in the fifteenth century. The truth is that the Pentagon feels much more at home in Saudi Arabia or South Korea or Taiwan than in places like Israel and India where there is a true political renaissance underway.

A strong internal police is necessary in any country. Police forces are especially necessary in fragile nations. But arming the feudal overlords in the manner we have done is something else. Asia, Africa, and Latin America have never known democracy or liberty or freedom. Those terms are empty and hollow. A few men or a few families own the country: the rest are serfs. There are few if any schools; few if any doctors; few if any opportunities to escape the slavery of ignorance, illiteracy, and disease. The jeeps of the Pentagon that roar through those villages bring no message of hope. The regimes we arm and support with lavish funds usually have no program of reform. Due largely to the Pentagon influence our heroes seem to be the dictators. That is one reason why the tides of history are running against us.

At home the military is more and more implicated in policymaking. Each branch of the armed forces has its own State Department.

The independence of nations is but one sign of ferment in the world. No matter what the Pentagon says, the feudal societies are doomed. Overseas the peoples' protests are being heard more and more. Hunger, disease, illiteracy, exploitation, and misgovernment—these are the enemies. The peoples of the world are going to be done with them. Revolution after revolution is going to be launched. Are we to credit every revolution to the Communists? Is every overseas reformer to be suspect?

Demands for reform and revolution are expressions of the world's unrest. The Pentagon and the CIA overseas search out men who temporarily crush the dissidents. But popular unrest is so deep that attempts to stamp it out only strengthen the Communists. The problem is not to quell the revolutionaries. It is to supply and support democratic *cadres* who will direct the reforms and manage the turbulent days ahead.

This requires a vast reorientation. We must be prepared to send to the blighted areas tens of thousands of teachers who will establish teacher-training schools. These teachers must speak the local language and be prepared to stay abroad for years.

We must have brigades of doctors and nurses overseas to help establish medical schools, nurse-training schools, first-aid centers, and hospitals.

Tens of thousands are needed at the agricultural level. The idea of a cooperative is as unfamiliar to the villages of Asia, Africa, and Latin America as Einstein's formula is to most of us. Yet cooperatives are the answer to many problems. Where are the men who can speak the languages of the world and who will make up our teams of teachers to show overseas villages how to farm and manage cooperatively?

Engineers and business managers are also needed. The Congo alone needs ten thousand. The enterprises established in the underdeveloped nations will be largely socialistic. Free enterprise that has served us so well is not a revolutionary tool in underdeveloped nations. It develops the sweatshop in immature societies; and sweatshops are new seedbeds of discontent.

Some of the new nations do not even have plumbers, let

alone architects of the free society. Technicians as well as political scientists must be trained. Many foreign students are being trained here, in Europe, in Israel, in Australia, and New Zealand.

Most of them however must be trained in their own nation. Shipping them overseas is a costly enterprise. Moreover those who study abroad must learn another language. Sending our teachers to overseas schools and institutes can educate hundreds where only dozens can be taught here.

In short we must be prepared to export hundreds of experts in task forces who speak the local language and who can show hungry and illiterate yet eager people how to lay the foundations of a free society.

The Communist bloc has detailed blueprints of a new society for each underdeveloped nation. These plans do not call merely for the assassination and execution of the feudal overlords and the democrats. Their project starts there; but it moves on to detailed plans touching every aspect of a society—from farming to medicine, from press censorship to music and dancing.

We have developed exportable houses that anyone who can read an instruction book can assemble. The Soviet bloc however has an exportable society with tens of thousands of experts, each speaking the local language, ready for overseas work. That is the measure of our competition—now that war has become obsolete.

Where are our troops for this kind of political contest?

If we were in the mood for this kind of adventure, we would have student advisers in all our high schools and colleges creating interest and curiosity among students and steering them into even the exotic languages such as Telugu, Tamil, and Mongolian. Yet over half of our high schools offer no foreign language. Of the leading eighty-three world languages we are prepared in a degree to teach some fifty. The rest however are not yet known to us.

This undertaking—the transformation of primitive pastoral societies to modern ones—is the nub of the cold war. These underdeveloped nations constitute the battleground. It is there that the contest will be won or lost. For that contest turns on the political balance in the world.

To help these new nations lay the foundations of a free society requires some money. But people and ideas are even more important.

Has the American sense of adventure, the American experimental attitude been dulled by the affluent society? Will a people who practice discrimination at home be eager evangelists of equality abroad? Are we sufficiently tolerant to permit our people and our aid to construct socialist societies in other nations? Is free enterprise, now greatly transformed in this country and only a shadow of its original form, still such a powerful symbol as to immobilize us from unorthodox work abroad? Is the orthodoxy that has caused the left to disappear at home and that has resulted in a polarization of political thought at the center and to the right going to paralyze us for revolutionary deeds abroad? Can we make "revolution" a respectable word or have we given the Communists a monopoly on it?

These are soul-searching questions concerning America that are as yet unanswered. There can be no doubt that the cold war would be easily won if we released abroad our technical skills, our humanitarian impulses, and the idealism of the Declaration of Independence. Are we so wedded to orthodoxy and the ease of the affluent society that we will lose by sheer default?

If the mood of this day reflected the spirit of the Declaration of Independence, the renaissance would have arrived. Then the ideas of equality would energize us and result in an outpouring of talents for work overseas in villages where ignorance, poverty, and filth pile high. Then the idea of "the consent of the governed" would become a principle worthy of honor in the most backward nation. It would take fire at home and bring into all phases of our foreign policy a concern for people rather than for power blocs and military bases. If the Jeffersonian ideas in the Declaration possessed us, revolution would be our slogan—revolution against feudal regimes as well as revolution against colonial powers. The problem of exporting revolution is extremely complicated. It requires dedicated democratic *cadres* who are native to the society being reorganized. It necessitates great flexibility in the political and economic patterns which are designed for the new nations. An attempt to remake a nation in the image of America might well be disastrous. For what was needed for the genius of our people might be ill-suited for others. Moreover the export of our institutions without the use of vast controls might do more harm than good.

Once the peoples of the world feel the force of the free society and see that it is built on the creed of liberty and equality, democracy can become the most contagious influence on all the continents.

5

Meetings with Remarkable Men
by G. I. Gurdjieff

*A Conversation on the book, by Professor
Roy Finch of Sarah Lawrence College,
Lord Pentland, and Lawrence Morris*

ROY FINCH: We are discussing today a book which has been read
for more than thirty years by people in different parts of the
world, but is only now being published for the first time in English. This book is entitled *Meetings with Remarkable Men*, and
it is by one of the most fascinating and remarkable men of our
century, G. I. Gurdjieff.

The general public has heard little of Gurdjieff—perhaps has
not even heard his name, but his ideas and teachings have had a
profound influence. He was born in 1877 in the Armenian city
of Alexandropol, near the Turkish-Russian border. His life was
spent in Asia, Russia, and France, although he traveled everywhere. He visited the United States several times. He died in
1949.

To discuss this long-awaited book, we have with us two men
who have had a long familiarity with these ideas: Lord Pentland, who is connected with a New York engineering firm, and
Lawrence Morris, a former foreign service officer in Washing-

ton. I wonder, Lord Pentland, if you would begin the discussion by telling us what the nature of this book is? Could you describe it to us?

LORD PENTLAND: By birth Gurdjieff was a Greek from Asia Minor. In his youth, about which nothing is known except what he himself wrote down in this book, he engaged himself on this series of journeys into the remotest regions of central Asia, where so many of the most ancient civilizations have had their source. In later years he lived chiefly in Paris, where he had immense influence as a teacher and writer about the ideas which he found there in Asia and which he had put together into a system intelligible to the West. It is a system of knowledge about man, and man's search for a real understanding of his situation on this planet. This is his second book, published fourteen years after his first. The form of the book, as Gurdjieff says in the Introduction, is from questions which were frequently put to him about his own personal life and these travels that he made, and particularly the question, "What remarkable men have you met?" To this, the book responds in a series of stories, each bearing as its title the name of one of the men he knew, and whose influence had left its mark on his whole life.

Gurdjieff calls them all remarkable, not because they are well-known people—quite the contrary, by ordinary standards they are average, with the average failings, and none of them has ever been heard of before or since. But they had the remarkable human quality, in their various walks of life, of not being satisfied with the answers that are handed out. They called themselves the community of Truth Seekers. Gurdjieff was the most remarkable of them all—an extraordinary man, as anybody who has read his first book will agree. These stories are all told very simply, with an oriental sort of feeling, which, if it's not an absurd comparison, takes one back to Omar Khayyam or the *Arabian Nights*. In a way, you could say this book is about Everyman's search.

FINCH: This is a man who strikes one as almost a legendary or mythical kind of figure. It's very hard to get a sense of factuality about this. You said that this is the only information that we have about his early life—that is, what is given in this book. I wonder whether you would call this an autobiography, Mr. Morris?

LAWRENCE MORRIS: It is, first of all, an autobiography—an autobiography in form, and a very human autobiography in the stories it tells. You find Gurdjieff, in fact, as a young man, before the great journeys of discovery that took him into central Asia, engaged in all sorts of exploits—from diving for coins thrown from the decks of ships at Constantinople to working as a bootblack in Rome. He was already traveling in search of knowledge, and he was completely unembarrassed by how he earned the necessary cash. In *Meetings with Remarkable Men* he is still unembarrassed, and it is this freedom from concern that gives the book its ring of inner truth. I found something very touching in the simplicity with which he speaks of his terror at walking across a narrow, swinging bridge without any handrails at all, over a gorge in the mountains of Turkestan, so deep that looking down into it was like looking down from the top of the Eiffel Tower—only more so. Still, in spite of what I've just said, it would be almost true to say that the important part of this autobiography lies between the lines. There is something baffling here. In reading you feel, in spite of finding all the complexities and absurdities that make up life at home, that somehow you have entered into a different world. After a while you say, "Where am I? What makes it seem so different?" And you begin to notice that all the familiar values you are used to applying to men and events are absent from this book. For our Western civilization is preoccupied with techniques for exercising power, both over our physical environment and over other human beings, and its values express these external concerns.

For Gurdjieff the only purpose in life that made sense was to explore, not central Asia but man's possibilities for self-development. By that he didn't mean some ethereal flower of the spirit. For him, physical activity and feeling and mind all had to develop simultaneously before, in any of us, there would be something substantial enough to contribute to this essential aim. This aim was the object of his own passionate search, a life-long search, and the subject of his teachings.

Much of this the reader may realize only some time after he lays the book aside. As Gurdjieff says in the Introduction, he has become adroit in concealing his serious thoughts under an enticing outer form.

FINCH: Certainly it is true that people who come on this book without any previous acquaintance with this man, or with his previous book, are going to be startled by the *Arabian Nights'* atmosphere of the book, and are going to wonder, as you say, what is this strange new world that we are coming into here. They may find that this world is rather impenetrable—it may seem to them that it is going to be impossible to understand anything at all about the book. Perhaps they will sense this element of strangeness and of different values; but I wonder if one of the reasons for this isn't the fact that the book doesn't talk about these ideas as if they were the private invention of Gurdjieff himself. In other words he isn't presenting his own philosophical system or developing a set of original thoughts of his own—in that sense he is not like so many of our supremely individualistic thinkers, but there is rather a different flavor here, as if he is uncovering something which has a kind of universal character which exists independently of him, and which he, somehow, stumbled upon.

One of the most interesting things about the book is the passionate quality of this search—the fact that this man persists—keeps looking—keeps traveling, as it were. One has to regard it, I suppose, on that level, as a kind of a spiritual pilgrimage as well as a factual account.

MORRIS: I am very glad that this aspect of the book has come up, because it is really essential. Now, you used the expression "stumbled upon." I think it's very seldom that what you can think of as laws—laws of nature, laws of man—are stumbled upon unless there has been a great deal of attention in that direction. You'll remember that the history of science shows men preoccupied for a long time with a question before they come to—not an invention, but a discovery. This book itself bears witness to the fact that it is not accidental that Gurdjieff stumbled upon any knowledge. He began when he was still a boy, finding himself baffled by events which he saw in his own life. He went to his teachers and they couldn't explain what had happened. He went to the library and read everything he could get his hands on. He still found questions to which the orthodox teaching of the world gave him no answer. He began to travel; he began to hunt for people who also had given thought. We find him going into the Near East—going into Egypt, going into central Asia, and moving progressively from his friends and first teachers to older men—to questioning the ancient religions, and finally feeling that there had at one time been a body of knowledge which was lost, but of which there were echoes in legends and ancient myths.

FINCH: You are suggesting that in very very ancient legends and myths there may be some truths which the modern world tends to overlook in its concern for the latest scientific discoveries. Gurdjieff felt this himself very strongly. As I recall, at one place in the book he says this in so many words; he speaks of the enormous significance buried in ancient legends—going back to the Sumerians, and so on. Now, in what way does this interest of his differ from the modern interest in mythology, where this is seen as a kind of psychological repository of interesting ideas which the ancient world had to express in this poetic form because they were not able to put it in the terms of modern science?

PENTLAND: Here you raise an enormously interesting question. Let's face it: this book is listed by the publishers as "occult," and that's a word that will put a lot of people off. I think we've got to ask ourselves, what is *occult*—what is beyond one's understanding? What is it that modern culture, even with the great importance and interest it gives to myth and ancient knowledge, is missing?

I think it means that there are a great many things which we pay lip-service to in modern culture, which in actual fact we evade.

MORRIS: May I take up what you were saying in answer to Professor Finch's question about where the difference lies between Gurdjieff's interest in ancient legends and the current and very common interest . . . everybody talks about ancient myths and everybody reads them. And yet, you feel very quickly when you come into the atmosphere of Gurdjieff's handling of them that here is something different. I was wondering, as you were talking, how, in a short form, we might express that difference. It seems to me that Gurdjieff was looking in these myths for the expression, in poetic form if you wish, of certain laws which hold for all men and which correspond to something beyond man. If these myths express a law, no matter how factually fantastic they are, they must contain a permanent truth. If you will compare the psychologist's use of myths, you find that everything that exists in psychology is, for him, true in his peculiar sense—that is, it is psychologically true—which is something less than the truth Gurdjieff was looking for.

In *Meetings with Remarkable Men*, we see Gurdjieff first coming to his point of view in the chapter about his father who, he says, exerted the strongest influence on his life of any human being. The picture we are given of his father is a very moving one. This man seems almost to have come out of some very early world. He is so simple, so natural, so human. Not only is this so in his own life; he is also a great depository of legend and myth which had come down under the shadow of Mount Ararat (where Gurdjieff lived as a little boy) from the days of the Sumerians—and, undoubtedly, from back before that. You remember, Gurdjieff tells in one amusing episode of how he lay all one night on a pile of shavings in his father's carpenter shop listening to a discussion between his father and the dean of the school there—who was also his first teacher—about the *Epic of Gilgamesh*, which had come down from Sumerian times. He heard it repeated so often that by the end of that night he knew it by heart. Many years later Gurdjieff came across a book in which he discovered that some of the early tablets had been discovered and translated, and he found this section of the *Epic* almost exactly as he had heard his father recite it. And yet it had come down to his father through an oral tradition, not written tradition. It had been buried over three thousand years and had come out almost without change.

FINCH: Are you inclined to accept this story without skepticism as being literally true? Is it possible that Gurdjieff, who is a very complicated man, is simply pulling our leg a little by telling us that the story told to him by his father was the identical story found on the tablet, so the old tradition proved to be that accurate?

MORRIS: Of course, that thought went through my mind when I read the book. I have no way of proving that that isn't the explanation, but there is one thing which tells me that he is not pulling my leg at this point, and that is the character of his father. There is in the tone, in everything he says about his father, a note of truth.

FINCH: This raises the question that Lord Pentland made about the occult nature of the book. I'm sure all of us feel that it is much more than that—that somehow the book has a much wider significance. I want to bring out what it is that distinguishes it from many, many apparently similar books. Obviously this book is much more than that, and this man is a lot more than that. I'd like to hear from you gentlemen just what more there is in this book.

PENTLAND: One is tempted to quote from the book itself, but I don't think that is why it is important—not for any one particular passage. In a way, everything that the book says has been said before. But what has not been done before is the book as a whole—the complete organic picture of man's possible growth, particularly man's emotional growth. A new way of living for the sake of understanding life. I think many more people will be refreshed and entertained by reading the book than will get all the author intended. Unless, perhaps, an echo of this new way of living life—not for what one gets out of it, but for the sake of life itself. Every moment—every little thing—becomes a possible turning point and then when accident intervenes, it often serves a higher purpose. What Gurdjieff himself said was that for ordinary people whose faith in accepted ideas has been shaken, this book contains constructive material for building a new world. That is a large statement. The burden of finding out whether it's true or not depends upon the reader.

MORRIS: I think the idea of common sense is also one that we ought not to pass without saying something about it. For Gurdjieff something was common sense only when it made sense to all the different elements in a man—to the mind, the feelings, and also to the body, and unless it was common to all those things, it wasn't common sense. Just think, for instance, how often in life we do something because our mind tells us this is the sensible thing to do, and in doing it we find that we violate our feelings. Gurdjieff never lets one fall into that kind of wasteful error. You can't put the feelings aside—in fact, they are the basis of common sense. It has to grow out of them. And yet, in our modern civilization, we regard the feelings as, somehow, secondary citizens. We say, oh well, they are subjective, they are ephemeral, they are changeable, they don't matter: the thing that matters is the intellect, and what can be measured and weighed, etc. This has been true for some three hundred years—that we give a lesser reality to the emotions on the ground that they are subjective.

PENTLAND: It also has to be mentioned that the book has a great importance to those who knew Gurdjieff, but only through his first book, *Beelzebub*. Many young people, for instance, have been excited by Gurdjieff's merciless criticisms of modern civilization, and I think they'll find this book a mellowing, as well as an enlightening experience.

FINCH: In Gurdjieff's book, remarkable men are remarkable because of their spiritual qualities, not because they are powerful or notorious in the limelight.

PENTLAND: Yes, one could say that, but that would be narrowing it too much and removing it too much, in an ideal sense, from the practical. Each one of them is remarkable in a different sense, first of all. He points out how one of them taught himself to love work. He taught himself never to be lazy—that any effort, whatever kind, is work. And then in the very next chapter he speaks of Yelov who came to the conclusion that as his thoughts worked both day and night, he might as well make them do something useful, so he learned a lot of languages with them. He said that learning a language wouldn't do him any harm and someday it might be useful.

FINCH: What you are saying is that these men were able to do things—quite remarkable things such as not being lazy, learning languages, and not working always for a reward, and so on, and even acquiring quite technical abilities. But I think there is even something more than that, too. . . .

PENTLAND: Certainly, what makes them all remarkable is what you call the spiritual sense. . . .

MORRIS: You were not using the word "spiritual" in the sense that a spiritual man is often thought of today, as a somehow ineffectual, nice person, who doesn't do anything wrong, but who doesn't accomplish anything either.

FINCH: I should perhaps say, more wholly human—more fully developed as a human being.

PENTLAND: Yes, and they were remarkable for different reasons and also for the same reason; for different reasons on a practical plane, and for the same reason on what you might call a higher plane.

FINCH: What do you mean by "higher plane"?

PENTLAND: I mean by that, not that they reached anything higher, but that their search was maintained. That as they came to one difficulty after another, as they became more disillusioned, it only served not to make them tired or tedious, but to awaken a new interest—to reveal to them, so to speak, a new peak which is to be climbed. This, I think, comes nearer to what Gurdjieff meant by "remarkable."

MORRIS: You notice, too, that in their lives they could not be thought of as conventionally spiritual people—they had all the weaknesses, all the traits of ordinary human beings. They came to a dissatisfaction with all the standard answers and the determination to do whatever they could to try to find a truer understanding of life and a development of themselves. What I wish to stress is that this is not some little special group but that these are the experiences of Everyman.

FINCH: I think there is another thing that probably needs to be said: we've been talking about the book and we've said what it contains, and we've said a few things about Gurdjieff himself. Now, I'm sure many of our listeners will be wondering what these teachings are.

MORRIS: If Gurdjieff is teaching in this book, it's in the same way —through life, through the situations that are created where people see something—he doesn't tell them what it is.

FINCH: That is, he refuses to play the role of someone who delivers the answers.

PENTLAND: Perhaps he knew too much to waste time playing that role. If he teaches, he speaks to a part of us which is not normally expressing itself. And he speaks as a question mark.

FINCH: I noticed in that connection one of these extraordinary common-sense remarks to the effect that it is a hundred times easier for a camel to pass through the eye of a needle than for anyone to give to another the understanding formed in him about anything whatsoever.

PENTLAND: And yet everybody goes on trying to communicate. How do you explain that?

FINCH: The book says something about that. It makes the point that was made many thousand years ago that what we are communicates more than merely what we say. The book says we communicate more through our being than through our minds. This may be one of the great things that Gurdjieff was trying to bring out. Certainly, this great distinction between knowledge and understanding that we've talked about here is one of the common-sense things that everybody knows and forgets. There is another one in the book which I think is very impressive that we ought to mention. When he was talking about the civil war in Russia, he was talking about how he and his friends passed through all this carnage and chaos, and were not molested. That is, by either side, with the Red Army and the White Army fighting each other; they not only survived in the midst of all this, but people also helped them. When he explains how this happened—why they were not just shot down by one side or the other, he says that in that civil war madness there was an instinct in human beings for distinguishing good from evil in an objective sense. This was not completely lacking even under these terrible circumstances of this civil war. The recognition of this deep capacity of people to distinguish good from evil in an objective sense—not in some kind of private, personal attitude —but in some deep way, seems to be another one of the great common-sense thoughts in this book. I wonder if we could say a word about that.

MORRIS: You might say that the effort to enable all men to go down through the layers of acquired opinions, second-hand notions of all the things one has been taught in school and acquired from newspapers, from books and from society—to go down through all of those layers to find deeply buried, but still alive, something objective and good, is the purpose of Gurdjieff's teachings.

FINCH: This is also identified by him with the word "conscience" —not a very popular word, perhaps, today, but there is a passage where he says not to do what people around us consider good or bad, but to act in life as our own conscience tells us. And then he says that the untrammeled conscience will always know more than all the books and teachers put together.

PENTLAND: Certainly I wouldn't want to explain what Gurdjieff meant by "conscience," and I think explaining it would miss the point, because conscience is an individual thing—something that each man has to seek and find for himself against all the conventions and suggestions which are reaching him all the time. What is it? In any case, I think what is understandable is Gurdjieff's idea that it is only by a sort of friction between this inward part—this most inner of the inward parts—and the automatic reactions and manifestations which a man is making, that he becomes aware of his own life and the possible sense of his own living.

FINCH: Yes; yet I think that for the person who may have heard of Gurdjieff and has a picture in his mind of somebody who was perhaps half charlatan, half unscrupulous rug-dealer or something like this, I think it is important to note that this book stresses that Gurdjieff himself lived by a standard of objective standards in a way, I think you will agree, that is altogether different from the way most people think of conscience. This is a side of him that will come as an important discovery to many people.

PENTLAND: It's a side that he didn't advertise. I suppose this is what is meant by common sense. I suppose it was necessary for the very large aims he had that he should appear mostly in disguise. If there are hints of his never departing from a certain discipline which he laid upon himself—a certain conscience, as you put it—they will only be seen by someone like yourself who is looking for them, who is taking the book more in the way that it is intended to be taken.

FINCH: There is one question that I have been wanting to ask all through this discussion, and that is why this book had to wait thirty years to be published in English, and I think almost as long to be published in any other language?

PENTLAND: It's answered for us in the translator's note to the book. It was felt that this book could not be withheld from increasing numbers of people in all countries who have become interested in Mr. Gurdjieff—in his teachings—and who have wanted to know what can be known about his personal life.

MORRIS: This book is not only a logical but a necessary sequel to his first book. You will remember that in the first book he states his purpose there. He said that his purpose was to destroy mercilessly in the minds of his readers all the views and opinions and associations about everything that had been rooted in readers' minds by centuries of custom. In other words, he was putting everything in question—leaving nothing untouched, unsuspected, untested. But, in that same section, he mentioned that in his second book he would offer some of the material for the construction of a new life, and show its soundness. Since the first book had quite a wide circulation, there are, scattered around the world, many people who now feel the need for this second step.

FINCH: This book was read aloud by some people who had the manuscript over some period of time. I'm curious to know if there was some special advantage to reading this aloud as against reading this silently to yourself.

MORRIS: This is part of a very ancient tradition. You have undoubtedly noticed, in the first book, that there is a certain style of repetition, due to the fact that it was originally conceived in this oral tradition. I think the reason why this was read aloud is we are all conditioned in our modern civilization—we read constantly. And a certain automatic mechanism of reading has been established by habit in us. We are not in the habit of *listening* to ideas of this kind. There is the possibility when we do so that ideas are not deflected by so many acquired prejudices and automatic associations. Perhaps also it may take us back to the state of childhood, where we have been told in the New Testament we must find our way, if we are to find the Truth.

6

First Amendment: Core of Our Constitution

by Alexander Meiklejohn

Dr. Alexander Meiklejohn, world-renowned educator, and recipient of the Presidential Medal of Freedom in 1963, was one of Pacifica Foundation's early advisers and a frequent consultant on its periodic problems of free speech. He was an implacable foe of every restraint on expression and worked continuously as a teacher, writer, and college president for educational ideas and practices which were not to win general acceptance for nearly a half century after he first began his challenging work. Dr. Meiklejohn continually stressed his belief that the First Amendment was intended as an absolute barrier to any governmentally imposed limitation on the expression of political opinion.

As the country moved into the McCarthy era, in the early days of Pacifica's experimental radio station, KPFA, Dr. Meiklejohn's voice was often raised in indignation at the state of mind both locally and nationally. For Dr. Meiklejohn the First Amendment was the essence of all that is best in America, and he spoke up for it when others were afraid to speak. His assistance to the Pacifica project was invaluable.

The following is edited from a talk Alexander Meiklejohn

*gave originally before a congressional committee in Washington
and broadcast over KPFA in 1953. It won KPFA an Ohio State
Radio Award.*

Mr. Chairman, I deeply appreciate your courtesy in asking me to
join with you in an attempt to define the meaning of the words,
"Congress shall make no law abridging the freedom of speech, or
of the press, or the right of the people peaceably to assemble, and
to petition the government for a redress of grievances."

Whatever those words may mean they go directly to the
heart of our American plan of government. If we can understand
them, we can know what, as a self-governing nation, we are trying
to be and to do. Insofar as we do not understand them we are in
grave danger of blocking our own prejudices, of denying our own
beliefs. It may clarify my own part in our conference if I tell you
at once my opinion concerning this much debated subject.

The First Amendment seems to me to be a very uncompro-
mising statement: it admits of no exceptions. It tells us that the
Congress and, by implication, all other agencies of the government, are denied any authority whatever to limit the political
freedom of the citizens of this nation. It declares that with respect
to political belief, political discussion, political advocacy, political
planning, our citizens are a sovereign and the Congress is their
subordinate agent.

Mr. Chairman, in view of your courtesy to me I hope that
you will not find me discourteous to you when I thus suggest that
the Congress of which you are members is a subordinate branch
of the government of the United States. In saying this I am simply
repeating in less passionate words what was said by the writers of
the *Federalist Papers* when, a century and three quarters ago,
they explained the meaning of the proposed Constitution to a
body politic which seemed very reluctant to adopt it. Over and
over again the writers of those papers declared that the Constitutional Convention had given to the people adequate protection
against a much feared tyranny of the legislature.

It is chiefly the legislature, the Federalist insists, which threatens to usurp the governing powers of the people. In words which unfortunately have some relevance today it declared that it is against the enterprising ambition of this department that the people ought to indulge their jealousy and exhaust all their precautions. And further, the hesitant people were assured that the convention, having recognized this danger, had devised adequate protections against it. The representatives, it was provided, would be elected by vote of the people. Elections would be for terms brief enough to ensure active and continuous, popular control. The legislature would have no lawmaking authority other than those limited powers specifically delegated to it. A general legislative power to act for the security and welfare of the nation was denied on the ground that it would destroy the basic postulant of popular self-government on which the Constitution rests.

As the Federalist thus describes with insight and accuracy the constitutional defenses of the freedom of the people against legislative invasion, it is not speaking of that freedom as an individual right which is bestowed upon the citizens by action of the legislature. Nor is the principle of the freedom of speech derived from a law of nature, or of reason in the abstract. As it stands in the Constitution, it is an expression of the basic American political agreement that in the last resort the people of the United States shall govern themselves. To find its meaning, therefore, we must dig down to the very foundations of the self-governing process. And what we shall there find is the fact that when men govern themselves it is they, and no one else, who must pass judgment upon public policies.

That means that in our popular discussions unwise ideas must have a hearing as well as wise ones, dangerous ideas as well as safe, un-American as well as American. Just so far as at any point the citizens who are to decide issues are denied acquaintance with information, or opinion, or doubt, or disbelief, or criticism which is relevant to those issues—just so far the result must be ill-considered, ill-balanced planning for the general good. It is that mutilation of the thinking process of the community against which the First Amendment is directed. That provision neither the legislative, nor the executive, nor the judiciary, nor all of them acting together has authority to nullify. We Americans have decided, together, to be free.

Mr. Chairman, I have now stated for your consideration the thesis that our American political freedom is not on any ground whatever subject to abridgment by the representatives of the people.

May I next try to answer two arguments which are commonly brought against that thesis, in the courts and in the wider circle of popular discussion. The first objection rests upon the supposition that freedom of speech may on occasion threaten the security of the nation, and when these two legitimate national interests are in conflict, the government, it is said, must strike a balance between them. That means that the First Amendment must at times yield ground. Our political freedom may be abridged in order that the national order and safety may be secured. In the courts of the United States, many diverse opinions have asserted that balancing doctrine. One of these, often quoted, reads as follows: "To preserve its independence and give security against foreign aggression and encroachment is the highest duty of every nation, and to attain these ends nearly all other considerations are to be subordinated."

That doctrine tells us that the government of the United States has unlimited authority to provide for the security of the nation as it may seem necessary and wise. It tells us, therefore, that constitutionally the government which has created the defenses of political freedom may break down those defenses. We, the people, who have enacted the First Amendment may, by agreed-upon procedure, modify or annul that amendment. And since we are, as a government, a sovereign nation, I do not see how any of these assertions can be doubted or denied. We Americans as a body politic may destroy or limit our freedom whenever we choose. But what bearing has that statement upon the authority of Congress to interfere with the provisions of the First Amendment? Congress is not the government—it is only one of four branches, to each of which the people have denied specific, unlimited powers as well as delegated such powers. And in the case before us, the words "Congress shall make no law abridging the freedom of speech" gives plain evidence that so far as Congress is concerned the power to limit our political freedom has been explicitly denied.

. . . Our doctrine of political freedom is not a visionary abstraction; it is a belief which is based in long and bitter experience which is thought out by shrewd intelligence. It is the sober conviction that in a society pledged to self-government it is never true that in the long run the security of the nation is endangered by the freedom of the people. Whatever may be the immediate gains and losses, the dangers to our safety arising from political suppression are always greater than the dangers to that safety arising from political freedom. Suppression is always foolish. Freedom is always wise. That is the faith, the experimental faith by which we Americans have undertaken to live. If we, the citizens of today, cannot shake ourselves free from the hysteria which blinds us to that faith there is little hope for peace and security either at home or abroad. Second, the rewriting of the First Amendment which authorizes the legislature to balance security against freedom denies not merely some minor phase of the amendment, but its essential purpose and meaning. Whenever in our Western civilization, inquisitors have sought to justify their acts of suppression they have given plausibility to their claims only by appealing to the necessity of guarding the public safety. It is therefore that appeal which the First Amendment intended, and intends, to outlaw. Speaking to the legislature it says: when times of danger come upon the nation you will be strongly tempted and urged by popular pressures to resort to practices of suppression such as those allowed by societies unlike our own in which men do not govern themselves. You are hereby forbidden to do so. This nation of ours intends to be free. Congress shall make no law abridging our political freedom.

. . . The purpose of the Constitution is, as we all know, to define and allocate powers for the governing of the nation. To that end three separate governing agencies are set up and to each of them are delegated such specific powers as are needed for doing its part of the work. Now that program rests upon a clear distinction between the political bodies—the legislative, executive, and judicial, to which powers are delegated. It presupposes, on the one hand, a supreme governing agency to which originally all authority belongs. It specifies, on the other hand, subordinate agencies to which partial delegations of authority are made. What then is the working relation between the supreme agency and its subordinates? Only as we answer that question shall we find the positive meaning of the First Amendment.

First of all then, what is the supreme governing agency of this nation? In its opening statement the Constitution answers that question. "We, the people of the United States," it declares, "do ordain and establish this Constitution. . . ." Those are the revolutionary words which define the freedom which is guaranteed by the First Amendment. They mark off our government from every form of despotic polity. The legal powers of the people of the United States are not granted to them by someone else —by kings, or barons, or priests; by legislators, or executives, or judges. All political authority, whether delegated or not, belongs constitutionally to us. If anyone else has political authority we are lending it to him. We, the people, are supreme in our own right. We are governed, directly or indirectly, only by ourselves.

. . . What are the intellectual processes by which free men govern a nation and which therefore must be protected from any external interference? They seem to be of three kinds. First, as we try to make up our minds on issues which affect the general welfare, we commonly, though not commonly enough, read the printed records of the thinking and believing which other men have done in relation to those issues. Those records are found in books, ancient and modern, in magazines of fact and of opinion, in documents and newspapers, in works of art of many kinds. All this vast array of idea and fact, of science and fiction, of information and argument, the voter may find ready to help him in making up his mind. Second, we electors do our thinking, not only by individual reading and reflection, but also in the active associations of public or private discussion. We think together as well as apart, hold meetings in order that this or that set of ideas may prevail, in order that that measure, or this, may be defeated. Third, when election day finally comes, the voter, having presumably made up his mind, must now express it by his ballot. Behind the canvas curtain, alone and independent, he renders his decision. He acts as sovereign, one of the governors of his country. However slack may be our practice, that, in theory, is our freedom.

What then, as seen against this constitutional background, is the purpose of the First Amendment as it stands guard over our freedom? That purpose is to see to it that in none of these three activities of judging shall the voter be robbed by action of other subordinate branches of the government, of the responsibility, the power, the authority, which are his under the Constitution. What shall he read? What he, himself, decides to read. With whom shall he associate in political advocacy? With those with whom he chooses to associate. Whom shall he oppose? Those with whom he disagrees. Shall any branch of the government attempt to control his opinions or his vote, to drive him by duress or intimidation into believing or voting this way or that? To do so is to violate the Constitution at its very source. We, the people of the United States, are self-governing—this is what our freedom means.

Mr. Chairman, this interpretation of the First Amendment which I have tried to give is, of necessity, very abstract. May I therefore give some more specific examples of its meaning at this point or that? First, in the field of public discussion when citizens and their fellow thinkers peaceably assemble to listen to a speaker, whether he be American or foreign, conservative or radical, safe or dangerous, the First Amendment is not in the first instance concerned with the right of the speaker to say this or that; it is concerned with the authority of the hearers to meet together to discuss, and to hear discussed by speakers of their own choice, whatever they may deem worthy of their consideration.

Second, the same freedom from attempts at duress is guaranteed to every citizen as he makes up his mind, chooses his party, and finally casts his vote. During that process no governing body may use force upon him, may try to drive him or lure him toward this decision or that, or away from this decision or that. For that reason no subordinate agency of the government has authority to ask, under compulsion to answer, what a citizen's political commitments are. The question, Are you a Republican? or Are you a Communist? when accompanied by the threat of harmful or degrading consequences if the answer is refused, or if the answer is this rather than that, is an intolerable invasion of the reserve powers of the governing people. The freedom thus protected does not rest upon the Fifth Amendment right of one who is governed to avoid self-incrimination; it expresses the constitutional authority, the legal power of one who governs to make up his own mind without fear or favor, with the independence and freedom in which self-government exists.

Third, for the same reason, our First Amendment freedom forbids that any citizen be required under threat of penalty to take an oath or make an affirmation as to beliefs which he holds or rejects. Every citizen, it is true, may be required, and should be required, to pledge loyalty and to practice loyalty to the nation. He must agree to support the Constitution but he may never be required to believe in the Constitution. His loyalty may never be tested on grounds of adherence to, or rejection of, any belief. Loyalty does not imply conformity of opinion. Every citizen of the United States has constitutional authority to approve or to condemn any laws enacted by the legislature, any actions taken by the executive, any decisions rendered by the judiciary, any principles established by the Constitution. All these enactments, which, as men who are governed, we must obey, are subject to our approval or disapproval as we govern. With respect to all of them, we who are free men are sovereign. We are the people. We govern the United States.

. . . Conflicting views may be expressed, must be expressed, not because they are valid but because they are relevant. If they are responsibly entertained by anyone, we the voters need to hear them. When a question of policy is before the house, free men choose to meet it, not with their eyes shut but with their eyes open.

To be afraid of ideas, of any idea, is to be unfit for self-government. Any such suppression of ideas about the common good the First Amendment condemns with its absolute disapproval. The freedom of ideas shall not be abridged.

7

The Problem of Death
by Alan Watts

Alan Watts, author of The Way of Zen *and many other books, is a noted interpreter of Eastern philosophies to Western audiences. His series of talks, regularly broadcast on Pacifica Radio since its inauguration, continues to the present day. The one that follows was given in January, 1953.*

The sense of individuality is the root of our concern for the survival of death. The sense of individuality, the sense of the ego, the sense of each one of us being a separate person, the sense of the continuing "I" who has "had" all our past experiences is something we abstract from the whole collection of experiences which we call the memory. We have no direct knowledge of an "I." The moment you try to be aware of yourself, you find yourself going around in a circle. The self of which you are aware is always memories, a combination of memories and abstractions from memories. Because, as human consciousness becomes more intense and the highly useful power of memory becomes very sensitive and vivid, it has the peculiar disadvantage—over and above its obvious advantages—of making its abstract creations so vivid that they seem to be real. Therefore the abstract feeling of the ego, which we get from memory, assumes for us a tremendous reality just because our memory is so vivid and our consciousness so clear and retentive. Thus what we pay for having the useful power of memory is the serious disadvantage of having a painfully acute sense of individual existence. Because that individual existence is an abstraction from memory, it is always something past, and is therefore in a process of decay. For past events are constantly slipping away from us, constantly dying, and as the past becomes more and more remote, so its contents are more and more inaccessible. It is because our egos are, in this way, purely *past* that we have a tremendous sense of anxiety and insecurity.

Now when you dwell in memory, you become identified with something past, in which no real satisfaction, no real life exists. As a result there is a constant sense of emptiness, anxiety, and frustration—and the only way of solving this frustration seems to lie in making the past continue. For our knowledge and our hopes for the future are based on the past. We have no first-hand knowledge of the future; we have only guesses based on what we remember. Therefore if we are mainly preoccupied with the past we become bound by time because the past and the future exist in relation to one another in rather the same way as light and dark, long and short. Because we, as egos, are past, our only hope lies in the possibility of being future. Hence our tremendous concern as to whether we're going to survive our hunger for more and more *time*.

For oriental cultures this concern does not exist in anything like the same degree. It isn't simply because there is a popular belief in reincarnation; it goes deeper than that. It is based on the dim realization, which is often much more emotional than intellectual, that the ego is not the real man. The real man is not this abstraction, this hangover from the past. The real man is the one who lives "now," in this eternal moment, and of whom we have no direct and immediate knowledge. *He* is the mysterious one—and this is not "I" because "I" is an abstraction and the real man is something altogether beyond "I." It is only this "now" that one's life—all life—actually, vitally, and fully *is*. Insofar as this point of view is ingrained in a culture, there is nothing like our concern for the survival of the individual.

Well, now, what *does* happen after death? We're still interested in the question, even though the reason for our interest is simply that we want to continue because our sense of ego, being past and dead, is impoverished. There is, perhaps, still remaining, an objective problem. What does happen to the individual when he dies? Well, obviously nobody knows. Certainly I don't claim to know, but I suppose that it is a matter on which one may speculate. For what they may be worth I, like everybody else, have my speculations, and this is roughly what I think. I don't believe that there is an individual survival of death. Our brains decompose when we die, and our memories probably decompose with them. At the same time, I don't think that we need be concerned with the possibility of annihilation, imagined as an everlasting endurance of unconsciousness. This concept doesn't mean anything at all. It's an attempt to visualize nothingness, and nothingness by definition doesn't exist. I imagine, then, that it would be something like this: You die, and as soon as the physical continuity of the individual has no further basis, that is to say there is no more conscious or unconscious memory, the experience which would "follow" would be the equivalent of the same experience you had when you were born, when you arose from what some people might call annihilation. Well, annihilation's funny stuff, isn't it, considering that you came out of it. You were annihilated before you existed, and if so, why should anybody be afraid to be annihilated after they die? For when there is the void—the complete blankness of consciousness—then there are still other consciousnesses surviving, and each one of these feels that it is "I" in exactly the same way as you.

It might, then, be rather like this: You die, you cease to exist as an individual consciousness—and then suddenly you wake up again, as a baby or some other kind of conscious being with no memory of any past. This has happened already, so why not again and again? Now in one sense this baby isn't you, because the memory—the principle of continuity—is gone. Yet it feels existing; it feels conscious; and if you think about that you will see that there's really no difference between these two ideas: (1) After death I shall be reborn again as another person, but of course I won't have any memory of the past. (2) When I'm dead, somebody else will be born. There's really no difference between the two statements.

In that sense, in a very strange way, you might be anybody. And, in this sense, you *will* be anybody—because anybody is "I", and they all have this same "private" feeling of existence. So long as there are any "I's"—and presumably there always will be—there will be no annihilation. Even if this globe and its inhabitants are destroyed by a comet or an explosion of the sun, the chances are that, after billions of years in the rotation of the eternal cycles, other living beings will arise somewhere else—and "I" will come to birth again. In other words, consciousness will come to birth again, and *you* will experience it because "you's" or "I's" will be experiencing. In the meantime, annihilation of individual life—even though it may occupy vast spans of time—will seem as totally nonexistent and brief as the interval between going to sleep and waking after a dreamless night.

If there is no survival of the individual, if memory does not continue in any shape or fashion, isn't it a meaningless and wasteful tragedy that lives which had so much promise were suddenly cut short? That person who in the course of his lifetime has accumulated a marvelous skill—in scholarship or sciences—should come to an end and all his store of knowledge and wisdom be dispersed to the four winds? But this objection is a result of not thinking deeply enough about the whole problem, that is to say, of not carrying one's half-formed or "half-baked" thoughts to their full and logical conclusion.

If we follow this wish, this craving, for the preservation of values, of the things which people have created, of the knowledge which they've accumulated, of the characters which they have begun to perfect, or whatever it may be—if we follow this desire on and on and on, we soon run into a nightmare. You know the sort of person who never throws anything away, who keeps every

piece of paper, who records everything, who photographs everything, who accumulates whole libraries of reminiscences, who
keeps drawers full of all sorts of sentimental treasures of past occasions—the program of their first dance, love letters, baby teeth,
valentines, locks of hair, theater programs, and other sentimental
reminders of good times? He accumulates a stupendous amount
of baggage which becomes a vast nuisance and expense every
time he has to move house. Such people actually spend a very
small amount of time going over these reminiscences and actually
enjoying the memories which these tokens evoke. Usually they
just let them lie and accumulate. And this is just the trouble with
any prospect of the indefinite continuity of the individual, which
means the indefinite continuity of memory—that it soon becomes
a kind of self-strangling mountain of dead stuff, very much in
need of a clean sweep.

Fantasies have been written about people who became im-
mortal and, having enjoyed the deathless state for maybe a couple
of hundred years, acquired at last an obsession to die, to be able
to forget and wipe out the whole mountain of memory. For there
can always be too much of a good thing. The most priceless treasures which have ever existed, the most glorious works of art, the
most inspired writings, the most gorgeous music, if they are preserved forever, become after a certain time demonic. The
continual preservation of the great works of man is in a way based
on a lack of faith in the possibility that such things can ever be
done again—or anything of equivalent value.

I'm not saying that we should immediately destroy the great
productions of art or of wisdom, but that we should not cling to
them excessively, because after a certain time they become
corpses living among us, blacking any creative outflow from other
people. There is nothing more marvelous in the whole world than
death, in the sense that every now and then it cleans the slate and
wipes out all memories, so that one becomes again entirely new.

Go back to your childhood, and recollect the sense of wonder
with which your unremembering eyes first saw this world. Remember, if you can, how you stared in amazement at the sun,

stared until it turned blue. Remember how you reached to try to catch hold of the moon, how things that adults consider trivial—small pots and pans, knives and forks, things lying around the kitchen—seemed to you quite marvelous.

And then, as you grew older you stored more of the sun and moon, of the pots and pans, and of the magical lights and shadows on the wall, in memory. Thereupon they became less and less important to you, less and less miraculous, because they were all familiar, and familiarity began to breed contempt. You lost the sense of living in an enchanted world, because those things lie upon your memory, so that whenever you walk out into the street and look at the trees, you know, "Well, that's just a tree." You look at the sun and, "Well, that's just the sun." To recapture the sense of wonder, you need greater and greater stimulations of the senses so as to revive them and penetrate the callouses which memory has grown over their sensitive surfaces.

If, then, it were possible to forget everything that one ever knew, and be reborn, one would once more see the world as the magical thing which it is to the eyes of a child. In this way, by the constant intervention of death, the constant breaking down of memory, the wonder of being alive is perpetually restored and one is preserved from what must be the awful boredom of the personal God. God, as he is popularly conceived in the Western world, is a being who knows and remembers everything and, having lived for always and always, knows, with Solomon, that there is nothing new under the sun. He can never be surprised. Of course, that God is mainly the invention of the inferior theologians. Even in the early myths in the Book of Genesis, such a God doesn't exist, for they tell us that when God first created the world, he made such oddities as great whales and—surprise!—"saw that they were good." He wasn't this know-it-all person who doesn't have a forgetery as well as a memory. He was delightfully human, until bad theology made a monster of him.

When you think of this theological monster, of a God who goes on living always and always and never forgets a single thing; who has seen all that can be seen and is no longer capable of being surprised, you can understand why the Hindu myth of God is so very different. For Brahma, throughout the incalculable ages of his life, has his days and nights, his millions of years awake, and his millions of years asleep—when the whole universe, which is really himself in disguise, vanishes, only to appear fresh and new as the cycle returns. Herein is the tremendous importance of following one's desires through to their logical conclusions. Do you really want, as an individual with a memory, to live forever? Do you really want to retain, to keep, for always and always, the very best things that you have experienced? For in the course of time they will become like those old photographs of dear friends and wonderful landscapes. Yes, there they are in color, and you look at them and they're beautiful; and you look at them again, and as time goes on you forget to look at them, and they're stuck away in a drawer, and the need to cling to the beauty of that face or that landscape with this little camera box has passed away. You are liberated from that memory. In exactly the same way, however great one's attachment to a particular human being, to a particular memory, in the course of time it would turn to ashes in one's mouth, because what we remember is actually, from the moment of its becoming past, already dead, already gone. It is pleasant to cling to those memories only to the degree that they can still convince us, by their vividness and by a certain unfamiliarity, that they're not dead already. In the moment when the event occurs, when, for example, we cast our eyes upon the landscape which so moves us that we have to grab it inside our camera . . . in the moment when we look upon it, we feel the whole thing is too momentary and life too brief for us to absorb the full delight of the vision. We feel we have to dwell upon it a little longer, so as to get everything out of it. Often the little camera box symbolizes our very souls—the attitude with which we go around wishing to possess, wishing to grasp this world all the time, wishing to get the most out of the things that we are enjoying. Precisely that wish compels us to cling, always, to these memory properties because the more you struggle, in the experience of beauty or joy, to get the most out of it, the more you frustrate and prevent enjoyment, the actual full assimilation of what you're beholding.

When we are concerned, in the midst of enjoying something, to retain it, we're doing something quite stupid. For we are trying to stimulate our nerves, by making efforts, to respond more sensitively to what they're feeling. Now you can't make efforts to increase the sensitivity of your nerves. If you try, for example, to see a distant object in clear detail, the more you strain with your eyes, the less clearly you'll see the detail. On the other hand, if you close your eyes and imagine black—that is to say, relax them for a while—and then just quietly open them and look, the detail will appear more clearly, because the more relaxed your nerves are, the more relaxed your consciousness, the more sensitively, the more clearly, you perceive things.

This is an analogue which can be applied to the whole mind. The less it is trying to remember, the more clearly it sees. But as one tries to hold things, as one clings to memory, then to that extent it becomes progressively the nightmarish business of grasping corpses. We are, as it were, people who have a beloved one always before us, dead, and we cling to the body trying to revive it with kisses, trying to breathe our own breath into its mouth—and there's nothing really more tragic, nothing more heartrending than the attempt to revive, with the power of one's emotions, that which has inevitably and finally gone. But were it not possible for memory to end, for things to be fully and finally gone, the thing which is really worthwhile about life could never be. And that is the element of wonder, the element of miracle, which shines from the most humble and prosaic things when regarded by eyes which have not seen them before.

8

Childbirth Without Pain
A Discussion

In 1960 WBAI broadcast a discussion of childbirth without pain. The participants were an expectant mother, a mother who two weeks before had delivered a child by the Lamaze method, a doctor and a nurse who taught and used this technique, and another doctor who questioned the applicability of the method. Soon after this broadcast a remarkable letter was received at WBAI—possibly the first letter in the history of radio broadcasting to commend a station for its extraordinary help during the process of childbirth. Here is the letter:

I have special reason to be very grateful to you: a little over three weeks ago you presented a discussion on natural childbirth. I listened rather carefully because I expected to give birth very shortly.—Exactly a week later—on a snow-stormy night—labor took me by surprise, without any possibility of getting to New York Hospital in time.

As much as anybody could possibly have learned from your radio presentation, I applied to those somewhat frightening moments—and gave birth to a healthy little girl, without any other assistance; mother and child being perfectly all right. I am sure you understand my special gratitude, because

I could not possibly have managed as well without you. Your sincerely grateful and appreciative listener.

M. B.

This is excerpted from the broadcast she heard:

DR. SEGAL: The Lamaze method of childbirth without pain is a method derived from the synthesis of Russian and French techniques for returning labor and delivery to formerly physiological, and therefore, painless processes. Who was Dr. Lamaze? I ask who he was because unfortunately he died in 1957, just as he was about to see the extension of his work made possible. Dr. Lamaze was a French physician who had an unusually deep fascination for his work. In 1950 he was aroused by the comments of a visiting Russian specialist from Leningrad, who spoke about the attempts in the Soviet Union to make childbirth painless by use of what they called psycho-prophylactic method. This seemed utterly incredible to Dr. Lamaze. Could women really give birth without pain? His own experience had led him to believe, as did physicians the world over, that only drugs could really be helpful. He visited the Soviet Union. He listened. He explored, attended clinics and, most important, he sat with a woman for six hours, observing her conduct her own labor with the active guidance of a midwife and the presence of the obstetrician. She delivered her child without pain.

Filled with enthusiasm, he returned to Paris vowing that he would do everything possible to give the same experience to French women. He put into practice what he had seen, making his own contribution to the theory and organizing a program for his own clinic and in other parts of France.

Since 1912 much attention had been given to the work of a woman researcher in Pavlov's laboratory in Russia. She demonstrated that pain is a cortical phenomenon—that is, that it is interpreted in the outer part of the forebrain. She showed that she could produce a conditioned reflex by means of a pain stimulus, and then could change it into a painless stimulus. She showed that the brain could suppress real pain. Just as important, the brain could also conceal a pain that has no physical cause. Just as the brain could conceive a nonexistent pain, so could it, through education, know that it does not exist. And so knowing, it could extinguish other previously experienced stimuli—that is, prevent them from appearing in the brain.

The first step in psycho-prophylaxis is education. For centuries contractions of the womb have been associated in the minds of women with pain. A reflex was created by the constant repetition of words denoting pain. This is spoken of as negative education, because of which women believe pain necessarily accompanies uterine contractions. By showing how popular ideas—and not necessarily accurate ones—can be responsible for setting up pain reflexes, by re-education in such areas, and by informing women about the processes going on in pregnancy, labor, and delivery, we can convert these processes into known actions. These known actions do not, of themselves, produce pain sensations. Through education you remove fear and raise the level at which pain can be perceived. In fact, through education we have produced what might be called a verbal analgesic—a pain remover—a pain preventer.

The second step in the psycho-prophylactic method is an active one; one in which the woman creates new, temporary reflexes; one in which she plays the main role, where she becomes responsible for making labor easier to bear. How is this possible? Let us take an everyday experience: a man is reading a book in a train. What conversation goes on around him? The man is conscious, for the most part, only of his book. The sounds of voices and of the train go into the brain and reach an area of inhibition around the area of excitement—in this instance, the reading area—and these sounds are not heard. What is it we do when we concentrate? Two things: by increasing the force of the excitement area, we put off inhibitions around it at the same time. We put up road blocks, we put up signs: GO NO FARTHER. This is the nature of nerve tissue; it acts like an induction system. The example of the reading man is one of an inactive force accomplishing something. With the woman in labor, however, we set up an active force. She learns consciously to do something at about the same time that something else is happening, in this case, at about the same time that the uterus is contracting. In the last three months of pregnancy the uterus contracts irregularly, and essentially with very little awareness by the woman. She is taught to recognize when these contractions occur. Having learned this, she is told to engage in conscious breathing at the same time that the contraction occurs. Later on, she is asked to tell herself aloud to breathe consciously as the contraction occurs. She thus forms a reflex consisting of the spoken word, the contraction, and the respiration. This is a special conditioning reflex.

I emphasize conscious breathing because, as you all know, normal breathing is done automatically and unconsciously. This new reflex can be achieved through diligent daily exercises. What happens in the brain? Having established this spoken-word contraction, respiration reflex, as soon as the uterus contracts, this conscious reflex directs the stimulus from the uterine nerves to a new area in the brain—the conscious-breathing area —instead of to the pain area. Result: a consciously determined maneuver for preventing pain. The first, education; the second, the spoken word—contraction, respiration reflex. The awareness of the *fact* of uterine contraction has been diverted to the *act* of conscious breathing. The breathing stimulus overpowers the pain stimulus. Full advantage of this is taken during labor. The patient is instructed in special kinds of respiration during different phases of labor from the beginning to the end.

We shall now try to elaborate some of the details, some of the objections, some of the experiences of this method of painless childbirth:

(*Introduction of people taking part in a general discussion: Mrs. M—— who is expecting a child momentarily; Dr. A——; Mrs. Rosensweig who gave birth two weeks ago; Mrs. Elizabeth*

Bing, who teaches the method to people in New York, and Mrs. Marjorie Karmel, author of Thank You, Dr. Lamaze.)

MRS. ROSENSWEIG: Dr. Segal said something about the "greatest joys of living because the woman participated in this creation of a new being"—something like that. I think that was the greatest thing that ever happened to me. I would call it "womanhood accomplished." I feel I have attained this great joy.

There is one interesting thing I would like to point out to the mothers who are listening; if I could do it, I believe anyone could do it who wants to, because all the factors were against me. I had a cold—a stuffed-up nose—I couldn't do those breathings properly. I didn't get my second lesson at all, and I got it in the labor room when Mrs. Bing called up the public health nurse and she ran in and taught me the transition breathing. Finally, when I got to the labor room, I was much more relaxed because of the position of the bed, and I began doing what I remembered, and then my doctor said, "Very good!" That "very good" took me through the whole labor until the public health nurse came up and taught me the next step. I felt at that point that I was in control; I knew what was happening. I could do it—and I did it!

There is just one other point: I had no medication at all, through the whole thing. And if I had it to do over again, I would do it exactly that way. In the recovery room I imagine I went in a little drunk—drunk on emotion—and my doctor then asked me if I wanted a very small dose of Demerol, as a tranquilizer, I imagine, and I took it. Judging from the effects that this Demerol had upon me at that moment, I felt that if I had had one drop of anything, it would have made me too relaxed— I couldn't have had the control during the contractions.

QUESTION: Was it really painless?

MRS. ROSENSWEIG: Yes—and no. When I was out of control, I felt pain—I was really hysterical. I was yelling at my husband, "Let's get in the car." Then I got to the labor room and I was under control. I had a slight discomfort, but I was on top of it every moment. I was working hard—I was straining, I was un-comfortable—but at that point there was no pain whatsoever—just a faint discomfort.

MRS. KARMEL: Was your husband with you?

MRS. ROSENSWEIG: He was with me up until I was eight centi-meters dilated, and then, apparently according to the hospital policy, he was not allowed in the delivery room. I felt that everyone was cooperating with me at this point, so, "Let's get the baby out," and maybe some other time he will be able to enjoy this wonderful experience.

MRS. KARMEL: Did you say your husband was very helpful to you?

MRS. ROSENSWEIG: Since I didn't have my second lesson—I wasn't properly conditioned—I forgot to do a few things. I was count-ing on him, at that time to say, "Rosy, do this . . . take that last breath . . ." and he didn't. He was reading a book. I was angry at that time and I started ignoring him. Later he told me that he remembered that I hadn't had the second lesson, and he was trying to read to tell me what to do next. Apparently he was so nervous that he ran down and called Mrs. Bing.

MRS. BING: Yes he did. He actually telephoned me and said, "We haven't got far enough with our lessons; what do we do next?" We talked for fifteen or twenty minutes, and I said, "This is the next thing to do. Now run back and see what you can do to help her."

MRS. ROSENSWEIG: I tried to do the breathing you taught me for the first stage: in through the nose, out through the mouth. Steady as I could possibly make it. But I had a clogged nose and this made me panicky. Then I decided, "To hell with my nose, I'll start on to the next stage." I started panting—as you taught. This panting is to be used through the contraction, and it is punctuated at the beginning and at the end by a deep breath—in through the nose and out through the mouth. This I started using in the hospital when I had my wits more about me—and it worked. Then the public health nurse came up.

MRS. KARMEL: I think the interesting point here is that in France and Argentina, and many of the countries where this method is really set up and working, you do have your trainer with you in the hospital. I think most women get panicky just at the sight of the hospital.

MRS. ROSENSWEIG: Did you?

MRS. KARMEL: No, actually I didn't. I was in such a hurry to get there. I thought it was marvelous to be there. I was in a French hospital for the first time, and it was very homey and friendly so I didn't panic. What you need when you come in is somebody there who says, "Now we know just what we are going to do." Start you off on the right foot. The women in America who have done it so far—many of them have the same feeling of, "What is actually going to happen when I get to the hospital— how will conditions be?"

MRS. BING: There is quite a bit of difference between the French and us in procedure. In France you are encouraged to come to the hospital very early because the atmosphere in the hospital is very conducive to the whole method; whereas we feel here, for the time being, that you are really better off at home. But it didn't work with you, I take it.

MRS. ROSENSWEIG: It did in a way. I didn't want to get to the hospital too early. I was afraid of receiving medication.

MRS. BING: We feel that since the method isn't very widespread in this country, that a woman is happier in her own home sur-roundings with her husband there—more relaxed (of course, when she has taken the full course)—than in the hospital where nurses might not be familiar with the method.

DR. SEGAL: Mrs. Rosensweig indicated her fear of getting some drug if she got to the hospital too soon—that possibly some-body would overpower her. This is understandable, and I have had this statement made by many patients who have gone through this technique. It is understandable, as I indicated, there must be a continuing, active, conscious participation on the part of the woman in the course of labor. Her fear of getting some medication—in fact she explained it when she received some Demerol after the child was born—she realized that had she received that Demerol during her labor, she would not have had control of the situation. And it is very important that she does have control of the situation from its very inception to the birth of the child.

MRS. ROSENSWEIG: One of the first things I did was call every hospital and asked, "Are you sympathetic to natural childbirth?" The hospital I went to—the public health nurse said, "We are using the Lamaze method; have you heard of it?" I chose the hospital because of this.

MRS. BING: Mrs. M——, did you have a question concerning the hospital?

MRS. M——: A lot of my questions have already been answered. I think Mrs. Rosensweig has done so well under some fantastic handicaps. You've completely wiped out any doubts I had as far as control is concerned. This has been the thing that's been on my mind for the longest time. I suppose the first question that comes to my mind concerning labor would be, "If I do lose control, can I get my control back?"

MRS. ROSENSWEIG: In the transition stage of labor, I was so exhausted I was sleeping between contractions. Many times I woke in the middle of a contraction, and it hurt. Then I had to pant real fast to get on top of the contraction. So, I believe you could say that I was out of control. But I regained my control mainly because I had this wonderful cheering section of the public health nurse, a labor nurse who called in a friend of hers to watch me, my husband, and finally the doctor. I think this encouragement helped me a lot, and the fact that I knew I was doing the right thing.

MRS. BING: How hard did you work beforehand to get to this control?

MRS. ROSENSWEIG: I'm ashamed to tell you, my dear teacher. . . .

DR. SEGAL: I think it's terribly important that we enlarge on the use of the word "control," as you used it. While it is very fine for you to understand yourself, and to know what it is that determined your decision to carry through with this method, this is not truly the basis for the method. "Control," as a psychiatric word, has a very sharp meaning. It is the people who are listening to us—particularly psychiatrists and obstetricians—who will pounce on that word and say, "Of course, that's exactly what we have been saying. These people who are being driven to do something—to keep control—do so because they have that sense of insecurity that you describe; because they are afraid of using drugs for fear of losing control. . . ."

MRS. ROSENSWEIG: But I'm afraid of pain—I can't stand pain. When I went into the labor room, there was a very nice nurse there, who was going to give me a shot. I saw a needle on the tray, and I said, "What are you giving me?" She said, "Don't worry, I'll tell you everything I'm going to do. This is vitamin K." When she came at me with that needle, I was frightened and I jumped. Then she saw that I was afraid of pain, and she gave me a very nice speech about, "Dear, now all of us can go through with this. If you feel you have to ask for medication because you feel pain, go right ahead—don't feel ashamed." I thought, "What a lovely person. I hope she is with me." Later on I said, "You didn't think I'd make it this far." She said, "No, I didn't."

MRS. KARMEL: I'd like to get back to the word "control." Now, you can't go through this without control, and what you want is control. If you look at it in terms of "personality" I know there is a lot of fighting going on about what kind of personality is suitable for this. I get a lot of letters saying, "I'm not a very aggressive person. Do you think I can do it?" I don't see what your personality has to do with your ability to learn to control a given situation.

MRS. M——: I want to say that I'm not afraid of pain. I don't like it, but I'm not afraid of it. I didn't go into this thing as an escape mechanism. Many women who go into this feel that here is a way to avoid an uncomfortable situation. I went into this feeling that here is a way to do something that is good for me in a physiological way, and good for my baby. I think that this attitude is going to give me any control that I'm going to have. It isn't because of the fear that if I lose control I am going to have pain. If I lose control, I'm going to have medication; and it is the medication and the anesthesia that are going to be wrong —one step after the other, the complete passivity that I want to avoid.

MRS. ROSENSWEIG: If I'm having a baby, I want to be acutely aware of everything that is happening.

MRS. BING: Lamaze says to be conscious of your contractions—to follow the contractions. The rate that they increase is the rate of your contractions. All the time you adjust to your contractions. I feel it's a scientific physiological process of adapting ourselves to our labor, and therefore staying in control of muscle groups that are being used in labor. We are being economical in the use of our muscles so we do not become exhausted and use up our oxygen. We allow the uterus to have the greatest amount of oxygen.

DR. SEGAL: I think it is important to be aware of the three words Mrs. Bing used: "control," "conscious," and "adaption." We haven't yet in our discussion set up the difference between an absolute and a conditioned reflex. An absolute reflex is one which you are born with, such as salivating when you see food. Conditioned reflexes are those which are established after our birth. Absolute reflexes remain with us the rest of our lives. Conditioned reflexes remain with us as long as we utilize them. That is why it is important to continue instructions up to the point of labor.

DR. A——: I'd like to speak about pain. So far everyone has taken the stand that if you use the method correctly, the patient will have no pain. I've spoken to many women who have had rewarding experiences in delivery, but most of them have, at some period during delivery, had some periods of rough going —you may call it pain, or whatever you will. Subsequently they generally tend to minimize the severity of what they felt. Now my belief is that most of these patients did have pain, which they were perfectly willing to put up with in order to achieve the goal they set out to achieve.

If most people realize that they will have pain, and that there is relief available in the form of small doses of drugs, I think it will be helpful. I think it will be a shock if they are led to believe there will be no pain and they feel something they can't distinguish from pain. I think this will help to lose control instead of keep control.

MRS. KARMEL: I agree with you, but it seems to me that when people start talking about pain, they can't stop and they feel they must harp on it. The statistics are that somewhere between 20 and 30 per cent of the women feel no pain at all. In France they say that with control, 90 per cent do not feel pain. Once she knows that, she knows what her expectation is.

DR. SEGAL: Don't forget that pain is in our heads—that it's subjective. We can train ourselves to the disappearance of pain and to the diminution of pain.

DR. A——: Mrs. Rosensweig mentioned the enriching and fulfilling experience of childbirth—if a woman wants it that way. But if a woman doesn't want this, there are other methods that are safely available. No one needs to feel she is being pushed into a mold. After all, there are some women who want painless childbirth without necessarily participating. I'm not completely convinced of this method, but I am certainly interested in it.

MRS. ROSENSWEIG: I'm curious: when a woman comes into your office for consultation, do you suggest using the Lamaze method, or do you just wait until you see if she asks about it?

DR. SEGAL: It varies. Some women ask me about it. And some say, "Now, I know about this natural childbirth and I want no part of it." I don't force her, but from time to time she will be hearing conversations in the office, and before long she will ask about it. Then I give her a book to read.

MRS. KARMEL: You mentioned natural childbirth. There are many doctors who think that the use of that phrase is a terrible thing because it gives the woman the impression that the success of the birth depends on her being a well-adjusted, natural person. That isn't fair to anybody in today's world. The woman feels that if she fails in learning the method, she is a failure in giving birth. In France and Russia, where this method is used, they never use the word "natural" because the method is a learned, an accomplished method.

DR. A——: Dr. Segal said something about returning childbirth to its once painless state, as though once there was a golden age, before the fall of Adam—you remember in the Book of Genesis it says that from this point onward women shall bring forth their children with pain. Now I don't believe that there is any evidence that labor was painless. This is a theory which we are entertaining here which proves to be successful in many instances, but is still a theory. What we do have is a method of deconditioning and conditioning—of making it painless now.

MRS. ROSENSWEIG: What I'd like to know is are we getting rid of the pain or are we getting rid of a sensation that is interpreted as pain?

MRS. KARMEL: Both.

DR. SEGAL: We must realize that pain is subjective—that pain is a sensation that can only be conceived and interpreted in the brain. We can understand what is going on, and by virtue of that understanding, cut down the intensity of the discomfort. That reminds me of a little verse:

> There once was a patient from Deal,
> Who said, "Although pain isn't real,
> If I sit on a pin and it punctures my skin,
> I dislike what I think that I feel."

MRS. KARMEL: Uterine contraction or no uterine contraction, a woman can cause herself whatever she may interpret as pain. She may be causing this by her lack of knowledge and by the lack of understanding and by the nervous processes in her own body. Now with this method you don't have the nervous process—and even if you do, you know how to get rid of it. You try to eliminate the pain you cause for yourself, and you get rid of any other pain you have. You keep your mind so active that the past influences you've had don't get in. But if you want to achieve painless childbirth you must work at it. You must be willing to give the time and the energy to the study of it.

9

Commentary
by William Rusher

The regular nightly Commentary series on all Pacifica Radio stations was designed to reflect the most diverse opinion spectrum possible, including uncommon as well as orthodox views. The following 1961 commentary by William Rusher, publisher of National Review, *set forth his reasons for declining to participate further in this series.*

For the past year representatives of *National Review*, America's leading journal of conservative opinion, have participated in WBAI's Commentary series along with spokesmen from a wide variety of other points of view. We have been grateful to WBAI for their hospitality and we hope that you have learned something even if you have not enjoyed our analyses of public questions. However, we have come to the reluctant conclusion that *National Review* must withdraw from further participation in the Commentary series. I might add that we are being joined in our withdrawal by George Sokolsky and Professor Russell Kirk and Ernest Van Den Haag. WBAI has asked us to give the reasons for our decision and we are happy to do so.

Let me begin by reading to you three sentences from the talk

with which I inaugurated *National Review*'s appearances on
Commentary a year ago. I said at that time, and I quote, *National
Review* declined the first invitations we received to broadcast on
this station because its programs at first seemed to us heavily
loaded with both open and concealed spokesmen for the cause of
Communism. We conservatives believe in free speech—so much
so, indeed, that we will not insult it by pretending that Communists are engaging in it when they talk to others. But, I went on to
say, WBAI is no longer serving as a handy platform for Communists and while that remains true we *National Review* conservatives will gladly appear on its programs to match our arguments
and our wits against the best the non-Communist left has to offer
—close quotes. That was what I said a year ago. In the months
that followed WBAI presented a broad range of able commentators—left, right, and center. But until recently it no longer included known Communists among them. Now it has resumed the
practice of inviting Communists to participate in the Commentary
series and, as I said a year ago, *National Review* is unwilling to
continue its own participation under those circumstances. Let me
emphasize that the issue is not whether Communists in this country should have the right to express their views. That question is
debatable but it does not concern us here. There are a score of
ways in which the American Communist Party today can and
does speak out on any subject that interests it—through its own
newspapers and magazines and from its own hired halls and soap-
boxes, but nothing in the First Amendment to the Constitution
obligates other Americans to make their communications facilities
available to the Communists—still less to treat a Communist as
just another participant in the discussion process. Do not be
misled, therefore, by the contention that some sort of necessary
service to liberty is involved in WBAI's decision to invite known
Communists to participate in this Commentary series or by the
argument that the appropriate response is to have *National Review* continue in the series and present an opposing point of
view.

National Review is always ready to disclose the dishonesty, not to mention the downright falsity of Marxist dogma, but the problem here runs much deeper. The Commentary series offers a platform to many distinguished representatives of varying viewpoints. To be included among them is to be recognized and accredited, by implication, as a person genuinely interested in the pursuit of truth through the processes of rational discussion and that a convinced Communist is not and cannot be. He is committed in advance to a particular concept of what is truth and he is ready to use any dialectical device, however dishonest, to further the success of his concept. He is therefore quite simply unfitted by his own choice to take part in the normal human exchange of honest views, honestly held and honestly defended. His participation in that process is from end to end one vast deception and those who enable him to commit it or who thoughtfully provide camouflage for it are to that extent his accomplices in the deception.

The deception is rendered still more complete in the case of Communists who appear on WBAI by the fact that the station does not identify these people as Communists even though they hold public positions in the Communist apparatus. Instead they are introduced to you under various circumlocutory titles—director of this, editor of that—titles normally recognized only by professional students of Communist organizations. Perhaps you heard one such speaker when he appeared on WBAI not long ago. You are scheduled to hear another very soon. Since they, of course, do not identify themselves as Communists and since WBAI itself does not so describe them, you are left to guess which, and all this is justified in the holy name of free speech. I will not spoil WBAI's fun or yours by telling you which of the voices you have recently heard on this microphone and which others you are soon to hear belong to card-carrying members of the American Communist Party. Suffice it to say that I have discussed those names with the management of this station and that no attempt has been made by WBAI to deny to me that they are precisely what I have described them as being. But I do suggest that if WBAI is truly interested in the discussion process and seriously thinks that Communists have something worthwhile to contribute to that process, then the very least it can do is identify Communists when it makes its microphones available to them.

But there is yet another reason why *National Review* is withdrawing from the Commentary series. WBAI is, as you know, owned by a tax-exempt foundation which is another way of saying that in the last analysis it can be supported by contributions which the donors can then deduct from the figure for gross income on their tax returns. The government permits this on the theory that the Pacifica Foundation, which owns WBAI, is an educational institution and is therefore entitled to special consideration as a matter of national policy. Now I do not for a moment doubt the sincerity of WBAI's motives in inviting *National Review* to appear on the Commentary series, but it is a fact that the participation of representatives of a pronouncedly conservative publication will go far toward reassuring the tax authorities as to the educational nature of Pacifica's WBAI and may have a soothing effect on the Federal Communications Commission as well if the station insists on broadcasting fifteen-minute chunks of Communist propaganda at irregular intervals on the same series of programs. Much as *National Review* has valued an opportunity to state the conservative case over WBAI, we are not prepared to serve in return for that privilege as a convenient set-off for an otherwise plainly noneducational endeavor.

Ladies and Gentlemen, it amounts to this. In our time the world must meet the challenge of a global conspiracy—a conspiracy which in the name of a pitifully inadequate view of life and history is seeking to brutalize mankind. If we have lost the will to resist that conspiracy, if we are narcissistically bent only on watching the intricate interplay of clashing ideas in our own minds, then it will not long matter who speaks to you on the Commentary series over WBAI. But *National Review* persists in believing that the Communist conspiracy can and should be resisted and we therefore decline to be a party to a deception that can only further it. With all due respect to different viewpoints, save one, and a parting salute to our colleagues and opponents on these programs, save only the growing number of Communists among them, we bid you a regretful farewell.

10

Documentary
Freedom Now!

"Freedom Now!" *was produced from tape recordings made in Birmingham, Alabama, and New York City by Dale Minor. The field recordings were made between May 11 and May 14, 1963, during the height of Negro demonstrations.*

"Freedom Now!" documents and dramatizes the struggle for racial equality in Birmingham. The program deals with demonstrations that led to an agreement between white and Negro citizens of Birmingham, the various interpretations of that agreement, the bombing of Negro homes, the Negro reaction to those bombings, and the Negro leaders' attempt to control the struggle for racial equality.

The events in Birmingham represent a crucial phase of the Negro's struggle in the United States. Birmingham may go down in history as the first turning point for United States Negroes. This larger significance is dramatized in "Freedom Now!"

Included in the program are the voices of: The Revs. Fred Shuttlesworth, James Bevel, Ralph Abernathy, A. D. King, Martin Luther King, Jr., and Bernard Lee; Birmingham's Mayor, Arthur Hanes; Police Commissioner Eugene "Bull" Connor; Birmingham financier Sidney W. Smyer; attorney Charles Morgan; a Black

Muslim leader, Jeremiah X; CORE field secretary in Birmingham,
Isaac Reynolds; and the voices of many Birmingham Negro and
white citizens. Attorney Charles Morgan was recorded in the
WBAI studios; all other recordings were made in the field.

The program was produced and edited for Pacifica Radio by
Dale Minor and Chris Koch. Technical production was by Bob
Kramer.

(*Music: "I've Got a Job."*)

ANNOUNCER: Pacifica Radio presents *"Freedom Now!"*

(*Music: "I've Got a Job."*)

ANNOUNCER: Forty days of organization and demonstration by
the combined forces of the integration movement under the
leadership of Dr. Martin Luther King culminated in the most
significant turning point in the entire history of the struggle for
racial justice in the United States.

RALPH ABERNATHY: Birmingham is on the front pages. It is on
every radio station. It is seen today all over the world. The
movement of freedom that is going on in the world today has
somehow leaped over the head of the state troopers. And it fills
the heart of every black American today, fills the hearts of those
on the plantations of Mississippi and the swamps of Louisiana,
in the fields of Georgia, in the hills of Alabama, and in this
magic city of Birmingham. And we are going to continue here
until the victory is won. (*Applause.*)

ANNOUNCER: Birmingham was chosen as the target of the integration movement, because, said Martin Luther King, Birmingham
is the symbol of segregation. The demonstrations were planned
the preceding winter when King was in the city holding work-
shops in nonviolent action. They began the first week in April,
1963, as an effort to bring about the desegregation of the downtown area. For four weeks the Birmingham effort followed the
pattern of earlier integration campaigns in the South; however,
two innovations changed the picture. They demonstrated in
mass numbers, and even more important, the masses were prin-
cipally composed of grammar and high school children. And on

May 3rd, precisely one month after the campaign began, violence began to shake Birmingham from its complacency. Adult bystanders, already angered at the arrest of the children, came off the sidelines hurling bricks and bottles when the Birmingham police turned police dogs and high-pressure water hoses on the youthful demonstrators. Birmingham's jails were beginning to overflow and Negro leaders were threatening to empty the schools and fill the jails.

JAMES BEVEL: And I'll say just like the students here in this town said to Bull Connor, we will fill your jails, the Negroes across the South, as I said to Mr. Kennedy, we will fill the American jails . . . not only Birmingham, but Alabama, Mississippi, Arkansas, Georgia, Chicago, and New York. We will fill the American jails, and tell the world, we don't have freedom over here.

ANNOUNCER: Before the week was over upwards of 3,200 Negroes would be jailed and a total of 16,000 Negro students out of school. Then on Wednesday Negro leaders, optimistic about negotiations then underway with leaders in the white community, and fearful of continued violence, called off the demonstrations. By Friday white and Negro negotiators had come to an agreement which included, on the white side, the dropping of charges against the demonstrators already arrested, and the establishment of a biracial committee to work out methods of establishing racial harmony and justice in Birmingham. Chief among the negotiators were Sidney W. Smyer, sixty-six-year-old white businessman, and the Rev. Fred Shuttlesworth, for seven years the leader of local integration forces. Mr. Smyer explained his impression of the substantive portions of the Birmingham accord, saying it provided:

SIDNEY SMYER: That ninety days after the Supreme Court decisions on the Birmingham city government, eating facilities in the stores will be desegregated on a trial or test basis. Within thirty days any remaining white and colored signs over drinking fountains and restrooms will be removed, and without delay fitting rooms (which always have been private and for the use of one customer at a time) will be desegregated. Employment opportunities for Negroes will be upgraded. Within sixty days at least one sales person will be employed in one store.

ANNOUNCER: Birmingham's Mayor Hanes addressed himself to the negotiations and the negotiators.

ARTHUR HANES: Gentlemen, here's what's happened, as usual. For forty days now or more we have protected the Negroes, aided and abetted and fomented and stirred up and agitated by people who have come to Birmingham, by people who in the past have been associated with organizations which were subversive. They have been constant companions, they have shared speaking engagements with known Communists, and they've come into our town and stirred it up, which is nightmarish and ridiculous. But as usual you tolerate and they push you, and I say it's asking too much of a city to prove that they are tolerant, and that they are a good city, and we've seen here in Birmingham a political mob, a mob to me analogous to a bunch of highwaymen who would ride up to a city and threaten it. And we say they are a bunch of weak-kneed Quislings in the city of Birmingham who are responsible for these entire outbreaks, bow down and say, "Oh please go away, we'll give you whatever you want." Now isn't this a great spirit of America? Isn't it a great spirit of those who founded this country? You know what they've done, they've adopted the old philosophy and swallowed it. "Better red than dead"; "Better back than fighting." You see.

ANNOUNCER: There were other factors and forces active in the negotiations and their conclusion. The Justice Department had been working for some time to head off the confrontation that occurred the first two weeks in May. On April 3rd, Burke Marshall, chief of the Department's civil rights division, asked Dr. King to hold off the demonstrations. King refused. From that time on the federal government began pulling strings to get some kind of negotiations between white and Negro leaders underway. One of the problems faced was finding leaders of sufficiently liberal cast on the race question to push and spearhead genuine efforts in that direction. We discussed some of these matters with Charles Morgan, a Birmingham attorney, and sole representative of the American Civil Liberties Union in that city.

CHARLES MORGAN: See, we didn't produce a Walter Reuther in labor even though we've got a large labor population. There's no Ralph McGill in journalism. There's no production of a Martin Luther King. We did produce Fred Shuttlesworth. We don't have a noteworthy tradition for the production of leadership. It's pretty well a steel-controlled town. It has been. Most of these problems could pretty well have been settled by U.S. Steel in a five-minute board meeting in Pittsburgh. But it never was done. U.S. Steel's subsidiary there is the largest private depositor in the banks, the largest private employer in the state, the supplier of steel to all the fabricating industry in town, the supplier of slag to the by-products industries, the greatest purchaser. Well now, I know enough, I think, to know that when a corporate policy is established "that you do X, Y, Z," or that the implementation of that policy is a rather simple thing to carry out. But as has been said there are many people who sort of feel like they played second-string short-stop on a third-rate farm club for some pirates from Pittsburgh. Now you've got this great leadership capacity there in industry, and this really may be our power structure. It may be that U.S. Steel is the power structure that you find lacking otherwise.

ANNOUNCER: Do you think U.S. Steel itself possibly had something to do with this agreement?

MORGAN: I'm reasonably certain that the president of their subsidiary there participated in the Senior Citizens——

ANNOUNCER: What's his name?

MORGAN: Wegel. Arthur V. Wegel. He talked in favor of the settlement agreement. But it's rather late when you're in the middle of the riot to settle the question.

ANNOUNCER: Mr. Smyer mentioned to reporters that Birmingham had a very happy relationship between the races prior to April 2nd. Is that true in your opinion?

MORGAN: No, it's certainly not true with the Negroes. But you see, when the community itself doesn't know how people feel, a man, an employee, has a constitutional right to lie to his employer. At least he does it. Now I'm not saying you do, or someone else does, but most folks say what people want to hear. Very rarely do you interview somebody and tell them that they're a pompous fool or something of that nature, even when you think it. Well, a maid's going to say the same thing to her employer and so's somebody else. They're going to say, "No, we're happy, Marse Tom, everything's fine! What problems we got? No, that's those other fellows—Shuttlesworth and King, those agitators." And then they take half their pittance of a salary and they contribute it to the movement.

ANNOUNCER: Mayor Hanes also had his own opinion of conditions of life in the Negro community.

HANES: You talk about economics for Negroes, their standard of living in Birmingham is higher than that of 100 per cent of the black people throughout the world outside the United States, and I'd say higher than 80 per cent of the white people outside the United States. The average household earnings. We have four swimming pools for whites and four for Negroes. Three out of the four Negro pools far excel all four white pools. Four and four, now how is this discrimination? Have a golf course for 'em. Cost the taxpayers $22,000 a year to subsidize it, for the Negroes to play golf. Now what is so wrong to ask them to play golf on their own golf course, which is the same as the ones the white people have? Or to go to school with their own kind? We have as fine housing projects here for 'em as you'll ever see. Five bedrooms, two baths, all utilities, $20 a month. Free food program for 'em, free medical programs, welfare, they work in our homes, and you have to get all of 'em totin' privileges or they won't work for you. You know what I mean by totin' privileges? Oh, bring a little sack to work with them, a little tote sack. You take a little bit of soap, and tote a little bit of . . . Oh, yeah, and they tote a little bit of this every time they leave your house. But we tolerate that, we understand it, that's the way the Negroes do.

ANNOUNCER: This is Mary Hamilton, eighteen-year-old field representative for the Congress of Racial Equality, one of the last people to be released from jail, Saturday evening.

MARY HAMILTON: Generally the case is when they see an organizer around, if they can, they will arrest you. So I had been ordered by the police to stay off the sidewalk. I had really stepped up on a ledge as the demonstrators were walking towards us, and I lost my balance, it was really this simple, I had lost my balance and stepped down to regain my balance, and the minute I stepped down on the sidewalk, I was nabbed and placed in the police car and I was arrested. At that time about eighty people were arrested. Two groups were placed in two different buses and we were taken to the city jail. These demonstrators were, the average age range, I would say, was about seventeen, although the ages ranged from about seven to thirty-five or forty. Now this was a demonstration in which Dick Gregory was arrested. All the girls were placed in a downstairs cell block. It then began to rain and so we all climbed up and looked out the window, so here were these children, a good two hundred children out in the rain, just being drenched . . . the rain was just coming in torrents. And people were milling about and the police were out trying to drive people away. There was plenty of room in the cell block in which I was in to put these children. But instead, the police preferred to leave them out. And it rained on those children two hours. So we began banging on the—they were steel doors. So a mob of policemen came in. One of them said, "Well, we know what to do with the whole group." And so they herded us all into these solitary-confinement cells which were about two by two. You could take two steps, two short steps in both directions. Had nothing in them but a little steel seat that came out from the wall. There were from 12 to 15 of us in each of these cells. We were left in there . . . a good two hours. Now mind you, the girls who were previously in this section had been in there two hours before that, without toilet facilities and water. So you can understand how uncomfortable they were. We were very uncomfortable still. And so after about three hours, we began banging on the walls of the cell. Of course there's a big noise and everything. And so the police came crowding in again. That's one thing that seems to be characteristic of these cops. They can never be alone, by themselves, and they always must come with their guns, their clubs, and their helmets. Anyway they all herded into the cell. And wanted to know what was up. And I told them, I said, "The girls have been in here for five hours without bathroom facilities and without water . . . and you can't treat people this way." And I just went on like this. So they took all the girls out except me and left me in there by myself. Well I was in there about two hours and then finally I had to leave. So I began banging. And so they all came in again. One of them said, "Well, I know what to do with her!" And he opened the gate and he came in and he . . . I thought . . . they had said, "Well, we'll take her shoes off of her." So I had thought that they were just going to ask me for my shoes. Well no, he just came in and he just snatched me, and he just encircled my body with his arm, and he took my shoes off. Well, by this time I was pretty angry and I guess I was trying to get out of—get out of his grasp and there was nothing I could do while he just slipped my shoes off. And he walked out and then he must of thought a minute, and he walked back in there and he snatched me, right in the front, and he walloped me with his fist up the side of my head so hard I was just stunned! And he was furious, you could just see it on his face.

ANNOUNCER: The releases made possible by parties to the Birmingham accord who posted bond to free the demonstrators from jail were slow even on a Saturday. Parents and friends stood outside the city jail as the demonstrators were freed, singly and in small groups throughout the day. I'm standing outside the entrance to the Birmingham city jail now. There are approximately a hundred people waiting here for friends, relatives, children to be released. They're being released very slowly. For the Negro leaders there can be no turning back or slackening of the pace. Dr. King is fond of quoting in this respect Gandhi's remark, "There go my people, I must hurry and catch up with them, for I am their leader." However, an alteration of that motto would probably be more descriptive of the power and temper of forces animating the American Negro today. Dr. King might more accurately say, "Here come my people, I must go faster, or be run over." Even within his own nonviolent movement, impatience is both evident and articulate. What would happen should King decide to slow down in Birmingham? The Rev. Fred Shuttlesworth answers the question.

FRED SHUTTLESWORTH: We have this second a truce in Birmingham made in the presence of a representative of the President of the United States. Birmingham is not going to back up on it as we go demonstrate again. And if 2,800 of us went to jail this last time, 4,000 will go next time. I've led this movement seven years and I think the Negroes have confidence in me. I'm not going to sell it down the river.

ANNOUNCER: This reporter tried to speak with Police Commissioner Connor, Bull Connor, as he is known in Birmingham, whom most Negroes blame for the violence that marked the last two days of the demonstrations. Commissioner Connor, however, had been too often burned by the northern press.

EUGENE CONNOR: Now wait a minute, I ain't talking for no New York newspaper.

ANNOUNCER: Well, couldn't you just give us a few words?

CONNOR: Not for anything in New York.

ANNOUNCER: Well, we just wanted to talk about the whole thing.

CONNOR: But I told you to start with I won't talk to no New York newspaper, or TV, or radio. No, I ain't getting no press at all . . . to hell with you . . . I've always got a bad press. What the hell's the press? Just a bunch of . . . if there's ever another war, that's what's going to cause it. You got that damn thing on? You know what's the trouble with this country? Communism, Socialism, and journalism.

ANNOUNCER: Saturday afternoon at a youth rally held in the 16th Street Baptist Church, to begin the next item on the movement's agenda, the voter registration drive, the Rev. James Bevel read aloud a circular, widely publicized, that morning, and broadcast once over a local radio station.

BEVEL (*Reading.*): The United Klans of America, Knights of the Ku Klux Klan, the Knights incorporated presents a public speaking, "White Citizens, Know Your Rights." The city of Birmingham, and the entire United States of America, which was created by your ancestors for your personal benefit is under attack. It is under attack by Jews and Negro Communist citizens! Two low races of mankind, the Jew and Negro, are trying and succeeding in their efforts to take over the country that your ancestors fought and died for. The Jew leaders have said, "We shall destroy . . . whether Americans like it or not." The Knights of the Ku Klux Klan rally will assemble on the grounds of the Moose Lodge at seven-thirty, Saturday evening. The Moose Lodge is located on the Bessemer Highway, Route 11. The date is May 11, 1963. There will be parking for automobiles. Mongrelizers, beware! The Klan is riding again.

ANNOUNCER: At about seven, Saturday evening, a threatening telephone call was received at the Gaston Motel, warning that that motel would be bombed sometime that night. Commissioner Connor's police were immediately notified. Their reply was reportedly: "If you see anything, call us." I talked to Rev. Mr. Bevel later Saturday night about possible trouble and its likely effect on the agreement.

BEVEL: They are supposed to make some basic change downtown Monday. And I think they'll make it. So I'm generally satisfied with the agreement. I wish it could all happen tonight but tonight you have a Klan meeting. This is a real problem, and a real dilemma for the merchants here. These bombings and things that have gone on . . . eighteen or so, this is a real dilemma for white people of good will. We have to recognize this.

ANNOUNCER: Our interview concluded at about eleven-thirty P.M. Afterwards three reporters sat in the coffee shop of the Gaston Motel, headquarters for Martin Luther King and the various elements of the movement. From eleven-thirty 'til midnight we talked shop, wondering aloud, and waited for something to break. At about midnight it did. At about midnight we received word that the home of Rev. A. D. King, brother of Martin Luther King, had been bombed. It was a ten-minute drive from the Gaston Motel in Insley, a suburb of Birmingham. By the time we arrived a crowd of some one thousand Negroes had gathered at the scene of the bombing. Before we left, the number had doubled. As we approached the scene of the bombing, we were given a preview of the rage that was to fill the hours before dawn, litter the streets with bricks, broken glass, and damage police cars, and flash headlines around the world. A tire on a nearby patrol car was slashed.

. . . Pardon me, could you tell me what's going on?

MAN'S VOICE: Two bombs exploded in Rev. King's house. Rev. A. D. King's house here.

ANNOUNCER: Was anyone hurt?

MAN'S VOICE: Martin Luther King's brother, that's who it was. There wasn't anyone hurt, I understand, but they damaged the house all on the front, because they made two shots at the house.

ANNOUNCER: I entered the house by the side door. Glass and broken timbers were strewn about on the floor. Nearly every window in the building was broken. What remained of the front end was lit only by police flashlights. There was a large crater, five feet across and three feet deep where the front porch once had been. . . . We're inside the house now and it appears that the building has been damaged 40 per cent of the way back. The living room is completely, absolutely demolished. Was anyone in the house at the time the explosion occurred?

MAN'S VOICE: The whole family. Five children, a wife, and a husband. And the wife was sitting in here.

ANNOUNCER: How in the world is it possible that no one was hurt?

MAN: Well, that's the reason why we are Christians. It's miraculous. . . . God's not going to let anything happen to us.

ANNOUNCER: The entire front of the house is open to the street.

MAN: It shook my house just like it did the house here. . . . I live right up the street there.

ANNOUNCER: You heard the explosion, then?

MAN: I was looking right at it and looking at the car when it passed by my door.

ANNOUNCER: The crowd outside was large and not a little angry. There were unruly elements in it. Slashing tires, hurling rocks at police vehicles, and shouting insults at the few policemen on the scene. But for the most part, it was controlled. Many of them sang. This was soon to change, and within minutes, Rev. Dr. King and his associates were struggling desperately to keep the angry crowd from turning into a rampaging mob. The incident that caused this change occurred just as I left the house and walked back out onto the lawn. Another bomb had just exploded in the neighborhood. Dr. King called for volunteers to guard his church.

A. D. KING: Right now I want fifteen or twenty men. I want fifteen or twenty men to go guard the First Baptist Church.

ANNOUNCER: The report of the second bomb was so loud that those present thought it was only a few blocks away. Our error was soon corrected.

P. A. SYSTEM: Please go to the motel immediately . . .

ANNOUNCER: The crowd, by now two thousand strong, began to rage and the local leaders of nonviolence worked frantically to head off a human explosion. With tremendous effort and a hairline margin, they succeeded.

A. D. KING: Everybody listen to me . . . Everybody listen to me . . .

(*Sounds of confusion in background.*)

ANNOUNCER: In the largely middle-class Negro suburb of Insley, violence was averted. Downtown, however, in the vicinity of the Gaston Motel, the inhabitants of the 4th Avenue bars, pool halls, and flophouses, uneducated, usually unemployed, socially disinherited, disowned by all, and responsible to none, went wild. By the time we arrived back at the motel, rioting had already littered the streets in that area and sent five policemen to the hospital, one with a serious knife wound. The explosion shattered the window of a grocery store across the street from the motel in front of which we're standing now. The whole plate-glass window is out. Isaac Reynolds, field secretary for the Congress of Racial Equality, was at the motel when the bomb exploded.

ISAAC REYNOLDS: I was lying on my bed watching television; about ten minutes to twelve, I heard a tremendous explosion and my glasses on my dresser were knocked off and I was thrown out of my bed. It threw my door open which was locked at the time. I got up and came out and found the lobby of the motel cloudy with smoke. And I went in to assist the people and I believe the sister of the manager was in the room asleep. It must have been God's help that she lived through it. There's a hole in the wall there. Her door was blown off. The wall in the room was completely destroyed, and yet she only had plaster marks and powder burns on her, and she appears to be seventy-five or eighty years old.

ANNOUNCER: Was she the only one that was injured?

REYNOLDS: Well, she was the only one that was injured during the explosion. The people here have gotten very excited and some policemen have been injured.

ANNOUNCER: How many?

REYNOLDS: I've seen four or five carried away.

ANNOUNCER: In the four-block area surrounding the Gaston Motel, the nightmare which began with the first bombing continued to rage. More policemen were injured. A white cab driver was pulled from his cab, beaten, stabbed, and his cab burned. The expected flood of violence miraculously never broke, but eddies and currents of it swirled through the streets.

MAN: They were berserk, they went crazy down there . . .

WOMAN: Who's gone berserk . . . the police officers?

ANNOUNCER: And in the middle of the terror, in a parking lot adjoining the motel, occurred one of the most memorable events of the night. A small group of Negro ministers, among them the Rev. A. D. King, in an attempt to arrest a situation which seemed to be rapidly reaching the point of no return, held an impromptu service.

A. D. KING: God is always on the side of right. Whoever it was who threw those bombs tonight, God knows the names. He knows their address. He knows the side of the bed that they sleep on. . . .

Please put off your hats, extinguish your cigarettes, and let us pray to Him who has brought us safe thus far.

Almighty God, who is the light, the truth, the way, we come at this hour, mindful of the kind of world in which we live. Oh God, we pray that thou would'st give us at this hour the spirit of patience. Give us the spirit of love. Give us the spirit of understanding. Have mercy, we pray. And bless our lives and bless this city in which we live, and bless our rulers tonight. Make them mindful of the responsibility that they have this night. Bless our governor and bless our nation. In Jesus' name we pray. Amen. Let us sing together: "We Shall Overcome." (*Singing.*)

ANNOUNCER: Dawn finally broke on the end of a nightmare. By five o'clock all was quiet. And by six those who wished were allowed to leave the area.

ANNOUNCER: A mass meeting held in the First Pilgrim Baptist Church, Sunday afternoon.

(*Singing.*)

ANNOUNCER: The Rev. Ralph Abernathy.

ABERNATHY: Mr. Governor Wallace has moved with his state men. But thanks be to God there is one higher than he. On the route in from the airport I listened to the White House in Washington, D.C., and President Kennedy said that troopers were on their way. (*Applause.*) And not only did he say that, but he said that he had authorized Defense Secretary McNamara to take the necessary steps, so if it became necessary, that the National Guard here in Alabama would be federalized!

ANNOUNCER: Washington, Monday, May 13. The *New York Times:* "President Kennedy last night dispatched federal troops to bases near Birmingham, Ala., for use if racial violence breaks out again. His action followed three hours of rioting early this morning in which 50 persons were injured. The rioting erupted after 2 buildings were bombed." In his Monday afternoon press conference Mayor Hanes had some rather bitter comments to make on the President's action.

HANES: You got bayonet brotherhood, gentlemen. They're going to tell the people of Birmingham: You'll love this Negro at the point of a bayonet, whether you want to or not. They are going to say you associate with him, whether you want to or not, and they're going to put a bayonet to the people's back and say give half of what you've got to the Negro. Gentlemen, this is Socialism of the rankest sort. And these troops are standing by as a bludgeon and a threat to the good decent American people of Birmingham, Alabama, to tell them if you don't do our will then, gentlemen, we're going to come in and force you to.

ANNOUNCER: Mayor Hanes, would you address yourself to the bombings last night?

HANES: I'll address myself to the bombings. Of course we have no idea who done it. We've got strong reason to believe, and I think the FBI will bear this out, these are not the bombings in the past that have been occurring in Birmingham. We know they were done, feel reasonably sure, were done by King and his crowd, and the Communists, to stir up trouble. You see King and his mob can't stay in business if everything is peaceful and calm and there is tranquillity. If there are no incidents for them to attach themselves to, to appeal to the people of the country to donate, and hold rallies in Madison Square Garden, and here and there and everywhere to raise funds. Then they have to create something, you see. I'm going to tell you gentlemen right here, as far as I'm concerned, in Alabama, Birmingham, Alabama, can be a firm stand for the rights of people locally to determine their affairs.

ANNOUNCER: Four hours before Mayor Hanes's press conference the Revs. King and Abernathy began a walk intended to make the rounds of the local Negro pool halls. The procession is now proceeding up 17th Street, Dr. King and Dr. Abernathy in the lead. And we are now entering a pool hall. We're descending a flight of stairs into the basement and we're now in a colored pool hall.

BERNARD LEE: May I have your attention, please. Turn your radio down back there. All right, I'm Bernard Lee; I'm one of Dr. King's aides and, of course, all of you know what happened Saturday night, and we were very much concerned. You saw some of us out in the street trying to keep the crowd down and stop the confusion that was going on. So Dr. King and Rev. Abernathy felt it very necessary to talk to you. Some of you were out there and this is the reason why he is here. Now Rev. Abernathy whom many of you know, who has lived in Montgomery, Alabama, and is now living in Atlanta, Georgia, will speak to you. He is an official of the Southern Christian Leadership Conference, and has been here in Birmingham with Dr. King on this situation, and he will speak to you at this time. Rev. Ralph Abernathy.

ABERNATHY: Thank you very kindly, Mr. Lee. The first thing I want to say to you is that we are involved in a struggle for freedom and we don't want to get the impression that we are cowards, because we don't need any cowards in our band. In fact, we do not want any cowards in our band. We intend to march on and to struggle on until freedom is won. We are not going to Los Angeles, California, to find freedom, but we are determined to find freedom right here in Birmingham, Alabama. Now we know that the time has come for that freedom. A few days ago all of us paid our income taxes, isn't that right?

VOICES: Right!

ABERNATHY: And did anybody tell us to wait: that the time had not come for Negroes to pay their taxes? We pay automobile taxes. We pay taxes on food, sales taxes, and other commodities, and we pay the same taxes as our white brothers pay. So we are determined to gain our freedom. But Gov. Wallace is not our leader, isn't that right?

VOICES: That's right! That's right!

ABERNATHY: Bull Connor is not our leader?

VOICES: Right! Right! Right!

ABERNATHY: . . . Then let us now hear the leader, Martin Luther King.

(*Applause.*)

M. L. KING: Thank you very kindly, my dear friends and co-workers in this struggle for freedom here in Birmingham, Alabama. We want to thank you for taking time out of your pool games to allow us to say these few words to you. Now, as has been said, we are engaged in a struggle—a mighty struggle for human dignity and, as you know after several days of demonstrations in a nonviolent, peaceful manner, we came to an agreement with the business and industrial leaders of this community. They made certain specific agreements in employment and in integrating the facilities in all these stores as well as some other things. And then came the Saturday night when the people who bombed the motel and the parsonage of my brother, Rev. A. D. King, revealed that they are trying to sabotage all that we are trying to do. These bombings were carried out by people who don't believe in freedom—who don't believe in democracy, and who don't believe in integration. And they feel that they can sabotage this whole thing by bombing homes and businesses, and by keeping terror alive in this community. But we must make two things clear. First, we are not going to stop in our righteous struggle to gain freedom here in Birmingham, Alabama.

VOICES: Right!

M. L. KING: We must also make it clear that we don't like these bombings and that something must be done about them. Now, as you know, on Saturday night after the bombing we did have a temporary reign of terror. Now, I can understand how impatient we are—I can well understand how these dread and deep-seated resentments well up in our souls. I can well understand how we are often driven to the brink of bitterness, and even despair, because of the way we are treated by policemen and highway patrolmen, and the way we are bombed, and our children are exploited, and we are exploited. I can understand how we feel, but we must make it clear that it is possible to stand up against all of these evils and injustices without fighting back with violence. Now, I believe in nonviolence as a creed. In other words, I believe that violence is immoral. But I go beyond that, and I hope you will see this—that not only is violence immoral in our struggle, but it is impractical. We can't win with violence. We make a much greater moral impact when we are the recipients of violence rather than the inflictors. That is when we are willing to receive violence if necessary, but we do not inflict it on anybody else. Now we must not beat up any policemen—as brutal as they may be. We must not burn down any stores. We must not stab anybody, for we have a greater weapon than all this. We have the power of our souls—the power of our standing up together and this amazing unity and this soul force are the things that will free us in this day.

So, tell everybody, your friends and your neighbors and your relatives, that this is a nonviolent movement; and that even if they bomb some more houses or businesses, that we are still going to stand up for our freedom, and yet we're not going to use violence.

Let us not become so angry that we lose our heads. Let nobody pull us so low as to make us hate them, or as to make us use violence. Let us go out on the wings of nonviolence and through this way we will be able to land in this great City of Freedom. God bless you, and thank you for this wonderful opportunity.

(*Applause.*)

ABERNATHY: Will those of you who are going to be nonviolent and follow the advice of our leader, who will not fight back, who will not throw bombs, who will not throw bricks, who will not use any knives, cut any tires, or do anything in the form of retaliatory violence—let us hear you say, "Aye!"

VOICES: Aye!

ABERNATHY: Let us now sing our great song, "We Shall Overcome!"

(*Singing of "We Shall Overcome" fades into . . .*)

ANNOUNCER: We are now proceeding down Fourth Avenue—the tenderloin area of the Negro section of Birmingham—and we are now entering another pool hall. This one seems to appeal to an older group of people than the last one we went into.

(*Crowd noises.*)

SPEAKER: May I have your attention for just a minute—could you fellows hold it up there on the crap table for just a minute?

ABERNATHY: . . . do nothing in any kind of way that will mar the beauty of our nonviolent movement. I want you to say it from the bottom of your stomach.

VOICES: Aye!

ABERNATHY: Let us now sing, "We Shall Overcome Someday," for this is the theme song of our movement, and it must be sung in every pool room and every tavern, in every church, whether it's Episcopal, Baptist, Methodist, or Presbyterian, throughout the South. We sing it in the jails wherever we go, and we must let them know all over the world that the Negro is going to overcome. Come on—"We Shall Overcome!"

ABERNATHY: Let's lock hands.

ANNOUNCER: Following that meeting, however, as Rev. King and his group attempted to proceed down 16th Street to visit more pool halls, police turned them back.

Violence, bloodshed, poverty, and oppression have long been the bread of black Birmingham, and brutality today has deep and well-entangled roots in that Alabama steel town. However, it is probably not insignificant that in the present range of opinion, Mayor Hanes is the pessimist and attorney Charles Morgan, the man who envisioned a decent future. What do you think the near future is going to bring for Birmingham in particular and other places in the South in general?

MORGAN: . . . I think the South will solve its problem. All across the South there are millions upon millions of white people who have a sense of fairness and a sense of justice. And they're never called on to do anything—they live lives just like anyone else but when they are, they can and they will produce. I think that it would be very difficult for instance for a person like me. Why, you see, from the time you're a child you grow up with a Negro in the house. It's been a paternalistic sort of relationship, but it's still a relationship—it is a relationship even if paternalistic. Now those days are dead. Those things are gone. They ought to be gone, but at the same time the relationship is still there. Nobody hates their own maid. Nobody hates their own yardman. Nobody really hates anybody they *know*. White people in the South don't know Negro lawyers. The Negro doctors during the demonstration ran an advertisement in the papers. There were forty or fifty doctors and dentists. The important thing of the advertisement was not that they backed the demonstration— that was important as far as the Negro community was concerned. But for the white community, it let them *know* that there were forty or fifty doctors in town. They don't know this. I think once Negroes are registered to vote, the barriers will break down much more rapidly because that's power. And we can demonstrate about a lunch counter all the time. Now Jeremiah X, who is a Muslim, had a pretty good quote in the *New York Times* that he had made in Birmingham.

JEREMIAH X: It's something that doesn't amount to anything to be able to sit down at a lunch counter and eat a hot dog with a white man. What we want is the lunch counter, and the store that the counter is in, and the land that the store is on. This is what we advocate. We're tired of being for handouts, and the chance to use the white man's facilities, we want something of our own. We want the back pay that the white man owes to the black man. This is what we want today.

MORGAN: . . . He'll get it by voting. . . . He'll get it by an equality of opportunity that he hasn't had. But the way he's going to get this is through court cases. Of course, through demonstrations, which bolster the community. The principal thing the Negro demonstrations do, is not for the white people, it's for the Negroes.

M. L. KING: . . . These persons were seeking to assassinate us. They feel that they can block this movement and this ongoing struggle for freedom with bombs. But it can't be done that way for we are on the move. Dogs can't stop us and bombs can't stop us. For we are on the way . . . to the land of freedom. And so we have a legitimate right to be disturbed and to be resentful and to have righteous indignation concerning what happened on Saturday night in these bombings. And they've got to stop! And I'm going to tell you this, they can be found, the people who did it. (*Applause.*) I remember a few years ago a young man who wanted to make some money put a bomb in a suitcase on an airplane. You remember that. It was a complicated, intricate situation, but do you know that our government, through the FBI, had the machinery to go through the intricate details and they found out who bombed that plane.

Now, if they can find that out, they can find out who's bombing these places down in Birmingham, Alabama. (*Applause.*) But now let me give you the other side: We've got to be calm. (*Amen.*) We've got to maintain our commitment to nonviolence. I'm giving you some difficult advice now. It's difficult to stand up amid the things that you've faced here in Birmingham across the years and be true to the creed of nonviolence. Let nobody pull you so low as to make you hate them. Let nobody pull you so low as to make you use violence against them. It may be necessary for the streets of Birmingham to flow a little more with a little blood before we achieve our freedom, but I give you this difficult advice: Let it be our blood and not the blood of our white brothers. And if we can do this——(*Applause.*) If we can do this, we, like Jesus Christ, will redeem this social situation. By bearing this cross, we will transform a dark Good Friday into a bright Easter morning.

The only thing that I can say to you tonight is keep your head high and keep on moving for freedom. We aren't going to stop; these shootings aren't going to stop us. These bombings aren't going to stop us. Let us go on. But I can say to you tonight, Not long! Go back with me if you will to the sands of Egypt. See God's children struggling to get out of the hands of an oppressive Pharaoh. Not long after that, . . . watch the Red Seas as they begin to roll back. . . . Watch God's children as they walk safely to the other side. How long? Not long. Go back with me to the scene on Calvary. And there you will see Christ on a cross, Caesar in a palace. But not long after that, that same Christian rises up to split history into A.D. and B.C. So that even the life of Caesar must be dated by His name. How long? Not long. I can say to you tonight as we are singing our song, "We Shall Overcome"—we *shall* overcome. Deep in my heart I do believe we shall overcome. Before the victory's won, some may have to get scarred up a bit, but we shall overcome! Before the victory is won, some may lose a job, but we shall overcome! Before the victory's won, we shall be misunderstood and called bad names, but we shall overcome. Before we get to the City of Brotherhood, somebody's home will be bombed, but we shall overcome. And I'll tell you why. We shall overcome because the arc of the moral universe is long, but it bends toward Justice. We shall overcome because Carlyle is right, "No lie can live forever."

We shall overcome because William Cullen Bryant is right, "Truth crushed to earth will rise again." We shall overcome because James Russell Lowell is right, "Truth forever on the scaffold, Wrong forever on the throne, Yet that scaffold sways the future, And behind the dim unknown Standeth God within the shadow, Keeping watch above His own."

We shall overcome because the Bible is right, "You shall reap what you sow." This is what we live by. This is my faith. And within this faith we will be able to go out and carve a tunnel of hope through the mountain of despair. With this faith, we will go out and adjourn the councils of hopelessness. With this faith we will be able to make a better Birmingham, and this will be the day when God's kingdom will be a reality, right here in this city, and so I say, Don't stop, don't get weary, walk together, children, don't get weary. There's a great camp meeting in the promised land of freedom.

11

Emotional
Involvement

by Ralph R. Greenson, M.D.

"Emotional Involvement" was a public lecture given under the auspices of the School for Nursery Years in 1962, recorded at El Rodeo School, Beverly Hills, California. It is condensed here from the full-length version, first heard over Pacifica Radio in November, 1962.

I enjoy having the opportunity to talk to people who are interested in psychoanalysis other than my patients who are forced to listen, or my pupils who have no choice.

My subject tonight is a rather complicated one. The title as you may know is "Emotional Involvement—Genuine and Counterfeit." Actually, my subject will be to describe for you disguised emotional uninvolvement. That's what I mean by counterfeit emotional involvement; and by genuine emotional involvement I mean both healthy and neurotic involvement. And even that doesn't tell you very much, so, rather than define my terms, let me try to illustrate what I mean by giving you a brief picture of people I have seen in recent times who portray one form or another of this particular kind of problem. I'll begin by describing to you a group of men I have heard about—almost always from women—and the women will tell me that they are spending time with a man who seems pleasant, entertaining, polite, courteous, considerate; who will take them to a good place to eat and some entertainment, and then would expect some kind of sexual satisfaction. And what puzzles these women when they describe these men is that these men don't talk—they won't talk about anything except trivia or gossip or some current event which is removed and remote and distant. And when they make any attempt to ask them about themselves, they are met with a rebuff. These men seem consciously to be saying, "I don't want to get involved. I'll walk with you, I'll talk with you, I'll eat with you, I'll go to the theater with you, I'll sleep with you, but I don't want to be involved." And they give the impression—and actually say—"Look, I've been hurt, and women are dangerous, and who needs it?" But they want everything else. They expect everything else. In fact, they demand everything else. And if you break off with them, they don't understand. They're not terribly hurt, because they've invested nothing. They are only nonplussed, surprised, resentful. Their attitude seems to be: no strings attached, i.e., no strings and no attachment—nothing. They are willing to give everything of themselves that is impersonal, but nothing which is personal.

I've heard this story so many times that I'm sure these kinds of men exist, although I can assure you they never come to me for any help. Why should they? They seem to have found a way of existing without being hurt, without being frustrated, and without being miserable. And they think they are living! These people that I am describing, this series, this group of men, are consciously uninvolved. This uninvolvement suits them, it is ego-syntonic; they have proved it.

I think I have heard similar stories occasionally about women—but much more rarely—and always obviously defensively. Women who are afraid. These men that I describe are no longer even afraid, or let me say more correctly, they are no longer *aware* that they are afraid. They have found a mode of living—uninvolved, invulnerable, and untouched.

Let me contrast this kind of a man with another, a man who comes to me for help because he is unable to remain and maintain an emotional involvement with a woman for a period of time—or even with a man, for that matter. And when he talks to me about it he talks with great feeling; he's upset, he's disturbed, he's bothered; he's lonely, he's miserable. He also seems to be complaining of uninvolvement, of an inability to maintain any kind of a human relationship that will deepen and broaden and be meaningful to him. But what a difference—it bothers him, he suffers from it. His uninvolvement is a conscious uninvolvement. He is not involved with human beings on a conscious level. When I talked to this man about how he lived he talked to me about his terrible loneliness. And only when he described to me in great detail how he lived, after many months, was I able to discover what seemed to be the basis for his problem. This particular young man was intelligent, and sensitive and perceptive; and he worked, he came to this town to get away from his family who lived in another city. And when he described to me how he lived and after his work in the office he went home and spent time all alone, day after day, and week after week, and month after month —I one day asked him to tell me in greater detail what was happening; at night, for example, when he couldn't sleep. And he told me about the apartment he lived in; he had money, and so he had a bedroom with two single beds, and it was well furnished, and he had some nice paintings, and he collected books. But one day he told me that he woke in the middle of the night and had to go to the bathroom to urinate; and so, he got up and put on his bathrobe and went to the bathroom. And I suddenly realized something; why did he put on his bathrobe? I realized he wasn't living alone; and that in that other bed, that other single bed in his room, somebody was living. And I talked to him. I said consciously he thought he was living alone, but unconsciously he wasn't; he was living with someone, someone who made him put on a bathrobe. And he said, "My God, my mother."

And so here's another example of a problem with involvement, emotional involvement, except of another sort. Here's a man who is consciously unable to be involved, but unconsciously *is* involved. In fact, it is the unconscious involvement, the unconscious fixation, you would say, the fantasy life, the unconscious or preconscious fantasy life of this man that keeps him from becoming involved elsewhere.

Let me give you another example of some of these problems. A woman calls me up, a forty-year-old woman, because she wants marital counseling. And I was rather leery about this because people come with the most fantastic expectations of marital counseling, but I heard she was referred to me by someone who I knew who knew about my work, so I agreed to see this lady about her marital problem, which was as follows: Very matter of factly she told me that she had been married for some sixteen years and she had a wonderful marriage; in fact, it was a perfect marriage, she and her husband got along like "clockwork." Everything went smoothly, there were no quarrels, there were no problems, there were no difficulties, there were no conflicts. It went smoothly, and she again insisted "like clockwork." And then suddenly, a week ago, her husband said, "I want a divorce." It isn't a funny story; it is rather pathetic because she was so startled by it. I asked her, "How could you be so surprised; didn't you have any indication?" And she said, "No, we had a perfect marriage." And once again, "Like clockwork everything went." I proceeded to explore the marriage, what happened in this kind of a marriage, how did they live together, what did they do? "Well," she said, "I took care of the house, and I cooked and I cleaned, and I took care of the children and he went to the office, and he came home, and I served the dinner, and I washed the dishes and he dried the dishes, and then we watched television and then we went to bed." And I said, well but there must be other things that happen. And she said, "Oh yes, and once a month we see his relatives and once a month we see my relatives, and . . ." I said, but there must still be other things that happen. "Yes, on Saturday night we go to the movies and once a month we entertain people." I couldn't believe this and I said again that there must be other things. And she said, "Yes, we are always together, we are inseparable. He travels sometimes and I always go with him; he would never be without me." And I tried to find what else there was in this relationship; what else did they do besides "being together." Oh, she then thought, aha, you are a Freudian. "Yes, we even have sex together, although the last two years we haven't had any." And I said, "Well—why?" And she said, "Well, I didn't ask, I didn't want to intrude."

I think this gives you a rather stark picture of what looks to be like a marriage and an emotional involvement, yet it's all fraudulent, it is all superficial, it is all phoney. All of this façade is only a screen for people who confuse spending time together with being related, with relatedness. It was shocking to me to see how little this woman knew about her husband; how little she was really *concerned* about her husband. She wanted to maintain this "clocklike" relationship; this mechanical, smooth-running, conflict-free relationship. This she considered relatedness. And she is like so many people who stress togetherness, who confuse togetherness with a relationship. "We were inseparable"—as though this means how we loved each other; instead of meaning: we were afraid to leave each other alone, or, I always needed someone to watch me, or I needed a baby-sitter, or something; who confuse the fact that physical togetherness is a wonderful addition to emotional, intellectual, ideational, verbal relatedness; but who instead replace emotional closeness by physical closeness. It's a substitute. They confuse physical contact for an emotional contact. They touch each other, but they don't really touch each other emotionally. So she is again an example of counterfeit, fraudulent emotional involvement which really camouflages an uninvolvement.

Incidentally, I told this lady that I thought I would like to see her husband and she was very hesitant about telling her husband but thought, well, maybe now that she had talked to me, she would change. "Well," I said, "I don't know if you can change." She said, "I will change." My heart sank and I said, well, fine. She said, "Well, I paid attention to you and what you asked me. I know, I know. I'm going to change," and she left. I'm sure, you know, that something is going to change, but how or whether it will be with any kind of greater capacity for relationship, I would certainly doubt.

Let me contrast this with another lady I saw some years ago. This woman was forty-five years old and told me that she had been referred to me by many of her friends who were very worried about her. They were worried about her because for the last many months—four or five months—she cried all the time. And every time she spent time with her friends she'd burst into tears and would cry. And when they tried to tell her to come out and have some fun, she didn't want to. Or when they were surprised that she wasn't interested in meeting some men, they were alarmed and anxious. And they told her: Look, you ought to go to see a psychoanalyst. And they persuaded her to come to see me although, she said, "I didn't feel I should see you." And I asked her to tell me why she cried. And she said to me, "Well, I've had two terrible experiences in the last half a year; I had an only child, an eighteen-year-old daughter, who was beautiful and intelligent and who was going to college, and she suddenly contracted polio and she died within three months. And while my husband and I were grieving about the loss of our only daughter and beautiful child, my husband had a heart attack and he died. And I had suddenly lost my whole immediate family. So I moved to Los Angeles because I have a sister here, my only living relative. And when I came to my sister I noticed she was cold and strange and distant to me. And when I tried to find out what was the matter she said, 'Look, I don't see you too often because my husband is jealous of it; he doesn't want me to.' So I cried, and I keep on crying, and when people talk to me and I talk about my husband or my daughter, I cry." And I must say I listened to her and I thought, yes, of course, she cried. What else should she do? This is a normal, healthy reaction to the loss of people who are dear to you. This is a healthy woman. This is a healthy involvement. Of course she should cry. It's only been five or six months. She used to cry a long, long time. Lucky woman that she can cry. And I said to her, "You don't need to go to an analyst; you only need to find some people who will let you cry," which wasn't as easy as you may think. But I ought to tell you I wondered what kind of friends she has. They worried me—these people who wouldn't let her cry. And I submit this lady as an example of a healthy, emotional involvement, a genuine emotional involvement as contrasted to every one of the other cases that I have talked about. She was fortunate.

All right—these are individual examples of people who have some kind of problem with emotional involvement. But now I would like not just to look at individuals, but to look more at society and see what you can notice and observe in people and groups of people who also seem to manifest a disturbance in their capacity and willingness to become related in a meaningful way to other human beings.

I want to describe a group of people who are at best called frantic—chronically intense people, they are *always* entranced; they are chronically enthusiastic—always. Something is the greatest or the worst or the best—but it is always a superlative, never less than a superlative. And if something isn't very good, then it's at least the worst! I'm sure you have met such people; it's hard to get away from them, because there's something contagious about them and they can be very charming—for an evening.

Incidentally, please don't think I am describing only other people—part of the time I think I am describing myself. And I'm sure all of us who listen and all of you who listen will find qualities of one or another belong to one or another of us—I don't mean to make an attack, and I deliberately exaggerate in order to make my points clearly. So let me go back.

These frantic ones, these chronically intense enthusiasts—it's very interesting to see how they operate. First of all, they are very quick to relate themselves, it seems. If you ever go to a party in their house, and they are great partygivers and partygoers, the minute you walk into such a gathering instantly you are called by your first name and you're introduced to everybody by their first name and your first name, and right away it's there: instant warmth!

And to really make sure it's instant warmth, then they give

you some alcohol and stir you around in the group, and now everybody is dissolved in this kind of an amorphous glow that looks like a relationship—except that you can't remember who these people are and what you're doing with them. It sounds familiar? They won't serve you dinner for two hours, until you're so plastered that by this time even the food tastes good and the people begin to look familiar, and then you wake up from such an evening and you wonder: really what happened? Now, are these people really involved? Not in the sense I mean. This is again a pseudo-involvement; a search for involvement, a frantic wish to become involved, but they can't really do it because it is indiscriminate; it is almost impersonal. And it goes on and on and on— and never stops. These people can never be quiet, and they confuse noisiness with joyfulness. If you make lots of noise, then everybody's been having a great time; and if you ever stop for a moment and be thoughtful, they say: What's the matter? What's wrong? And you say: I'm thinking. "Oh, don't tell me that." That means you're not interested—because they demand your constant attention to them in this very, very superficial way. These are people—above all—who have this terrible need to be popular. And that is this inability to discriminate between friends, acquaintances, strangers, and enemies. If you're there, you're my friend, in fact you're my dearest friend and I call you "honey" and "darling." And this is a typical sign that they call anybody and everybody darling and honey. And this goes for the husband, the children, and even the people they despise.

And again I think you can see by this, that underneath this that looks like relatedness, can't be—or it wouldn't be this indiscriminate; and it wouldn't be as quick. It must be that they feel a lack of the ability to be related and this hunger for relationships— and that is what it is: a hunger for relationships which demands that you feed them in some way or other; and they are fed by having lots of people around.

Let me describe another group of people whom I would call —they are very different but have a similar problem—I would call them the sleepwalkers, the quiet ones; just the opposite from these noisy, loud, frantic, instant-warmth people. Ah! the peace-of-mind people, the peace-of-mindlessness people—where everything has to be peaceful at any price, even the price of living; where the whole attitude of being with people or relating to people has to do with "killing time," finishing one day after another, in going from one day to another. These people actually are disguised apathy-and-boredom people. What looks like tranquillity is really a kind of apathetic boredom. They are also "togetherness" people, and confuse physical proximity for any kind of a relationship, and spend a great deal of time watching television, eating, drinking—and above all, together with someone; and also, usually, accompanied by some tranquilizer—Miltown, thorazine, etc. These people are actually—undead. If you look at how they live you will see they are only undead. This blandness hides a terrible inertia and a lack of fantasy and a lack of imagination. And you know, mental life without thinking and without fantasy and imagination is really poor, very poor. These people, incidentally, I have described before, they do a lot of things together, and it's interesting they *can* feel, but never to each other directly in a one-to-one relationship, and never alone; but put on the television and they will sit and watch it together and cry about the person on the television set; they can cry about a movie, about a television show. The curious kind of peculiar uninvolvement where only indirectly in this kind of a way have they dared to let themselves feel under the safety of television or the Miltown—which I think are pretty much the same thing. I do. And again, I don't want to run down all television shows; there are some which really stimulate you and really entertain you, but the vast majority, you know, just distract you; and I think they are a kind of Miltown taken in with the eyes instead of by mouth.

I want to take up a last group—and those are the pseudo-sexual people. It's become popular in our society for people to behave much freer sexually than they used to. And now you find a very interesting group of people who apparently are prone to have sexual relations, but they have sex without passion and also without guilt. It's an amazing thing, they can be unfaithful and readily admit it and apparently without any remorse, any regrets, or any guilt. And also if you listen to their sexual adventures—which they are quite willing to tell you—you find they are so boring, which is remarkable; it used to be that sexual stories or adventures were exciting; not with this particular group of people. They, again, are boring because they're indiscriminate; this is not a person falling in love with another person and trying to woo or court or conquer them or seduce them. No, it is only another conquest in a series of conquests or another step in some kind of a ladder that leads nowhere, or some kind of a collection—you add certain trophies or people to your collection, and you have the impression when you listen to these people that they are a kind of orgasm collectors, and that this is what they are after and nothing more, and that people happen to be attached to it—well, they are there, but by and large they're replaceable and changeable. They happen to be the extra part that is attached to the thing you're after; and they seem to be interested in certain organs and not in people. I may exaggerate slightly, but only slightly. But it's a degradation of the whole meaning of sexuality and of passion; as I said, these people are not passionate; they don't love, they don't become infatuated. They just feel some bodily needs and try to find some kind of a person to satisfy them with—and this is how they live.

Again, I describe it to you because you can see what happens. The interpersonal, human part of the relationship has become a gadget—a gadgetlike replaceable thing. If this person doesn't fill that purpose and it's worn out—you change a car every few years, so you change the person every few years. And this is how you go on.

Now—all these examples have to do with my subject of emotional involvement or uninvolvement. And when you look at this a little more intently, which I now propose to do after these many examples—what am I really describing? What is involvement? What is this emotional involvement?

It has to do with the care or concern or regard or interest in human beings. It has to do with relatedness to people. Obviously care, concern is derived from love in its broadest sense, in its perhaps most sublimated sense, if you will. Because caring and concerning—being concerned, has to do with the nonsexual, nonromantic part of a relationship. You can care for someone you love. That's marvelous. You could also care for someone in whom you are not interested, sexually or romantically—and that's also marvelous. Or another order of relationship. And this is what involvement refers to: it means you recognize that every human being is a unique individual and that you can discriminate and distinguish between them, and they are not interchangeable. There's a difference between sweetheart and friend and acquaintances or enemies. They're *not* all the same and you do not behave the same way to them. You don't call your wife "honey" and your enemy "honey." There's a difference. And you do not expose yourself or talk in the same way to your enemy as you talk to your wife, or your dear friend, or the casual acquaintance. It is the most flabbergasting thing to see people who have the ability—if you want to call it—to talk to the milkman or the taxi driver who's driving them, and tell them the intimate things about their life without awareness that this is bizarre or strange or peculiar. Any time you go for a ride in a train or on a plane—aren't you amazed by people who sit down next to you and pour out so much about themselves? I say that because they don't know I'm a psychoanalyst, I'm just sitting there. I'm amazed how ready some people are to tell intimate things about themselves without any awareness, without any sense of discrimination, without any feeling for the mutuality or the lack of mutuality in the relationship. And that's another characteristic of relatedness or involvement. It's a two-way relationship in more than one way; it's two way in that this kind of involvement has a great deal of mutuality in it; there must be an important aspect of reciprocity in it. You can't be related to someone who is indifferent to you. That's another problem. There must be a back and forth, and there is in all these involvements always giving and taking; never one—if it's only one there's something wrong, something missing.

Sharing has also to do with a willingness to be hurt and to

have a relationship endure even if you are hurt. Emotional involvement means that someone is a friend even though he was nasty to you or mean or cruel or angry or thoughtless; and yet, you can remember when he wasn't, or other qualities, and you're not willing to discard the whole relationship because of it. You're willing to endure pain for someone who matters to you. This, I think, is a very important ingredient of emotional involvement. Sure, it means a willingness to understand; but it also means a willingness to be misunderstood at times. It is based, as you can see, on some kind of trust for this other human being. And you will immediately say to me, and I immediately think of it: well, trust!—you go around trusting and you're going to get hurt. These are the suckers. And it is true. The biggest trusters in the world are the biggest suckers in the world. They're the gullible ones, they're the credulous ones. But let me tell you, by and large, they are far more happy than the cynical ones and the suspicious ones. Do you know any suckers? Think about it. They've usually had a lot of good experiences—I'll get into that later.

But the other part of this involvement has to do with being willing to take—and I say it in a peculiar way: being willing to take. But I want it emphasized that there are some people who are quite ready to give but have great difficulty in taking, which limits the involvement and limits the mutuality, and is a problem. It has to have both in it. And there must be this willingness to give the other one the pleasure of giving you. You see what the ones who don't take don't realize. They're not being noble, they're not being abstinent, but they're depriving the one who wants to give you something of the possibility of giving.

And then there are friendships and all kinds of human relationships in which people when they are in trouble, won't tell you their trouble, and you resent it, and say, "Why? Why didn't you tell me? Why didn't you share this with me?" Well, they thought they wouldn't burden you, but in a sense they're depriving you of the possibility of being a good friend to someone you cared about.

All of this involvement as I describe it to you hinges on the willingness to risk. This is the key point. The emotionally involved people are willing to risk being hurt; they're willing to risk painful emotion; they're not playing it "cool" but "hot." It matters to them; and if it matters, that means there can be difficulties, conflict, disappointment, misunderstandings, betrayals, death, infidelity. All of this can happen when you care. And so to be involved you must be willing to experience these emotions, because any of these involvements are not placid or necessarily calm, and there are ups and downs, and there are bound to be painful interludes; any kind of relationship that matters—I have never heard of a good relationship that didn't have some pain in it; if it was painless, it was not a very good relationship. People say: We had a marvelous marriage, we never quarreled. Frightening! Yes. With friends, they'd say: We had a marvelous relationship; we never had a harsh word between us. Well, no harsh words, no friendship. Now, all of this risking and being involved means that you are willing to expose yourself and be hurt because you have something to hold on to; and what you have to hold on to in all of this is the memory of what this relationship was in addition to what's happening now, at the present moment of pain.

And now I want to take a more microscopic look at this problem of relatedness. When I began to look at people—not only my patients, but at people I knew—I realized I could divide them into two big groups; and what were these two groups? I realized it had to do with this problem of involvement—I could describe people who were involved essentially with other people, and their problems came from the miserableness of their involvement; and then I could describe a whole other group of people who were different, whose main interest was not involvement with people but who searched for security and safety. If you want love, you have to risk. If you want safety, well, fine—to hell with people. You want the safety.

The involved ones are afraid of rejection; this terrifies them—to be rejected, because then they will be forlorn and miserable and depressed; and they're terrified of unfaithfulness and infidelity, and they can be miserable and they can be angry. Whereas the uninvolved—the safety-oriented people—are not afraid of rejection but are afraid of destruction, of self-annihilation. It's a cumbersome term, it would take me too far afield to describe it in any more detail. What they want to preserve is their own integrity; whereas the depressed ones—and I am talking about the involved ones—have integrity as long as they have someone they care about. The involved ones are ready to empathize and sympathize; and the secure ones are those who are the loners, who play it alone, play it from the outside; they're often self-contained, self-centered. Again I am exaggerating these differences to make my point; we are all mixtures of this, incidentally, so I reassure everybody—including myself.

The involved ones, since they are riskers, are apt to be more liberal in every kind of a way—including politically. They're willing to take a chance. Whereas the insecure ones—the ones who need so much safety—are much more conservative. The involved ones are apt to be gullible, the suckers; the uninvolved, the safety ones, are suspicious, cautious, cynical. The involved ones always seem to be close or live never too far where they can't be touched and become sad; even the healthy ones—they can feel sad easily. And the uninvolved ones are very prone to become mistrustful and suspicious.

How does one understand this? What is this difference? How do you understand this? You see the problem is the following: The basic or first emotion that the human infant has to cope with, the first affect, is anxiety—fear. The first emotional reaction of the newborn is panic, and in the first days he lives very close to panic and every pain is panic-producing or can be. One lives in the early days and weeks and months of life very close to panic, which is fear; and this is the feeling of being overwhelmed and of losing your identity or your integrity, losing your ego function—it's a terrible feeling. But slowly the child learns by increasing his thinking capacities, memory, judgment, anticipation; slowly the child learns that you don't have always to get overwhelmed, you can use a little bit of anxiety as a signal to warn you of bigger anxieties. It's a tremendous step when you master anxiety, and can feel a little scared—but not panicky; when you can feel "oh-oh, something might happen" before it happens and you are over-whelmed; when this happens—when you have mastered anxiety to this point, then you have the capacity to love somebody. Then, if you care about somebody, if you are aware of somebody who brings you pleasure and joy (and I'm talking now about very young babies)—once you can master the anxiety, then even when these people hurt you or are absent, you can remember them. Now the capacity to feel sad is based on the capacity to remember somebody who is absent—but he's there in your memory—and even though he deserts you and she (let's talk about a mother deserting a baby) is not present, instead of going into a panic this baby can remember: there was a good mother who used to come and feed me, and now I am miserable and depressed and sad. I think it's a tremendous accomplishment when the baby, instead of getting panic-stricken when the mother isn't there, gets depressed and sad. And what I'm talking about is the accomplishment of this particular feat: the ability in times of stress to feel, as I say, de-pression or sadness rather than panic. And this is all based on having mastered anxiety. I think it's a step in maturity; I'm not alone in saying this, that it is a step to feel sadness and depression instead of panic. And you can see this when you work with pa-tients or observe people, that where anxious people begin to im-prove, one of the signs of improvement is that they get depressed. And people are far more treatable when they are depressed, inci-dentally, than when they are in any other state. (Of course, you know, happy people are untreatable. Don't worry.)

So, the analytical point of this whole story has to do with the fact that there is a piece of progress involved in mastering anxiety and going from panic and anxiety as a signal to depression and sadness, and the ability to remember somebody who hurts you, about whom you are ambivalent, and still to remember them, to long for them. This makes it possible to cry, incidentally; when you can allow yourself to feel this longing. People never cry when they're frightened, only after they're frightened. As you know, anybody who has been terribly scared will not cry until they see a protective figure; and then when you come you say, "Don't worry,

I'm here," now they can cry. It's very interesting, children who can be scared to death, panicky and white and pale won't cry until they see mother; and when they see mother: boo! And it's quite an accomplishment in an analysis when a patient dares to cry. That means at least at the moment they don't dread or fear you.

Yes, it is the capacity—even though you are ambivalent—to remember and to long for the good person, that part of you which was once good. I think it is a higher state of development, I think essentially it means that the sad person is able to hold on to people even though he is frustrated and miserable, and I think it is based on their ability to handle their anxiety without becoming panic-stricken.

Now you can see this difference all along the line, not only in relationship to single people, to people you know, but to the world—to the concern for humanity. This is my last point: that the involved people are not only involved with their families, their friends—but also with mankind, with humanity; it matters—they pay attention. They have a sense of responsibility to the rest of the world. They have a kind of concern, if not a guilt, for what happens in the rest of the world. And they want to do something, to help. I want to contrast them with the others who look at the rest of the world as dangerous; watch out, they're out to get you. "We've got to be prepared and strong." Look, I'm no hero, but I can't *believe* that the rest of the world is out to get me—or us. (I've doubted it at times; but I won't get into this.) The related people can't forget the relatedness, even when it has to do with the Negroes in the South, or Africa, or wherever you will; whereas the others are always willing to forget: "but they're dangerous, they're dangerous, be careful, be careful, be careful." They want to play it safe; they play it "cool."

Of course, it poses a tremendous question: How do you bring up children, then? What's the emphasis—safety or love? Do you want your child to be related to the world and to suffer the blows of fate, whatever they may be; or do you want him to survive? And I think this is a basic question; I don't think we always have to ask it consciously, but whether you ask it or not it's always there: What do you want? I make a plea that we should bring up our children with a capacity to love and to be involved, and that any survival which does not have emotional involvement isn't worth anything.

12

The Philosophical
Vacuum
by Ayn Rand

Ayn Rand, author of the best seller The Fountainhead, Atlas
Shrugged, *and other books, and an editor and publisher of the
philosophical journal* The Objectivist, *broadcast on Pacifica Radio
two series of lectures on her political, ethical, and philosophical
views. The following is selected from an early broadcast.*

In my last broadcast, I discussed the moral vacuum of our age,
created by the final collapse of the morality of altruism. I stated
that altruism—the morality which regards man as a sacrificial animal who has no right to his own life and must exist in selfless
service to the needs of others—has run its course and has led to its
ultimate climax: the collectivist-totalitarian state; and, faced with
the full, nightmare reality of their altruist ideals in actual practice,
but lacking the courage to check their basic premises, the modern
intellectuals have abdicated their leadership, have abandoned the
realm of the intellect, and have left Western civilization morally
disarmed before the advancing Dark Ages of the collectivist
brutes. I stated that the present world-crisis is the last stage of the
conflict between capitalism and Socialism, that Socialism is the

204/ THE EXACTING EAR

inevitable result and expression of the altruist morality, that capitalism and altruism are incompatible—and if civilization is to survive, men must fight for a system of free, uncontrolled, *laissez-faire* capitalism and for the morality of rational self-interest, which had been its unacknowledged root. If civilization is to survive, it is the morality of altruism that men have to reject.

Today, I will discuss the *philosophical vacuum* of our age— the *intellectual* shambles which is being rapidly translated into the *physical* shambles of the world around us. . . .

All our modern schools of philosophy—such as Pragmatism, Logical Positivism, Existentialism, and all the rest—grew out of Kant and are playing less and less intelligible variations on his theme. The essence, which they all have in common, consists of holding as an absolute that there are no absolutes, that reason is a superstition, that reality is unknowable, that man has no mind, that science is a game of arbitrary constructs which have nothing to do with facts, that objectivity, truth, logic, and proof are impossible, and that all this has been logically proved.

These are the *neo-mystics* of today, whose sole distinction from the old-fashioned mystics is that their loudest proclamations consist of announcing their opposition to mysticism. But there is not a single proposition among the modern tenets I have just named, which an old-fashioned mystic would not heartily endorse: he has been preaching them all for centuries. And modern philosophical publications are filled with the voices of old-fashioned mystics, gloatingly attesting to this fact, proclaiming the defect of reason, and celebrating the downfall of their eternal enemy: man's mind.

Reason is the faculty which identifies and integrates the material provided by man's senses—the faculty which gives him his knowledge of reality. If men decide that reality is unknowable, it makes no difference whether they choose to stumble on as zombies moved by supernatural voices or as zombies moved by the secretions of their glands. It makes no difference whether they reject the mind in favor of revelations or in favor of conditioned reflexes. The result is the same: when a gang that regards itself as a special elite, exempt from the "limitations" of logic and reality, demands your obedience at the point of a gun, it will make no difference to you whether you are forced to obey the decrees of another dimension or of dialectical materialism. It will make no difference whether you are burned at the stake because you are regarded as a spirit whose flesh is of no significance, or are shot by a firing squad because you are regarded as a chunk of flesh, whose consciousness is of no significance. You are not a man in either case: you have no mind.

The leading philosophical school of neo-mystics is Pragmatism. According to Pragmatism, there is no such thing as a specific, *objective* reality that exists independent of man, there is only a flexible, plastic, indeterminate chaos which man's consciousness can "organize" into anything it finds expedient. Thus man does not *perceive* reality, he *creates* it; he creates it in whatever form he regards as practical. What, then, is our standard of knowledge or truth? Truth, say the Pragmatists, is anything that works. For instance, if you *want* to believe in God and this belief helps you to feel better, then God *does* exist. If you *don't* want to believe in God and this helps you to feel better, then God does *not* exist. Truth, they claim, is to be judged by its consequences. How do we judge the consequences? Blank out. By what standard or principle are we to act? There are no standards or principles, they answer; try anything, you can't know whether it will work or not until you've tried it, play it by ear, by rule-of-thumb, by hit-or-miss, fish around, you'll stumble onto something—standards and principles are impractical. It is unscientific, they claim, to be bound by such unrealistic concepts as reality or facts; a "fact" is anything that you find it convenient to believe.

If you want to sum up the essence of Pragmatism, it is contained in the title of an old popular song, "Wishing Will Make It So."

It is only by means of abstractions that man can hold a long-range view and a long-range control over his own activity. It is specifically man's power of abstraction that Pragmatism attacks, wiping out man's *conceptual* knowledge, reducing him to the *per-*

ceptual level of an animal and to the concrete-bound range of a savage.

The other major school of modern philosophy, Logical Positivism, goes still further: it denies the validity of the perceptual level of knowledge and brings man down to the sensory level, the level of mere sensations unintegrated into perceptions, which is below the range of the animals but might be the range of insects. Logical Positivists claim that man can be certain of nothing; they grant that he experiences some sort of sensations—but what these sensations are, what they mean and where they come from is inaccessible to his consciousness and is to remain unknowable. Any concept used to identify these sensations, they claim, is unprovable and uncertain; for example, you can know that you experience something, but you cannot know whether it is a sensation of color or of sound or of heat or of smell. Whether man's sensations do or do not come from an objective reality, whether such a reality does or does not exist are questions which Logical Positivists dispose of by pronouncing them to be meaningless. Among the concepts which they consider meaningless and seek to abolish are: entity, essence, mind, matter, reality, thing.

What then does man's knowledge consist of, according to Logical Positivists? Words. Words detached from reality, disconnected from facts, denoting nothing. Words as an arbitrary social convention. Knowledge, they claim, is merely a matter of how we use language—and there are no rules for the use of language—and it has nothing to do with reality. Where, then, did language come from? Blank out. What, then, is science? The creation of arbitrary constructs by means of arbitrary sounds. To be exact, one would have to say by means of inarticulate sounds, because words which do not refer to anything are inarticulate sounds. Can we be certain of the conclusions of science? Certainly not, answer Logical Positivists. "Certainty" is the one concept they are out to destroy; certainty is the thing nobody may claim; certainty, for man, is unknowable. What then does science give us? Science, they answer, gives us "percentages of probability." How does one estimate probability where no certainty is possible? Blank out.

How does one calculate percentages of the unknowable? Blank out. What is the difference between 1 per cent and 12 per cent of the unknowable? Blank out.

If you think that I am exaggerating—if you wish to see for yourself the full extent of the devastation brought to the realm of the intellect by present-day thinkers—I will read to you a quotation from a modern philosopher, who attempts to claim some sort of certainty for man's mind and is criticized by a great many of his colleagues for claiming unwarrantably too much. This quotation is from a work entitled *Perception* by H. H. Price:

> When I see a tomato there is much that I can doubt. I can doubt whether it is a tomato that I am seeing, and not a cleverly painted piece of wax. I can doubt whether there is any material thing there at all. Perhaps what I took for a tomato was really a reflection; perhaps I am even the victim of some hallucination. One thing however I cannot doubt: that there exists a red patch of a round and somewhat bulgy shape, standing out from a background of other color-patches, and having a certain visual depth, and that this whole field of color is directly present to my consciousness. What the red patch is, whether a substance, or a state of a substance, or an event, whether it is physical or psychical or neither, are questions that we may doubt about. But that something is red and round then and there I cannot doubt. Whether the something persists even for a moment before and after it is present to my consciousness, whether other minds can be conscious of it as well as I, may be doubted. But that it now *exists*, and that *I* am conscious of it—by me at least who am conscious of it this cannot possibly be doubted. And when I say that it is "directly" present to my consciousness, I mean that my consciousness of it is not reached by inference, nor by any other intellectual process.

Thus, in the twentieth century, speaks a *defender* of man's mind.

Observe that in pleading for certainty, he offers assurances that his certainty was *not* reached by any *intellectual* process.

Anything reached by an intellectual process would be axiomatically regarded as uncertain.

Such is the end of the track, of the sidetrack to which philosophy has been switched by Immanuel Kant, the champion of "pure reason."

Is it any wonder that the last convulsion of what is still alleged to be philosophy is an open, explicit collapse into a prephilosophical, prehistorical cult of mystic faith, in the form of a doctrine entitled Existentialism? Existentialism, today, is the most fashionable school of—well, one cannot say of "thought"—among the intellectuals. Existentialism announces that man's mind is not a tool of knowledge but a distorter of and an obstacle to knowledge, and that a deeper knowledge of the *true* truth about the *real* reality has to be achieved by other means. What is that knowledge? I will quote from a book proudly entitled *Irrational Man* by William Barrett, a professor of philosophy and a leading Existentialist: "It is not the kind of knowledge that man can have through reason alone, or perhaps not through reason at all; he has it rather through body and blood, bones and bowels, through trust and anger and confusion and love and fear." Close quote—and close the door on modern philosophy. *This* was its obituary. In the light of this, it does not matter that the rival trend and fashion attracting modern intellectuals is Zen Buddhism, the oriental twin-brother of Existentialism.

If you are shocked by the present state of the world, ask yourself what one could expect, if such is the state of the world's philosophers.

Do you care to observe the power of philosophy? When you hear candidates in political campaigns, particularly in presidential campaigns, declare that we must not be bound by any rules but must be bold, daring, and not afraid to make experiments—and if the experiments don't work, we'll try others that will—you are hearing the voice of Pragmatism. Only remember that it is your life, your money, your taxes, your future, your business or profession that are being experimented with by men who intend to find out only from the consequences—from your destruction—whether the experiment was practical.

When you see the senseless, planless, purposeless, range-of-the-moment jumble of our foreign policy, you are seeing Pragmatism in action.

While American scientists are producing weapons such as the H-bomb, while bureaucrats are holding the discretionary power to decide when that bomb is to be dropped, while the American public is being battered into chronic anxiety by predictions of global destruction—the American philosophers are struggling to solve the problem of whether the red patch before their eyes is *really* a tomato.

This, I submit, is cultural bankruptcy.

Now observe a significant fact: the intellectual trend which has brought us to this state, the school of antimind, antiman, antilife—or the mysticism-collectivism-altruism axis—has been gaining momentum since the nineteenth century, has been winning victory after victory, and is, at present, our dominant cultural power. If truth and reality were on its side, if it represented the proper philosophy for men to live by, one would expect to see a gradual improvement in the state of the world with every successive victory, one would expect an atmosphere of growing confidence, liberation, energy, vitality, and joy of living. Is this what we have seen? Is this what we see around us today? Today, in the moment of their almost total triumph, the voices of the mystic-collectivist-altruist axis are rising in a single, long wail of despair —proclaiming that existence on earth is evil, that futility is the essence of life, that disaster is man's metaphysical destiny, that man is a miserable failure, depraved by nature and unfit to exist.

This was not the way that the reason-individualism-capitalism axis greeted its triumph in the nineteenth century, and this was not the view of man nor the sense of life that it brought to mankind.

Consider that contrast. And before you give in to the prophets of doom, observe that throughout all history this alignment of fundamental adversaries has been constant, always with the same results: reason, freedom, self-esteem *versus* faith, force, self-destruction.

The philosophers are the men who determine this choice for the rest of mankind. But when there are no philosophers any longer, it is up to any man who cares to think and does not want to surrender his life without a struggle, to assume the responsibility they have dropped and to pave the way for a rebirth of philosophy.

I shall give you an illustration of the choice, a brief preview of the future which either camp has to offer you. First, I shall let you hear the voice of an advocate of faith. I shall read a quotation from a paper published by an Alumni-Faculty Seminar of a prominent university:

> Perhaps for guidance in time of trouble, people will turn not to human thought, but to the human capacity for suffering. Not the universities with their thinkers, but the places and people in distress, the inmates of asylums and concentration camps, the helpless decision makers in bureaucracy and the helpless soldiers in foxholes—these will be the ones to lighten man's way, to refashion his knowledge of disaster into something creative. We may be entering a new age. Our heroes may not be intellectual giants like Isaac Newton or Albert Einstein, but victims like Anne Frank, who will show us a greater miracle than thought. They will teach us how to endure—how to create good in the midst of evil and how to nurture love in the presence of death. Should this happen, however, the university will still have its place. Even the intellectual man can be an example of creative suffering.

This is the voice of mysticism.

Now let me read you a quotation from *Atlas Shrugged:*

> Some of you will never know who is John Galt. But those of you who have known a single moment of love for existence and of pride in being its worthy lover, a moment of looking at this earth and letting your glance be its sanc-

tion, have known the state of being a man, and I—I am only the man who knew that that state is not to be betrayed. I am the man who knew what made it possible and who chose consistently to practice and to be what you had practiced and been in that one moment.

That choice is yours to make. That choice—the dedication to one's highest potential—is made by accepting the fact that the noblest act you have ever performed is the act of your mind in the process of grasping that two and two make four.

Whoever you are—you who are alone with my words in this moment with nothing but your honesty to help you understand—the choice is still open to be a human being, but the price is to start from scratch, to stand naked in the face of reality and, reversing a costly historical error, to declare: "I am, therefore I'll think."

Pauline Kael: On Movies

Pauline Kael, film critic and author of I Lost It at the Movies, *was a controversial speaker on Pacifica for many years. Her outspoken, witty, sometimes devastating film criticism unfailingly aroused audience reactions of equally strong opinion. Her frequent disapproval of Pacifica's policies found its way on the air, on occasion, and widened the areas of controversy. Here is an excerpt from one of her many programs, which totaled a million words!*

Miserere and misery me. To be truthful, I had an uncomfortable feeling about *Sundays and Cybèle* even before I saw it. Too many people were calling it a masterpiece—and among them were people who never acclaim the films I like. It isn't anything so simple as snobbery; it's a matter of intuitions developed from experience. Too many people were calling it "artistic"—and if you observe the way new work is received in almost any art form, it is generally the pretentious, the imitation-romantic which are so enthusiastically received. It is one of the simplest truths of criticism, whether of literature, painting, music, or film, that art almost never appears to be artistic. New work in any field is much more likely to seem rough or crude or confusing or upsetting; it says something new by being different from what people have come to accept, by defying the notions of what art is; it makes demands on our responses, on our understanding. Generally speaking, the more it alters our vision of that particular art form, the more important it is as a work of art. A film so widely acclaimed as artistic gives rise to the suspicion that it stays within those old limits of what a lot of people have come to think art is.

The people who would once have said "how sweet, how pretty," now say "how artistic"—and this may represent a deterioration in taste. For there is a great deal to be said for the honest, old-fashioned desire for delicacy and charm and prettiness—there was something genuine in its disingenuousness. But the new cry "how artistic" generally means that the work looks very new and tricky and is somewhat incomprehensible. But not enough to bother anybody, because in the Marienbad decade it is fashionable to assume that the less you understand, the more artistic it is anyway. A movie that is totally incomprehensible can be acclaimed as "pure film."

As a motion picture, *Sundays and Cybèle* is negligible. It looks beautiful because of the exquisite photographic skills of Henri Decae. (Some of the sequences are almost recapitulations of what he did for Claude Chabrol in *Le Beau Serge*.) But as the misty landscapes follow each other, and the audience oohs and ahs, the experience begins to seem like going to the performance of a play at one of those matinees when the ladies in the audience are less concerned with the content or acting than with the star's wardrobe, and each new ensemble is greeted with sighs of appreciation. I have been at the theater also, at Kazan productions, when the audience applauded the elaborate sets. I don't think that the audience ever responds this way to the images in a good movie: if we are moved by the breathtaking beauty of a shot in *La Grande Illusion,* say, or *A Day in the Country,* or *The Rules of the Game,* it is because of the emotion that Renoir has given us, has made us feel about this moment in the lives of his characters. *Sundays and Cybèle* is bathed in beauty, but it's a formal, meaningless kind of beauty that makes a rather mushy story seem far more important than it is. The beauty is not integral to the story, nor are the various elements in the story integrated with each other.

I wouldn't spend so much time on this film if it weren't for the peculiarly hushed tones in which people speak of it. It is, to be precise—something *Sundays and Cybèle* never is—not so much the film itself that is worth analysis, but rather the way this kind of forced marriage of elaborate cinematography and soft sentiment can appeal to modern audiences.

I detest retelling plots, but I'd better outline this one because it has so many of the newly fashionable elements. Reduced to the bare elements of trauma, psychic injury, child as earth goddess and so forth, it may be revealed to have a remarkably fancy skeleton—but one that resembles no living creature. At the opening there is perhaps the fanciest trauma on film: the aviator hero machine-gunning a convoy and the terrified face of a little girl about to be killed. Then it is after the war, and the hero, the amnesiac victim of his plane crash, is a man without identity, living with the nurse who took care of him and now loves him. He sees a child, the twelve-year-old Cybèle, who is forlorn and about to be abandoned, and he and she form a relationship—a peculiar love relationship which is generally misunderstood, and no wonder! He is somehow cured of his fears. But the grown-ups, those terrible dirty people who don't understand all this and think he's going to attack Cybèle, kill him.

It's all so hokey and erotic and symbolic that it's really very unfair for the film-maker to show us all this peculiarly romantic infantile eroticism and then tell us it's all just in the dirty minds of insensitive people. I can't think of any other movie which has presented so much ambiguous material and then insisted on its purity. When a romantic fairy tale shifts into unconvincing tragedy, it's a presumption on the part of the film-maker to blame the disaster on dirty-minded adults. It is he who has failed to resolve the film. He wanted to have a poetic make-believe movie and a tragedy besides.

The director, Bourguignon, fills the screen with lovely trees, not to mention anything else lovely he can get in the image—icy lakes and, in the interiors, birdcages and sculpture. There are, although they are irrelevant to the story line, tricky mirror images, and every time someone goes up or down in an elevator, it becomes an occasion for a camera étude in moving horizontals. The pretentious mush of the story is surrounded with so much cold calculation. This film is so fancy that the hero carries bits of glass in his pocket, just so the images can be exquisitely distorted when someone looks through the bits of glass. This prismatic elegance, a familiar enough cliché of bad experimental movies, is somehow supposed to be linked to childhood; and the flamboyantly sophisticated camera work is supposed to result from the innocent eye of childhood. The eye of Cybèle, Patricia Gozzi, has all the dark, moist, winsome, heart-catching pathos of a Keane painting. Look, I'm lovely and lonely and lost. Bosley Crowther was accurate when he wrote that *Sundays and Cybèle* has been "angled to be a rhapsodic song of innocence"; what's astonishing is that he meant this to be praise.

The elements of the story are rather like those bits of glass. When we learn that the hero has lost his memory, we expect the plot to hinge on this: amnesia is such an opportunistic convenience that it's hard to believe it would be used at all unless it will prove necessary to the story, as in *Random Harvest* or *Spellbound.* Here it is simply a flossy addition to the story; perhaps, as Penelope Gilliatt suggested, "Brain damage seems to have a peculiar poetry for film makers in the sixties." The story of *Sundays and Cybèle* wouldn't be substantially different if the amnesia were omitted and the hero were simply neurotic or unhappy or infantile. The amnesia, like the pebbles tossed on the icy lake, adds to the romantic atmosphere. Nor am I happy about being presented with that trauma either—that explanatory device which, as usual, explains nothing, but which makes the audience feel so knowing and educated and perceptive. (This is the mechanism that Manny Farber calls "the gimp.")

Sundays and Cybèle has an obvious source—René Clément's *Forbidden Games*—but what a difference there is between the two works! *Forbidden Games* also begins with the plane and the strafing. It is clear and definite and we see exactly what happens. And later, when the two children conceal their play from adults, when the boy steals for the girl, the meanings arise out of the material; they are not labeled and stuck onto it as they are in *Sundays and Cybèle*.

At the end of *Forbidden Games* when the six-year-old girl is separated from the boy—her only friend and love—separated in that film also through the treachery and stupidity of adults, she wanders off in desperate search of him, and her cry of "Michel!" tells us that she is completely lost, that she has lost her identity in losing her only connection.

But when Cybèle formulates it for us, when she says, "Now I'm nobody, now I have no name," everything is made both explicit and false. For what she has lost has been a contrived sort of fairy-tale image—a zombie playmate who could not possibly have provided her with an identity. Neither one has any base in reality: he is as blank as she is tenderly sensitive. They are both too old for the game they're playing.

What happens to a director who with his first feature sets out to make a subtle masterpiece? Can he ever come down to making a good movie? How can he ever learn the art of the film—which is to tell a story, be it simple or complex, as simply and beautifully as possible—if he starts by rejecting simplicity and by cheating on the meaning of beauty? Part of the greatness of film artists like Renoir or Griffith or Murnau or Dreyer or De Sica is that each time they move the camera it is for a reason; they don't just fiddle around to make decorative compositions. And if you ever saw one of their characters going up in an elevator, you would know that something was going to happen when he got to the top.

14

Koinonia

A Talk
by Rev. Clarence Jordan

Koinonia is a religious, interracial community in Georgia. The remarkable talk about it that follows was broadcast by its founder in 1957.

I grew up in the state of Georgia, and very early became aware of a tremendous struggle going on in the hearts of people. I saw it in the life all about me. There were people professing a loyalty to Jesus Christ, and yet there was an unrest there. He would teach men to love one another as themselves. He would teach that red and yellow, black and white—all are precious in His sight; and yet that was not a reality, and in my own home there was always that tension between the gospel of Jesus and the environment in which we found ourselves. As I grew up, I wanted to try to reconcile that into a whole, and growing up in a rural area, I decided to go to a college, and try to come back to my people, somehow or other, in Christian love and brotherhood.

Later, as I finished the University of Georgia, I became aware that men do not live by bread alone, but by those words proceeding from the mouth of God. I went to the Southern Baptist Seminary to learn what these words of God might be, all the while dreaming of a time when I could go back to Georgia and seek to set up a fellowship that would be true to these things that were taught by Him.

In 1942 this became a reality when another family, Marvin England and his wife and children, who were from South Carolina also had something of this same vision. So we went down and found an old rundown four hundred-acre farm in the south-western part of Georgia. Now, we didn't choose that particular farm for any reason other than that it seemed to be fairly typical of the whole South. The white-Negro population ratio was about typical of the whole South, the old farmstead was about what you would find anywhere in the South. It was a fairly typical, average situation, and that's what we wanted, for we felt that we would be experimenting. And an experiment would be of value only insofar as it was carried out under typical conditions.

We had agreed on several fundamental principles. One was that as we read the New Testament it became clear to us that God is the Father of men irrespective of their race. And we agreed that we would hold to that, regardless of the consequences. Second, we agreed that the way of Christ was not the way of nonviolence, but the way of active good will. Now, I might digress a little bit there to say that I don't believe in nonviolence. These white Citizens' Councils are applying a tremendous amount of nonviolence against Koinonia right now. There's a little bit of violence going along with it, but on the whole, they're depending upon the boycott, which is nonviolent. Jesus taught more than that, not just nonviolence, but active good will. And so we agreed to commit ourselves to actively trying to love even those who are opposed to us, and to overcome their evil by doing good—and I could cite you a lot of opportunities that we have along that line. Then, third, we committed ourselves to the equality of the believers, economically and otherwise, so that meant of course having a common purse. It meant the renunciation of all common property. Into our fellowship we would accept people as equals, but we could not see how they could come in if property were dividing them. So one of the requirements for membership is that you have no earthly possessions. Jesus said it's hard for a rich man to enter the kingdom. We haven't even had one to apply, but we just don't want him to have any trouble entering it, so we just unload him at the door.

Now, things—property—have a tremendous ability to separate people, and so we wanted to get rid of that divisive wall that grew up between people, between the rich and the poor, and we just thought if we were going to be one family, that we would pool all that we had and make distribution on the basis of need, and not on the basis of greed, or knowledge, or power, or skill, or influence.

So these three basic things we felt were important; with these in mind, we went to this old, rundown farm, and started in. We had hardly gotten on the place when we had some Negro visitors and we invited them right in. We were very happy to have them. We sat down and ate, and we could not control who came and who went, and about the same time some white neighbors dropped in, and they saw what was going on, right there in south Georgia, and their mouths dropped open. It reminded me of the entrance to Mammoth Cave. Well, I knew there would be some trouble after that, and a day or two later a couple of gentlemen came—uh, said they had been sent by the Ku Klux Klan, and they said, "We want to come right to the point with you. We want to let you know that we don't let the sun shine on folks that do things like that here." And I, I put on my broadest smile and stuck out my hand and said, "Well, I'm just so happy to meet you. All my life I wanted to meet some people who had power over the sun." And I said, "We will be watching it with great interest tonight." And sure enough, the sun did go right on down as usual . . . no Joshua there at all. That was about fourteen years ago. Yes, right at the very beginning.

As time moved along, we thought, now, we've got to overcome the evil with good, and so we tried to outline a program of agricultural missionary activity so that we could reach out to the people and be a blessing to them. I had graduated from Ag College, and of course, knew all of the answers to all agricultural problems, you know, and I was ready to just spout information any time. But, I wasn't quite prepared to cope with the actual problems of farming myself. So every morning our missionary activity consisted of getting on the top story and looking out to see what our neighbors were doing, and we did the same thing. If they were plowing, we plowed. If they were planting, we planted. And for a year or two we were that kind of agricultural missionaries absorbing all that we could from our environment. I remember on one occasion I had learned in college how to farm scientifically, and unfortunately, the mule that we had hadn't had the same course that I had. He didn't know anything about scientific farming. And I was trying to get him hitched up one day, and there was a neighbor watching me, and the old mule just wouldn't stand still, and I couldn't get the bridle on him—I couldn't get the collar on him, I couldn't get the hamstring tied, and on and on it went. Finally a neighbor farmer says, "You know, I don't think a preacher ought to have to plow a mule."

I says, "Why not?"

"Well, a preacher ain't suppose ta cuss."

I said, "Man, what do you think I had two years of Hebrew for?"

Well, as we moved on, we did learn a lot about agriculture, and we began to put our theory and our practice together; we became more and more skilled; and we introduced scientific poultry farming into that area. We wrote to a man up in Virginia and told him we were trying to introduce a better strain of poultry in that area and wanted the finest chickens he had. And he said, "I'm interested in that." And we'd sent him a check for fifty biddies, fifty little chicks, and we'd devised a little homemade breeder that would take care of fifty. He said, "I want to give you the chicks." So when they came, much to my amazement, instead of it being fifty chicks, it was five hundred. Well, you can imagine, for a while it was like Old McDonald's farm. It was "here, chick, there, chick, everywhere, chick, chick." We raised those chicks all the way from babyhood all the way up to, uh—ladyhood—womanhood, I guess you'd call it. They're all pullets. We did have a few casualties. We lost about six one night when I crawled into bed on them, and several went to roost in the oven and my wife baked them without knowing they were in there—built a fire in there. But we had good luck, and later on those hens began to lay. I never saw anything shell out like they did. They'd just line up to get on the nest, and people would come from all around to see those chickens lay. They'd never seen anything like that before. One old farmer said, "I want to see those patented nests you all got down here." I said, "Patented nests?" He said, "Yeah, I hear you all got some patented nests." I said, "No, come on out and look at them." So we went on out to the chicken house. And he said, "That ain't the kind of nest they told me you all had." And I said, "What kind did they tell you we had?" He said, "Well, they said you all had a nest here that had a sliding bottom to it and a little chute at the back. And said the ol' hen'd sit down and lay and the egg'd roll down in there, into the chute and right inta the basket. Then the old hen'd get up, and look all around and wouldn't see the egg, and think she hadn't layed the egg, and sit down and lay again."

Well, well, anyway, as a result of that, the poultry idea spread, and now our section is one of the largest egg-producing centers in the state. When we moved into Georgia fourteen years ago, Georgia was importing approximately nineteen million dozen eggs from other states, and now it's getting pretty close to meeting its supply. Another thing we thought we could do was to introduce better dairy cattle into that area. There were quite a few coffee cows running around down there. Do you all raise these cows up here? Do you know what kind of cow a coffee cow is? That's a cow that gives just enough milk for a cup of coffee. Another thing that we noticed was, that there were a lot of Negro families, particularly with a lot of children, and not a milk cow anywhere around. So the idea occurred to us that perhaps we could set up a cow library, where a family could come and check out a milk cow and take it home and keep her until she went dry and bring it back and check out another one. So, for a number of years we operated the most unique library I know about, a cow library.

Now, we also had, along that time, our difficulties, because of the race situation. One neighbor, about three or four miles from us, was very bitterly opposed to us, had fought us all the way, teeth and toenail, until one day he had an outbreak of blackleg in his cattle. Now, blackleg is something that kills very quickly, and the only cure for it is inoculation. The agent was away, the veterinarians were away, so he couldn't get anybody to do it, and somebody told him we could do it. Well, he came with his head hanging down, very apologetically, and asked if we could do that job for him. Well, I went and inoculated his cattle. When it was over he said, "Well, how much do I owe you?" I said, "Not a thing, not a thing." He said, "Well, I oughta' pay ya." I said, "It's our privilege to do it for you." "You mean you'd do it for me for nothin'?" "Certainly, you of all people for nothing." Well, it seemed to touch him, and he couldn't understand how somebody who'd opposed us as bitterly as he had would be responded to, and now he, he is one of our closest friends. Now, that's why I say I don't believe in nonviolence. Nonviolence would have said, "All right, old boy, I've got you over the barrel. Let your calves die. You've been mean to us, we'll be nonviolent to you." No—and then what? No—well, I know what I'm saying. I'm just trying to push this point very strong, because I believe it is the actual expression of good will. That is the strong thing in the Christian approach to it, or it is the second mile, it is that extra push of good will that does overcome and destroy evil.

Well, back to my story. Now, there was, as time moved on, a good bit of opposition. It came from several sources at first. It came from some of the patriotic organizations who were opposed to our pacifist stand. It was back during the war, and we had quite a great difficulty. We were accused of being German spies, we were accused of having contact with the Japanese. The Grand Jury was called into session at one time to indict us for treason, and the FBI, naval intelligence, and various others were called in to make a thorough investigation, and it looked like at one time things were going to be very, very difficult for us. Finally as a result of these investigations, however, we were cleared, and the war was over, and that kind of died down.

The next group that took it up was led by the county school superintendent. The thing that got him all riled up was that since there were no buses to transport Negro children to school, we were running our own automobile in order to carry them to the public school. The county superintendent heard about it and became greatly incensed, and tried to stir up all kinds of opposition to us. He failed to win his point, and finally he wrote a letter to my father, who lived in a little town about fifty miles away, posing as a friend of mine, telling my Dad that I was in very great danger, and that he, the county school superintendent was my friend, and that he would like to ask my father to use his influence to try to get me to move away before something happened of a very bad nature. My father, who was rather aged, at that time had a bad heart condition—was not at all supposed to be excited. I came by soon after he had received that letter. He was quite excited and asked me what was going on. And I told him everything was all right, and he was greatly worried about my family and children, and finally I asked him why he was so excited—so worried. And then he showed me this letter from the county school superintendent. Well, I left immediately and headed back to Americus, and without even going to my home, I went straight to the office of this county school superintendent, and here I tell a story that I'm not at all proud of. I'm thoroughly ashamed of it, but I suppose we have to tell our weaknesses along with our strengths. I went to his office, and told him that I had just come from Temton and had read his letter to my father. And I said, "I want you to tell me why you are so bitterly opposed to us."

And he said, "Well, it's because you eat with the niggers."

And I said, "Now, wait a minute, fellah, we're followers of One who ate with anyone—publicans, sinners, the outcasts. And as long as we are His followers, we will eat with anyone. Even if a man sinks so low that there is no other man between him and hell, we'll still eat with him." I said, "We'd even eat with you."

"But," I said, "you are not complaining because of whom we have as our guest. There's something else bothering you." And he went on and named a few other things. And finally I said, "Come now, tell me, what's your trouble?"

And he said, "Well, I'll tell you. You oughta know. You grew up in this area." He said, "You know the colored people do our work for us, and if we educate 'em they all going to leave here." And he said, "I don't intend ta sen' an educator."

I said, "Well, I do. And every morning at eight o'clock our old car will leave our place, heading toward the school which you supervise, loaded down with Negro children." Then I said, "Before I leave now, I want to say to you that I am a follower of Jesus, try to be, but if you ever write one more letter to my Dad, I'm going to ask the Lord Jesus to excuse me about ten minutes while I beat the hell outa you." Well, weighing 200 pounds, and he weighing only 135, I could speak like that. But I . . . I know that was not the right attitude, but I must confess it did accomplish the purpose. No other letter came from his hand, and that was the end of that particular phase of that activity.

Another group took it up soon after that, and that was the local Baptist church. Up until this time, we had all been members of the church, trying to work within it, and to bring it around to an attitude of love and of brotherhood. We had never pressed our views, but had always been outspoken about them. One time a student from India visited us, and he became very much interested in Koinonia, and interested in Christianity, and asked if he could go to church with us. We took him to church, and people somehow mistook him for a Negro, and the church became incensed, and the following Sunday a resolution was introduced by the deacons of the church excluding all who were members of Koinonia from membership in the Rehoboth Baptist Church. My wife was the only one of the Koinonia people there, and the accusations were that we had had Negroes—we had eaten with Negroes, we had visited Negro churches, and that we had brought a member of the Negro race into that church, contrary to its practices and policies, and had broken up its spirit of unity and Christian fellowship. "Therefore," they said, "we recommend that these ones be excluded from membership."

My wife got up and said, "I'd like to make a motion that these recommendations be adopted." Well, the people who were against us didn't want to vote with her, and those who were for us didn't want to vote for the recommendations. It was a church that was quite torn when the preacher called for the vote. My wife immediately stood in favor of turning herself and the rest of us out on these charges. And the rest of the people, some who had gathered for the first time in fifteen or twenty years who'd heard there was to be a big scrap going on there, began to wonder how they should vote. They couldn't see themselves standing with her, and yet they were anxious for the motion to carry.

Finally, a few people straggled to their feet, and then he called for all those opposed, and nobody stood. And he said, "I declare the motion carried." Well, at that time everybody got quiet, and then they got a little more quiet, and then they got a little more quiet, until finally there was just kind of a suspension of animation it seemed there, and for perhaps several minutes it was as though everyone was even afraid to breathe. And then someone started sobbing—and then another—and then another —and for about five minutes the whole church just sat there weeping. And then very quietly they, one by one, they got up and tiptoed out and got in their cars and went home.

On Wednesday, the chairman of the Board of Deacons who had drawn up the resolution came down to Koinonia, called me aside, and he said, "Rev. Jordan, I wanta talk ta ya." He said, "There's an awful lot of tension in the community. I don't know what's going to happen. There might be some physical harm befall you and your family." He said, "I heard you're going away speaking tomorrow somewhere, and I came down to ask you not to leave until things die down a little bit." And I promised not to leave, and then he started to go away, and I saw he was still tremendously concerned about something. I said, "Mr. Bowen, is there anything else on your mind?" And he said, "Oh, well, nothing specially." I said, "Kinda unspecially, is there anything bothering you?" "Well," he said, "yes, there is." He said, "You know, I haven't slept a wink since Sunday. I've heard the clock strike every hour of the day and night." I said, "What's your trouble?"

"Well," he said, "I go to bed, and I lay there and toss and roll for hours." And then he said, "If I nod or doze, someone comes in the room and they start singing and it just wakes me so wide awake I just can't go back to sleep. And if I do doze off again, they come back and start singing, and it just wakes me up again." And he said, "I've heard the clock strike every hour." I said, "Can you make out what it is they're singing?" "Oh, yes," he said, and then he started weeping, just weeping profusely. I said, "What is it?" He says, "It's, it's 'Were You There When They Crucified My Lord?'" Then amidst his tears he said, "Brother, I was there. And worse than that, I was helping do it." And he said, "I came down here to ask you to please forgive me."

Well, I put out my hand, and I said, "Man, I grew up in this section. I know how people feel about it. I forgave you before it ever happened." He said, "You mean it?" I said, "From my heart I mean it." "Well, then, will you pray that God will forgive me?" I said, "No, I won't pray that." He said, "Why not?" "Well," I said, "because when you felt you had sinned against me, you didn't send anybody. You came yourself, and you asked for forgiveness, and you got it. Now, don't send me to plead your case before God. You do it." He said, "I'll do it. Let's do it now." And so we knelt down, and he asked God to forgive him. And when he got up, he took my hand and squeezed it tight. He said, "Brother Jordan, I want you to know I'm sticking wi' ya." "Now," he said, "what must I do?" He said, "I must go up there and take my letter out of the church. I can no longer be a member of that church." Now, this was the chairman of the Board of Deacons who'd just turned us out. We hadn't argued with him, we hadn't even said anything to him—had had no contact. I said, "No, sir, I don't want you to take your letter out of that church."

"But I can't be a member of a church that won't let you be a member," he said. I said, "Well, I appreciate that, but I want you to go back up there and so live as to get kicked out."

Well, he got the point. He said, "I'll do it." And he went back and, if ever there was a divine irritant, he was. He gave them the works for the next year or so, until he died. He was a very old man at that time—lived about a year afterward, and he certainly preached the gospel to those people that we would never have been able to have done.

Well, we, even after we were turned out, we thought we should go right on back and still try to overcome evil with good, and the next Sunday we were right back in our places as usual. We figured that mechanical membership didn't mean anything. What did it matter if you don't have your name on the books? It didn't bother us, so we went right on back. Well, Thursday after that Sunday the preacher came down and he says, "I wanta' ask you to never come back to this church any more at all. I thought when we turned you out you coulda caught the hint." I said, "Well, now, Reverend, what's our sin, now? What's our charge? What've we done?" "Oh," he said, "nothing, except that we turned you out, and we thought you ought to stay away!" "Well, we said, 'If we are saints, we need the fellowship, and if we are sinners, we need the gospel.' In either event we ought to be there."

But he couldn't quite classify us as either, and said, "I just wanted to ask you to stay away, anyway." So, we agreed that if he would let us come back one more Sunday and tell the people why we were staying away, that it was not because we were angry with 'em—that we were not mixing feelings with hate, but that we would stay away out of consideration for a preacher who could not preach with us in the audience, that we would stay away. "Well," he said, "can't you just withdraw without making that statement?" I said, "No, no, we couldn't because we want the light to be turned on this." He finally agreed, and so that next Sunday we made that statement to the congregation, and since then have not been in attendance at the church. Many of the people came around afterward, saying, "Well, we want you to know that they might keep you out of the church, but they can't keep you out of our homes and out of our hearts. We want you to come to see us."

I tell you that, not to reflect bad or evil on anyone, except to show you the tremendous struggle going on in the hearts of Southern people. I don't think they are vicious devils. I think they are people with the good and the evil, and it's pulling against them. There is this struggle between an ideal and a tradition. It exerts such a tremendous pull in their lives, and they want to do what they know Christ teaches, and, yet, they're not strong enough to break with the traditions in which they found themselves.

That brings us to something of our present situation, and then I shall give you the opportunity to raise some questions. Several months ago, I was asked to come to Atlanta to help some Negro students get some courses that they weren't able to get in any of the Negro colleges. I talked with them and found they were absolutely sincere and had gone as far as they could. They were not out to test any law or anything. They simply wanted the courses. Their plan was to get in line the next day at the Georgia Business College for white people and just try to register like any other normal, American citizen would. Well, that had much to commend it, but I felt it would be better to go first to the president of this college, tell him what the problem was, and see if he couldn't find some answer to it. We went to his office. He received us very graciously. We laid the problem before him, and he said, "I sympathize with you. I hope we can work out something." And he called in the registrar. The registrar saw immediately it might set off a bomb, and he said, "No, we just can't accept you." Just put his foot down on it.

The president suggested that we go over to the chairman of the Board of Regents of the university system and talk with him. The president called him up and made an appointment for us, and we started over to his office. Before we left we promised the president of the college that we would not make any public statement—we would bring out no publicity about it.

Just as we stepped out of his office, the whole vestibule was jumping with photographers and reporters. I don't know how they'd gotten hold of it, but flash bulbs going off everywhere and reporters wanting to know this and that. Well, we went over to talk to the chairman of the Board of Regents, and he was also very sympathetic, but felt that it was something he would have to take up with the board. I then left to go back to Americus, and before I could get back, I found that the governor of Georgia had already called up the sheriff down there to find out what this Jordan fellow was up to. The headlines of the Americus paper came out with the fact that an Americus man was trying to get two Negro students into the university system of Georgia. Well, that night all kinds of anonymous, threatening phone calls came through, cars came by shooting, a shot was fired into our roadside market, and it looked like we were going to have a hot time in the old town that night.

Well, shortly after that, a roadside market was dynamited, a considerable charge of dynamite was thrown into it, blowing the top and sides off of it, doing considerable damage. And men came and started an avalanche of insurance cancellations. Every insurance policy that we had was canceled, and then the boycott began. People refusing to sell to us. Now, this had been the most difficult thing of all to deal with. It's fairly easy to fight an enemy that you can meet, but it's hard to fight the strangling economic pressures that are brought against you. Somebody said that twentieth-century people no longer feed Christians to the lions—they just don't feed 'em. Just try to cut their economic roots, and I could go on and on how one business after another has refused to do business with us, not because we're a bad risk, not because we've had unpleasant business relationships at all, but each one saying, "Now, understand there's nothing personal with me. I think the world of you people, but it's either my business or—or else. So many people are saying they won't trade with me if I continue to supply you with poultry feed, or gas, or something." And I have repeatedly put it up to them, "Well, you are facing exactly the same question we are facing." And they'd always ask right off the bat, "Are you a member of a church?" "Yes, I'm a Baptist." Down there, everybody who isn't either a Methodist or Baptist, somebody's been tinkering with him. It's taken for granted that you're kinda like a state church. Well, I always say,

"You're facing the question we are. Will you be true to your convictions, or will you sell out to your business?" Now, I said to this fellow who is supplying us with gas and oil. "We know how to do business in Georgia. We know how to be popular. We know how to break this boycott. All we got to do is get up on the courthouse square and yell "Nigger" a few times, and holler "White supremacy" and go the rounds. We know the language, and we know how to do business, but with us it's a question whether we will be true to—to the highest and noblest, regardless of the cost to ourselves, and that's your problem too."

I said to him, "Now when this thing is over, will you be more satisfied having lost a good bit of business, maybe a little of your business, maybe having to move into a little wretch of a home? But having stood by that which is right, would you feel better that way? Or when it's all over to feel that you've sold your principle and sold your friends and sold your soul? For a little bit of business profit?" But as yet I haven't found a businessman in our country who's made that decision. Nor have I found a professional man. There is one minister, just one, who is trying to make it, and he's having one hard time. The other ministers have sold out. The lawyers fell like a bunch of tenpins.

Even my own brother. When a good bit of legal pressure was brought against us, I went to my brother Bob and said, "We've got to have some help." I showed him this injunction and various other legal papers that had been brought against us. He said, "Clarence, these charges are not at all true; they are trumped up things. They've—it's a stacked case." I said, "I know it is. I don't need any legal advice to point that out to me." He said, "They're after you because of your stand on the race question." I said, "That's right. Now, that's why I need *you*, a Baptist deacon, and a lawyer, to help us in this situation." He said, "Well, now, I'll give you all the advice you want, but I cannot accept the case."

"But, Bob," I said, "aren't you a Christian?"

"Oh, well, yes."

"Don't you love Jesus?"

"Well, yes. Up to a point."

"Would that point by any means be the Cross?"

"Yeah, yeah. Up to—the Cross."

I said, "Bob, I admire your frankness in this situation, but I seriously question your discipleship. For Jesus said, 'Except a man take up his cross and follow me he cannot be my disciple.' Now I think in all honesty you ought to go to church next Sunday and tell the people you are not a follower of Jesus Christ."

"Well," he said, "if all of us did it there wouldn't be anybody left in the church."

"Well, maybe there wouldn't. Maybe we could get along without those kinds of churches anyway, I don't know."

"But," he said, "Clarence, if I were to take that stand I'd lose my home, I'd lose my practice, I'd lose my business."

"I know all that. You'd lose the same things we're having to lose. Then you could come on to Koinonia and join us, for our requirement is that you have nothing. You'd be a prime candidate for membership. Then we could be *true* brothers, not just brothers in the flesh, but brothers in the spirit." He said, "I'm not prepared to take that stand."

Well, we finally did succeed in getting one lawyer in Atlanta to take the case and he has certainly stood by us.

Well, I need not go into all of it. It has taken several forms. One the physical part of it, such as the dynamiting, shooting, and so forth. On one occasion I was coming home over a rather lonely country road and a truck blocked the road over a little one-way bridge. I noticed what was going on and had slowed down considerably up the road. As I came around the curve when I saw the gentleman get out with a shotgun I remembered Jesus' injunction that when they persecute you in this city, flee to the next, you know. And I also remembered that if a man smite you on your right cheek, turn to him both heels, and I put it in reverse and backed out of that situation very quickly. I didn't see any point in arguing with a man who could win the argument with a slight pressure of his forefinger. I don't even know whether he shot or not. I was traveling at supersonic speeds and the sound probably wouldn't have reached me anyway.

Well, the physical side of it has somewhat died down now, but the legal and economic side of it still continues very, very severe. It's almost impossible for us now to either buy or sell our products anywhere in the county. We have to just go outside of it where we're not known, or where the pressure has not been applied to people who deal with us. The state of Georgia has applied all of its legal machinery of every department to try to get rid of us. They're trying now to get rid of our corporate charter, and whether or not we can exist as a corporation there any longer I just don't know. Time will tell about that.

Just a few hours before I left, I learned that a petition was being circulated through the county asking us to leave the county. If they are petitioning us, well, we can disregard it. The only one I know that the petition would have any effect on would be God. That's where we get our orders from and I don't think He'd give them much of a hearing. So I don't know of anything to do but stay. Some very important battles have already been won. If we can see it through financially I think we got a pretty good chance. It's quite a hard job to make a living just farming, without all of these other obstacles. But for everything that the opposition has thrown at us, somehow new things have opened up. They practically stopped the local trade with the roadside market, but now through peacemakers and others, a mail-order business is developing, and I don't think that even the most rabid of the local rabble-rousers can stop Uncle Sam's mail from going right on. They've stopped us from getting gas locally, but the American Baptist Social Service Council loaned us $1,000 without interest to buy some big storage tanks, and now we can go down to the Gulf and get a whole trailer load of gas at three-four cents a gallon cheaper than we were buying it anyway. Every time it seems that we've been kicked upstairs. Now, that's why I'm so optimistic about it. I know that we are not an isolated little phenomenon down there. I know that we are part of a whole worldwide surge toward this kind of thing, and we feel ourselves borne up on a tide of a world movement that's going on. And I don't think that the local people are

on the losing end of it. Now, they might lose large among themselves, but they're very insignificant in the worldwide picture.

In all of the thing, in the whole crisis, I have not heard one
word from any one in the whole sixty people of Koinonia even
hinting that we should give up. We have had to take extra precau-
tionary measures. We've had to put somebody on watch at night,
and it means staying up all night every so often. Of course, the
person on watch is not armed with anything but a flashlight. But
we find that light is a very powerful weapon at times. Now, we
have had a tremendous burden, and I'm not saying that you don't
get jittery and you don't get on edge, but there has not been one
slightest indication on the part of anybody that it's time to quit.

15

Stories of Cronopios and Famas

by Julio Cortázar

*In these stories, the Argentine novelist and short-story writer,
Julio Cortázar, divides the world, traditionally enough, into three
separate categories: the* famas *(Very Important People), the*
esperanzas *(Hopefuls is too nice a translation for them, because
what they hope, of course, is that they become famas), and the*
cronopios, *the rest of us, the flies in the flywheel of progress, and
the true heroes of these tales. These selections were among the
many* Stories of Cronopios and Famas, *read first in 1960 for Pacifica by the American poets Robert Kelly and Paul Blackburn.
The translations from the Spanish are Mr. Blackburn's.*

Turtles and Cronopios

Now it happens that turtles are great speed enthusiasts, which
is natural.

The esperanzas know it and don't bother about it.

The famas know it, and make fun of it.

The cronopios know it, and each time they meet a turtle, they haul out the box of colored chalks, and on the rounded blackboard of the turtle's shell they draw a swallow.

On the Preservation of Memories

To maintain the condition of their memories, the famas proceed in the following manner: after having fastened the memory with webs and reminders, with every possible precaution, they wrap it from head to foot in a black sheet and stand it against the parlor wall with a little label which reads: "EXCURSION TO QUILMES" or "FRANK SINATRA."

Cronopios, on the other hand, disordered and tepid beings that they are, leave memories loose about the house. They set them down with happy shouts and walk carelessly among them, and when one passes through, running, they caress it mildly and tell it: "Don't hurt yourself," and also, "Be careful of the stairs." It is for this reason that the famas' houses are orderly and silent, while in those of the cronopios there is great uproar and doors slamming. Neighbors always complain about cronopios, and the famas shake their heads understandingly, and go see if the tags are all in place.

The Narrow Spoonful

A fama discovered that virtue was a spherical microbe with a lot of feet. Immediately he gave a large tablespoonful to his mother-in-law. The result was ghastly: the lady ceased and desisted from her sarcastic comments, founded a club for lost alpine-climbers, and in less than two months, conducted herself in such an exemplary manner that her daughter's defects, having up till then passed unnoticed, came with great suddenness to the first level of consideration, much to the fama's stupefaction. There was no other recourse than to give a spoonful of virtue to his wife, who abandoned him the same night, finding him coarse, insignificant and, all in all, different from those moral archetypes who floated, glittering, before her eyes.

The fama thought for a long while, and finally swallowed a

whole flask of virtue. But all the same, he continued to live alone and sad. When he met his mother-in-law or his wife in the street, they would greet one another respectfully and from afar. They did not even dare to speak to one another, such was his perfection and their fear of being contaminated.

The Particular and the Universal

A cronopio was about to brush his teeth standing next to his balcony, and being possessed by a very incredible gaiety to see the morning sun and the handsome clouds racing through the sky, he squeezed the tube of toothpaste prodigiously and the toothpaste began to emerge in a long pink strip. After having covered his brush with a veritable mountain of toothpaste, the cronopio found he had some left over, started to flap the tube out the window, still squeezing away, and strips of pink toothpaste fell over the balcony into the street where several famas had gathered to discuss municipal scandals. The strips of pink toothpaste landed all over the famas' hats, while up above, the cronopio was singing away and, filled with great contentment, was brushing his teeth. The famas grew very indignant over this incredible lack of self-consciousness on the cronopio's part, and decided to appoint a delegation to upbraid him immediately. With which, the delegation, composed of three famas, tromped up the stairs to the cronopio's apartment and reproached him, addressing him like this:

"Cronopio, you've ruined our hats, you'll have to pay for them."

And afterward, with a great deal more force:

"Cronopio, you shouldn't have wasted your toothpaste like that!"

Eugenics

It happens that cronopios do not want to have sons, for the first thing a recently born cronopio does is to be grossly insulting to his father, in whom he sees obscurely the accumulation of misfortunes which will one day be his own.

Given these reasons, the cronopios turn to the famas for help in fecundating their wives, a situation toward which the famas are always well-disposed, it being a question of libidinous character. They believe furthermore that in this way they will be undermining the moral superiority of the cronopios, but in this they are stupidly mistaken, for the cronopios educate their sons in their own fashion, and within a few weeks have removed any resemblance to the famas.

Their Faith in the Sciences

An esperanza believed in physiognomical types, such as for instance the pugnosed type, the fish-faced type, those with a large air-intake, the jaundiced type, the beetle-browed, those with an intellectual face, the hairdresser type, etc. Ready to classify these groups definitively, he began by making long lists of acquaintances and dividing them into the categories cited above.

He then took the first group, consisting of eight pugnosed types, and noticed that, surprisingly, these boys divided actually into three subgroups, namely pugnoses of the mustached type, pugnoses of the pugilist type, and pugnoses of the ministry-appointee sort, composed respectively of three, three, and two pugnoses in each particularized category. Hardly had he separated them into their new groupings (at the Paulista Bar in the calle San Martin where he had gathered them together at great pains and no small amount of coffee with sweet cream, well whipped), than he noticed that the first subgroup was not homogeneous, since two of the mustached-type pugnoses belonged to the rodent variety, while the remaining one was most certainly a pugnose of the Japanese-court sort. Well. Putting this latter one aside, with the help of a hefty sandwich of anchovies and hard-boiled eggs, he organized a subgroup of the two rodent types, and was getting ready to set it down in his notebook of scientific data, when one rodent type looked to one side and the other turned in the opposite direction, with the result that the esperanza, and furthermore everyone there, could perceive quite clearly that, while the first of the rodent types was evidently a brachycephalic pugnose, the other exhibited a cranium much more suited to hanging a hat on than to wearing one.

So it was that the subgroup dissolved, and as for the rest, better not to mention it, since the remainder of the subjects had graduated from coffee with sweet cream to coffee with flaming cognac, and the only way in which they seemed to resemble one another at the height of these festivities was in their common and well-entrenched desire to continue getting drunk at the expense of the esperanza.

Never Stop the Presses

A fama was working so hard in the raw-tea industry that he didn't-have-time-for-anything. Thus this fama languished at odd moments, and raising-his-eyes-to-heaven, frequently cried out: "How I suffer! I'm a victim of my work, notwithstanding being an example of industry and assiduity, my-life-is-a-martyrdom!"

Touched and depressed by his employer's anxiety, an esperanza who was working as a typist in the accounting office of the fama got up enough nerve to address himself to the fama, speaking like this:

"Gray day, fama fama. If you solitary occasion work, I pull solution right away from left pocket."

The fama, with the amiability characteristic of his race, knitted his eyebrows and extended his hand. A miracle! Among his fingers, there the world lay caught, and the fama had no reason to complain of his luck. Every morning the esperanza came in with a fresh supply of miracle and the fama, installed in his armchair, would receive a declaration of war and/or a declaration of peace, or a selected view of the Tyrol and/or of Bariloche and/or of Porto Alegre, the latest thing in motors, a lecture, a photo of an actress and/or of an actor, etc. All of which cost him ten pieces of silver, which is not very much bread if you're buying the world.

Education of the Prince

Cronopios hardly ever have sons, but when they do have them, they lose their heads and extraordinary things occur. For example, a cronopio has a son, and immediately afterward, wonderment invades him, and he is certain that his son is the very peak and summit of beauty and that all of chemistry runs through his veins with here and there islands of fine arts, poetry, and urban architecture. Then it follows that this cronopio cannot even look at his son but that he bows deeply before him and utters words of respectful homage.

The son, as is natural, hates him fastidiously.

When he comes of school age, his father registers him in 1-B, and the child is happy with other little cronopios, famas, and esperanzas. But he grows proportionately worse the closer it comes to noon, because he knows that when class is out his father will be waiting for him and upon seeing him will raise his hands and say divers things, such as:

"Grade A, cronopio cronopio, tallest and best and most rosy-cheeked and most particular and most dutiful and most diligent of sons!"

Whereat the junior famas and junior esperanzas are doubled up with laughter at the street-curb, and the small cronopio hates his father with great pertinacity and consistency, and will always end by playing him a dirty trick somewhere between first Communion and military service. But the cronopios do not suffer too much from this, because they also used to hate their fathers, to such point as it seems likely that this hate is the other name for liberty or for the immense world.

Place the Stamp in the Upper Right-hand Corner of the Envelope

A fama and a cronopio are very good friends and go together to the post office to mail several letters to their wives who are traveling in Norway, thanks to the diligence of Thos. Cook & Son.

The fama sticks his stamps on with prolixity, beating on them lightly numerous times so that they will stick well, but the cronopio lets go with a terrible cry frightening the employees, and with immense anger declares that the portraits on the stamps are repugnant and in bad taste and that never shall he be obliged to prostitute his love letters to his wife with such sad pieces of work as that. The fama feels highly uncomfortable because he has already stamped his letters, but as he is a very good friend of the cronopio, he would like to maintain solidarity with him and ventures to say that, in fact, the twenty-centavo stamp is vulgar in the extreme *and* repetitious, but that the one-peso stamp has the fuzzy color of settling wine.

None of this calms the cronopio who waves his letter and exhorts, apostrophizes, and declaims at the employees, who gaze at him completely stupefied. The postmaster emerges and hardly twenty seconds later the cronopio is in the street, letter in hand, and burdened with a great sorrow. The fama, who has furtively posted his in the drop-box, turns to consoling him and says:

"Luckily our wives are traveling together, and in my letter I said that you were all right, so that your wife can read it over my wife's shoulder."

16

Commentary
by Lewis Hill
(*October, 1949*)

Some radio commentator or other makes a practice of beginning his stint—so I have heard—with the fulsome declaration that There's Good News Tonight. In the world of radio commentary it is categorically impossible, in my opinion, that there could be good news more often, say, than one night out of a hundred. I am not certain, myself, that I can remember ever having begun a commentary with the feeling that there was really good news of any lasting, fundamental nature about the world commentators are supposed to discuss. Many will feel that this admission displays a woeful blindness to a world paved with good intentions. So be it. Some must be blind, in order to be led. But tonight, in any event, is an exception. There is actually some news of what we might term national and international import which to me seems radically good—good for the world, good for me, and for everyone who cares a busted dime about the shape of tomorrow.

One such piece of news appears in the current issue of *Harper's* magazine, in an article by writer Bernard DeVoto. People who read *Harper's* regularly tell me that DeVoto writes an article every month, a book every year, and is one of those chaps who make their livings as public scolds. Whether making his living now or merely indulging his disposition, he ranks as a professional bellwether, like the Muckrakers of old.

There is one important fact about professional bellwethers which distinguishes them clearly from both prophets and rebels. Prophets have no country, and rebels are hanged. But a public scold like DeVoto, while he may embroil himself in the issues of the day—in writing; and even challenge the probity of public officials—in writing; still, the professional scold draws a healthy paycheck for it—for writing, that is; and has a comfortable home and the most respected associations; and is feted at various banquets on his fiftieth birthday; and lives an honored life full of honorary degrees quite in contrast to the terrible things he says in print. This is axiomatic even with bellwethers more terrible than DeVoto —with the likes of Milton Mayer, for example, who leads a most comfortable and even privileged life on the strength of all the terrible, terrible things he says in print. So it came as no surprise to hear that the current issue of *Harper's* contained another good old-fashioned piece of muckraking by Bernard DeVoto, whose monthly column is called, I believe, "The Easy Chair." Everyone is full of words when he sits in an overstuffed easy chair.

But when I looked at the terrible article I rejoiced, yea, I stood and cheered. The subject is the FBI, and the development of the secret police mentality in America. DeVoto looks, with the fashionable verbosity of such publications, at the gossip-mongering of the FBI, the demand it brings to the loyal citizen that he spy on his neighbor, the demagogic secrecy with which it conceals the sources of its alleged evidence, the fantastic fiction and irresponsibility of its alleged evidence when revealed. All this enrages bellwether DeVoto, as might be expected. But he then says, by George, that there's only one thing to do about it: refuse to answer any questions asked by an FBI man, or by any other government agency investigator. Say, instead: If it is my duty as a citizen to tell what I think, know, imagine or have heard rumored about my neighbor or anyone else, I will do so under subpoena in a court of law in the presence of the accused and his attorney. I will not do so anywhere else, and particularly not with you, O college-graduated flatfoot in the service of fear and dishonesty. So much, in paraphrase, says DeVoto.

I do not at all suggest that this should form the basis for a new optimism toward the course of world history. But I do say it is refreshing. It makes me feel good because it relates a typically vast, intangible public fact to the possibility of relevant personal action. The FBI is a contemptible institution and the whole country knows it, despite its constant propaganda. Even those who have the biggest stakes in the commie witch-hunt blush over incidents like the Coplon exposé, and mutter of expediencies and unfortunate necessities, never daring to speak for the principle of such an institution. Of course not; for the secret police of any state are the most instinctively detested of all the state's arms of power. But the question remains, what can be *done* about it. DeVoto's solution is the only one. It is always the only solution in a relationship with the state which violates the integrity and conscience of man. Refuse to cooperate. Say, No. Say, I for my part will not.

It is not, in this particular case, that DeVoto has inaugurated any challenge. He has not proposed the violation of law, but rather the restoration of law—one of the good and vital laws of our overly legalized society; the one that guarantees the accused knowledge of his accusers, of their accusation, and the right to face them in public. The fact is the FBI exercises no legal compulsion whatever. It possesses no legal authority to ask you questions about your neighbor. DeVoto is perfectly aware of this fact, as he is also aware of his responsibility to his editors to turn out a kind of stuff that will have a general appeal. The encouraging thing to me is precisely that DeVoto's article would not have appeared, in the inscrutable nature of the commercial publishing world, were there not his own and a shrewd editorial opinion that it will ring the bell with millions. I hope it does. Even in an easy chair one can say No to an FBI man. In fact, that's just the place for it.

Still another refreshing piece of news, in my jaded outlook, concerns the successor to the pulpit of John Haynes Holmes in the Community Church of New York. That Church, and Holmes, have a long history some of you may know. It is New York's big-

gest, richest, and most fashionable center of congregational worship. Holmes in his many years as pastor has shaken a finger more
than once at intolerant ways, but never like his successor on a
recent date. The new pastor of Community Church (Holmes having retired on his age) is Donald Harrington. Be darned if the first
thing Harrington did on installation in the pulpit wasn't to raise a
nasty question about individual freedom, in the most worldly
sense. And in a way, I'm afraid, that *did* break the law—at least
what one federal court says is the law. And not content with this,
Harrington thereupon dared the FBI to come and get him.

Here is the saying of the law which Harrington breached: If
a man believe in his conscience that it is wrong to submit to conscription for war, and right to refuse to be conscripted; and if
another man believe that the first should follow the voice of his
conscience above all other voices, the second man must keep silent, and must abstain from any speech or action which might
encourage the first man to follow his conscience. Do you believe
that that is the law? But I assure you it is. Early this year a young
man named Charles Rickert, believing that to hand himself over
to the state so that the state can make war with him is an evil,
refused to register under the Selective Service Act. He was arrested and so forth. After this had occurred, another young man, a
certain Larry Gara, a college teacher, counseled Rickert to hold
fast to his conscience for conscience sake. Gara was arrested and
is now in federal prison.

Don Harrington, the new pastor of Community Church, got
up in his rich, respectable pulpit the other day and said that he,
personally, urges all young men who are inwardly moved to follow Christ in the matter of war to refuse to register for the draft.
If Gara is guilty, said Harrington, I am guilty.

Well sir, I am refreshed. Every year in these years of vanish-
ing freedom a batch of men are clapped in prison for being inwardly moved to follow Christ in the matter of war and refuse
conscription for war. They are mostly obscure folk; you never
hear of them. But here is a man in the respectable setting of a
New York pastorate, with all manner of opportunity before him to

make a great career talking vaguely about civil liberties. He chose, instead, to talk concretely. He hates war—who doesn't? But in that event, what does one *do* about it? Harrington's solution is direct and final. One gets up on his haunches and says No. And one deliberately spreads the idea that others, everyone who has haunches to get up on, should say No. Let governments do their damnedest then (and you may be certain they will do their damnedest)—they won't make war. This appears to be the essence of the message from the fashionable pulpit of Community Church, New York.

I like that. It reminds me of some of my capacities. It renews my own suspicion that I am a moral creature, responsible for my acts, and with the miraculous capacity to assume such responsibility. And the sudden thought visits me, as it must have visited DeVoto after years of uneasy interrogation with FBI men: My gosh, what's wrong with me, *I* can say No too. If it's wrong, how can I expect anyone else to say it's wrong if I don't? . . . Et cetera: and thus giddy with new expectations of myself and the world, I go on to contemplate the good news about Garry Davis. O there's good news tonight!

You may have read about young Davis in the paper today, or heard about him on radio. *Time* magazine currently relates a part of his latest adventures. Suppose we review the case briefly, agreeing beforehand that when one not only proclaims himself a world citizen, but acts like it, he must naturally expect to find the world a strange and often inclement place.

You remember that Garry Davis is the son of a well-known dance orchestra leader in this country; and further, that he was a bomber pilot, killed a few thousand people, was decorated and all that, and emerged from the war clean-shaven, an honored citizen, pretty well off. He was having a good old G.I. time in Paris, I guess, when one day, while walking round a corner, he had a disastrous collision with a thought. It's been nagging him ever since. You first heard of him a couple of years ago when he formally renounced his American citizenship, not, he declared, in contempt of America but as the only concrete, practical step he could take toward transcending the nationalism that caused World War II. He was, he said, a World Citizen. Here at home, as I remember, his father denounced him, the Secretary of State frowned and coughed, and the newspapers had a whale of a time with it. With flourish and fanfare young Davis set up court in Paris, issued World Citizenship identification papers, enlisted the sympathy of intellectuals all over the world, and had quite a movement going for a while.

As I recall the French government was somewhat slow in awakening to its opportunity. Davis was unwelcome in France for a time—I believe he had to go to Belgium. But someone in the French foreign office, on the public relations staff, had a better idea. Davis was brought back. France welcomed Davis. President Auriol himself welcomed Davis. You get the idea. France too loves peace, espouses brotherhood, believes in ideals—as everyone knows. And think how little to lose, how much to gain, in welcoming a confused young man whom the newspapers have publicized as a symbol of the peace cause, the brotherhood cause, and who cannot possibly do anything about any of those causes. In the months since, Davis has lived a busy life in Paris, somewhat like a boutonniere on the diplomatic lapels of the French government.

But far off in Indochina peace-loving France was, and still is, engaged in war, against the brotherhood of natives. A colonial war, a noble effort to continue centuries of colonial exploitation. And in France there was a young man, like Donald Harrington, Larry Gara, and Charles Rickert in this country, who believed that it is wrong to hand oneself over to the state so that the state can make war with one. Like Gara and Rickert here, the young man in France, Jean Moreau by name, was thrown in prison.

It was at this point—a wholly commonplace point in the workings of the modern state—that Garry Davis became less confused. Someone told him about Jean Moreau, and do you know, it was a very puzzling thing. The President of France had welcomed him, Davis, because of his high principles, because of his personal dedication to the ideals of peace, brotherhood, reason, and conscience. But those were the very principles that young Jean Mo-reau believed in—and certainly he had the same high personal dedication that the French government had praised in Davis. Well, says Davis, there must be some mistake. How can Moreau be guilty of a crime if, for the same thing, I am regarded as an international hero? So, just to clear things up, Davis wrote a letter to his good friend President Auriol. He quoted the first article of the Declaration of the United Nations:

> All human beings are born free and equal in dignity and rights. They are endowed with reason and conscience, and should act towards one another in a spirit of brother-hood.

Obviously, since France signed this declaration, the government must believe that young Jean Moreau, born with a conscience, possessed the right to follow it, especially if its promptings were in a spirit of brotherhood. The government must simply have overlooked something, and would wish to release Moreau imme-diately.

Some time passed, and Davis had no reply from President Auriol. But the French press abused him for "meddling in internal French affairs." To that accusation he replied in these rather quot-able words:

> If the privileges I enjoy [residing in France without papers] have been bought by moral convictions—because Moreau was born in France does that make his conscience different from mine? . . . Should I count my blessings smugly while another counts the bars between him and my liberty? I am here only by the grace of the French peo-ple. Should I not continue to express and act by the same convictions which I believe the French people consider valid. Indeed, if I did not defend these convictions I should be betraying the confidence which both President Auriol and the French people have placed in me.

But still no answer from the President. Davis thereupon said, as Harrington said in New York: If he is guilty, I am guilty too.

The press accused him of attempting to undermine the defense of the West. For after all, by this time Davis was leader of a widespread movement. Let me quote him directly again in his reply to this accusation:

> Where then does peace start? And of what does this precious defense consist? Is it the defense of atom bombs, deadly bacteria, biochemical weapons, tens of thousands of warplanes, hundreds of warships, tens of millions of machine-guns and flame-throwers, billions of bullets? . . . Does this frantic preparation for final destruction in the name of "defense" afford [the governments] the security they desire? I do not mean to be presumptuous, but for me it does not, and I am led to believe that they are simply misdirected in their reasoning. The lessons of the first two world wars are all around us. For me, and no doubt for many of us, the era of violence is dead, though not yet buried. We will only evolve and surmount our terrifying problems on a higher level: the "reason and conscience" recognized by the United Nations itself; and it would seem that the sooner we individually and then collectively learn of the tremendous force of Non-Violence in its most positive active sense, the sooner we shall be able to emerge with true freedom into our One World civilization.

And do you know what Garry Davis did then? He went down to the prison where Moreau was held and politely asked to be admitted, since he was guilty if Moreau was. The paddy wagon came to get him. He was jailed on the charge of "being in France without a permit," and after eight days brought to trial—that was just yesterday. According to *Time* magazine, when the magistrate examined him, Davis asked bluntly: "Does the French government believe in reason and conscience?" To which the magistrate replied: "I am a simple functionary. I follow my orders and do not question my superiors."

Among Davis' various statements to the press, one expressed a hope that the French government would not try to force the responsibility of dealing with him on some other government.

This posed an extremely difficult problem for the public relations experts of the Foreign Office. Reports from Paris yesterday said Davis had been sentenced only to the time he had already spent in jail—eight days—and set free. Whether France intends to deport him remains to be seen. Deport him whither? A World Citizen?

The story of Davis is of course rich in the abysmal cynicism of the modern bureaucracy, and in the futility and helplessness of the state trapped by its own expediencies. But if we enjoy that rich taste we can indulge in it without searching so far, and it is not this that makes me feel so good about Davis' story. What I find so refreshing is, again, the way it illuminates and reaffirms the extraordinary relevance of personal principles in matters of the public destiny. Garry Davis, like Donald Harrington and Bernard DeVoto and thousands less lionized, has got hold of a basic fact, a basic equation. The responsibility for the principles on which the world handles its practical affairs lies literally and entirely with him. This does not mean that his view is necessarily a universal one, or his power of enforcement comparable to that of a state. It does not mean that as an individual he can presume to blueprint the world's society. It means simply that there are no principles in society unless he himself, directly and personally, asserts them and persists in them wherever his life touches practical affairs. Liberty is not an abstract question: it's as real as steel bars and concentration camps. Peace is not abstract, but as real as flame-throwers and the local Selective Service board. And the responsibility of the individual is as real as a diplomat's lie. Gertrude Stein once told an American general in Germany that the only thing wrong with the Germans was that they had not learned sufficiently to disobey—to say No. The general agreed . . . but he didn't know what he was saying. The power of the individual to disobey is the one power which governments, FBI's, and generals, cannot contend with. It makes me feel good to notice that people as diverse and yet as commonly derived from settled and respectable backgrounds as those I have been discussing, take hold of this basic fact and put it to use.

The opportunity is always with us. And in that opportunity there is hope. The more I read the news and comment on it, the more suspicious I become that where we are concerned with the history of society, and the problems of changing society . . . we are dealing first in the quality of the individual. If there is a problem, it is a problem of the transformation of the individual. I suspect that the idea of a mass of people having a character of its own—the American mass, the Russian mass—is simply a spectacular fiction. The blueprints, the policy planning, the official pronouncements which propose to do something with masses of people—these also are by their inherent reference fictitious.

I wonder then if ultimately the individual, whether in Berkeley, California, or in Hankow, China, will not experience some of the sense of helplessness and frustration I do unless and until he decides that the reality of society lies in his own inward nature, and that change in society can only be the product of his own inward transformation.

17

From *An Autobiographical
Novel*

by Kenneth Rexroth

*Kenneth Rexroth, poet, author, and critic, was instrumental in
bringing to Pacifica Radio the major and unknown poets of America and other countries. From Pacifica's earliest days, Rexroth
appeared in hundreds of interviews, soliloquys, poetry readings,
and discussions about poetry, literature, the condition of the arts
in the United States, and his own personal observations of our
times. His autobiographical novel was first spoken spontaneously
on Pacifica in regular weekly broadcasts over a period of many
months. The following is a chapter from it.*

My trip around the world with Harold had aroused my curiosity
about the Southwest, which we had never reached. So I only
stayed in Chicago a couple of weeks, and then took off through
Kansas and southern Colorado to Taos and Santa Fe. On the way
down I visited Haldeman-Julius in Girard, Kansas. He had a large
stock of a Little Blue Book on diet which he couldn't get rid of. I
bought the lot at two cents a copy and had them shipped ahead.

On West Madison Street and Bughouse Square, Eddie Miller once made a good thing pitching a similar book from the Lindlahr Naturopathic Sanitarium. If the stiffs in Chicago bought them, I could envisage an even hotter pitch that would sell them to the weed monkeys.

Taos was under the bitter cloud of the presence of D. H. Lawrence, a miasma which has only recently begun to die away. Lawrence may have been an apostle of love, but his immediate followers hated each other like poison. They spent their time quarreling and organizing the innocent bystanders into their several factions. I went to a couple of parties at Mabel's where everybody shuffled around full of sugar moon while tame Indians hammered on tom-toms—a weary orgy of skinny or overweight millionairesses, hitchhiking hobohemians, disordered anthropologists, lady imagists from the Middle West, and a select number of very mercenary Indians. During these brawls the Master periodically stormed out of the room in white-faced, red-whiskered rage whenever anybody used a dirty word. However, he magnanimously ignored the considerable amount of gumming-up that went on in the inglenooks of Mabel's stately home. I won't say I was disillusioned—every genius to his insanity—but I didn't cotton to it either.

The only people in the Lawrence set with whom I could make friends were "Clarence"; the Danes; Knut Merrild, still one of the finest human beings I've met in my life; Meta Lehman, who seems to have fallen out of all the memoirs and who was much the nicest woman in Taos, being very similar in personality and appearance to Shirley before her T.B. cure; Jaime de Angulo, and Witter Bynner, who didn't get along any too well with Lawrence anyway. Most of them I met at the first parties at Mabel's, but from then on I visited them in their own homes.

Much more interesting were the painters who had their own well-organized world, carried on much less, and seldom mixed with the Lawrence set. The majority of the first generation of Taos painters had lived in Chicago. They had already achieved a distinctive style, a kind of virile Impressionism, and were painting some of the more interesting pictures of the day. They knew the country thoroughly, and had traveled all over its mountains on horseback. And they knew the Indians a good deal better than the professional Indian worshipers, although they, too, were corrupted by the same sort of Theosophical nonsense which was a blind, bigoted religion with the others.

Two of the second generation of Taos painters were very good indeed—Willard Nash and Andrew Dasburg—and with them I formed fast friendships. I believe that Dasburg is one of America's better painters. His style is temporarily out of fashion, but I think his pictures are still popular on an invisible market, uninfluenced by dealer-promoted fads. Willard gave me the run of his studio, and I painted several pictures alongside of him with great benefit to myself. I left all the pictures behind me, and thought no more of them. Over twenty years later I discovered one of them in New York on the wall of a poetess who was visiting in Taos for the summer and had picked up some paintings in a junkshop.

The local Indianism began to infect me. The first Indian painters were just becoming known in those days. There was one at Taos who wasn't very good, and another at Santa Domingo who was the best of the lot. The others, who have since become famous, were not nearby, but off in the Zuni or the Hopi pueblos. I did my best to make friends and they were friendly enough in their turn but we didn't communicate much. I'd come to call and we'd sit and talk very little and, when we did, just pass the time of day. It was all very Indian.

The poet Hal Somers had a handsome secretary, a young Navajo girl whose father was the richest man in the tribe. She had been East, not to an Indian "college," but to one of the better girls' schools, and was a great deal more communicative. Since she didn't fit the local stereotype, she wasn't popular around Taos. We became good friends.

Much the solidest writers and the ones incidentally who knew the most about Indians were Mary Austin, Witter Bynner, and Alice Corbin Henderson. They may not have been quite as advanced as the Lawrence set, and any one of them would have been horrified at the suggestion that they were biblical prophets. But they were far more civilized people. Witter Bynner was just beginning to translate Chinese poetry. He was the first person I had ever met with whom I could share my own interest. He had a very sensible Chinese informant, and had never fallen victim to the outrageous ideographic theories of Ezra Pound and Amy Lowell. He introduced me to the major Sinologists in French and English, in those days still a rather limited study, and recommended a Chinese student at the University of Chicago who was a great help to me the next winter. He also helped me to shift my focus of interest from the poetry of Li Tai Po, in those days considered by most Westerners China's greatest poet, to Tu Fu. For this—an hour's conversation in a sun-baked patio—I have reason to be eternally grateful to Witter Bynner. Tu Fu has been without question the major influence on my own poetry, and I consider him the greatest nonepic, nondramatic poet who ever lived. In some ways he is a better poet than either Shakespeare or Homer. At least he is more natural and intimate.

Tu Fu comes from a saner, older, more secular culture than Homer and it is not a new discovery with him that the gods, the abstractions and forces of nature are frivolous, lewd, vicious, quarrelsome, and cruel, and only men's steadfastness, love, magnanimity, calm, and compassion redeem the nightbound world. It is not a discovery, culturally or historically, but it is the essence of his being as a poet. If Isaiah is the greatest religious poet, Tu Fu is not religious at all. But for me his response to the human situation is the only kind of religion likely to outlast this century. "Reverence of life" it has been called. I have saturated myself with his poetry for thirty years. I am sure he has made me a better man, as a moral agent and as a perceiving organism. I say this because I feel that, above a certain level of attainment, the greatest poetry answers out of hand the problems of the critics and the aesthetician. Poetry like Tu Fu's is the answer to the question, "What is the purpose of art?"

Alice Corbin's role in the development of American poetry

has almost been forgotten. She was unfortunate in being survived by more ambitious people. Actually it was she, not Harriet Monroe, who made *Poetry* magazine available to the best modern verse. And it was she who was responsible for what little modernist poetry there was in the early editions of the Monroe-Henderson anthology. She was a more civilized woman than Harriet Monroe, both in her literary taste and in her human contacts. Harriet lived and died a provincial suffragette with the manners and tastes of a crank. She was convinced that a glorious future awaited young American poets who would write bad sonnets about dynamos, and confident that time would vindicate her judgment that George Dillon was a better poet than T. S. Eliot. I found it impossible to sit in the same room with her for five minutes without losing my temper. Alice Corbin, on the other hand, sought me out, invited me to dinner, tactfully suggested that I bring her some of my work the next time I came, and devoted hours of conversation and several long letters to discussing it with me on my terms—she certainly belonged to a different school of poetry—and in the sanest and most helpful manner possible.

Mary Austin was a type I had never known well before, a thoroughly professionalized and successful woman writer. We didn't have much in common in a literary way, but talking about life and letters she helped me to realize that it was possible to adopt literature as a profession with the same dignity that you adopt medicine, and in turn demand the same respect from society. In addition, Mary Austin knew more about Indians, and more about Indian song especially, than anybody else in the country, except Frances Densmore and Natalie Curtis Burlin, whom I never met. She understood my interest in the, so to speak, non-Aristotelian syntax of Indian and African languages a generation before Whorf. She played cylinder records of Indian songs for me, and gave me a long list of books to read when I got back to Chicago. She knew people all over the Southwest, especially off the main lines of travel; people in remote valleys in central Nevada and east of the mountains on the California line, around the Four Corners, on the Tonto Rim, and tucked away in box cabins in

Utah, like the one in *Riders of the Purple Sage*. She gave me all sorts of addresses, both Indian and white, and many of them I used. All these people, as a matter of fact, gave me names and wrote letters for me all over the intermountain country. In addition, I had a list of names of more or less political Indians given me by Chief Little Bear, who was a friend of Kep Thorpe's and a most effective one-man lobby in Washington for all the Indians in the country. He was himself, I think, a member of the Sac and Fox tribe.

There is one thing wrong with this narrative: I can't keep straight who lived in Taos and who in Santa Fe, back in those days. It seems to me that Bynner, Alice Corbin, Mary Austin, and Andrew Dasburg all lived in Santa Fe. I know they did a few years later. On this trip I did a considerable amount of shuttling back and forth, and it's become confused. Certainly Santa Fe was much the better place. Not only did Taos have all the fakery of an art colony, but in addition, the people lived in mud huts with little or no plumbing and were all badly infected with the absurd theosophy of highbrow Indianism. To this day they circulate petitions to protect the sacred rights of the pueblo to get its drinking water out of polluted irrigation ditches.

It wasn't long before the scene began to pall on me. The painter Hal Somer's secretary was going back to Window Rock and then north to the San Juan on a visit with her parents. I went along. In those days the Navajos were a good deal less embittered and ethnocentric. John Collier and his Taos friends had not fouled up their economy. Nobody in the family inquired about my intentions toward their beautiful daughter. I was made completely at home, as though I had been born and raised in a hogan. Maybe, but I drew the line at sleeping in one. My girl and I slept outside under a pile of quilts and sheepskins. Except for Nanda Devi, she was the most accomplished lover I have ever known, and she was at least as beautiful. She wore the Navajo fashion of those days— hair in two big wheels, black velvet blouse with little silver conchas, silver belt, full-back satin skirt with rainbow stripes above the hem, and bright red moccasins. Underneath all this she wore nothing. Whenever she came near me, the thought of her body made me a little dizzy. She had three perfectly ravishing younger sisters. They were even more beautiful. On the trip to the San Juan, which took a good many days on horseback, they let me know they were quite available. However, they had not been to Smith College. They had not only never learned the use of modern plumbing, but had grown up in a world in which water in any form was not abundant. They dressed in exactly the same way as my girl, and whenever they came near, the thought of their bodies made me dizzy, but in a different sense. Evenings around the fire of roots of mesquite and greasewood, I always sat upwind.

However, I learned that this blemish was situational. After several days' riding we entered a rocky arroyo, and the horses caught the smell of the far-off muddy San Juan. The whole party broke into a furious run. Horses loaded with women and babies, pack animals with coffeepots and Dutch ovens clattering and banging, off they went at the long rocking run of Indian horses, leaping over boulders and whinnying like birds. I tried to draw in my horse, and had expected the Indians to do the same. On the contrary, they were all shouting, kicking with their spurs, and whipping on the pack animals with their quirts. My animal jumped over five-ton boulders like a jackrabbit, oblivious to what might lie on the other side. After about an hour's run, still mounted, still running, people began to undress on horseback. When we hit the river, saddles were thrown off, packs dumped, and panting, sweating stock, men, women, and children plunged into the brown swirling water. There we all stayed till nightfall.

We camped for a week in a little box canyon near the Bends, where there were peach trees planted by the Indians but left untended and only visited at harvest. Scattered amongst them were a few cherry trees, already loaded with ripe fruit. My girl and I lay around nude in the flickering shade of this orchard, made love, gorged ourselves on cherries, and read *The Canterbury Tales,* which she had brought along. I imagine this was the strangest brief love affair that savage orchard had ever seen. At last the group headed on up the river and we parted when they turned

back south up the Chaco. I went on with a pack horse and another zebra dun. In the pack was the box of health books. Carefully cradled in one of the saddle bags was a tame Gila monster
which I had bought from one of my girl's little brothers.

In the first little town, maybe Durango, I set up shop. I didn't
have a regular keister, so I put the box of books on a folding camp
chair which I got at the general store. On it I put a candle and a
big bright navel orange. It was getting along toward dark. I stood
there for a while fondling the Gila monster stretched across my
chest with his nose nuzzling my ear. After I had collected a small
crowd I lit the candle which burned steadily in the hot, windless
twilight. Then I slowly peeled the orange in one continuous spiral.
Then I broke off a piece of peeling, held it close to the candle,
skin side toward the fire, and snapped it back between my fingers.
When the oil of the orange hit the flame there was a little explosion of blue fire. I put the Gila monster down on the stand and got
him to mumble at my fingers, and began my pitch.

"Ladies and gentlemen," said I, "would you all stand just a
little closer? It will serve to shelter the candle from any vagrant
breeze of the evening that might spring up and I would under no
circumstances wish to block traffic and cause any embarrassment
to the local guardian of law and order, otherwise known as the
town clown. However, ladies and gentlemen, do not stand too
close. Do not, in sudden moments of interest and passion, belly
up, so to speak, against the stand and irritate or annoy the little
animal. As you know, having grown up in this country, although
the Gila monster is one of the most lethargic of all living reptiles,
he is nevertheless subject to fits and starts of sudden wrath, and,
as you further undoubtedly know, the bite of the Gila monster is
more venomous than that of the cobra of India, the tiny jewellike
but deadly coral snake, or the instantly fatal fer-de-lance of the
jungles of the tropics. Compared with that of the Gila monster the
bite of the largest diamond-back rattler is but a scratch. Furthermore, these notorious snakes strike like lightning and instantaneously release their victim, unless, as sometimes happens, their
fangs become embedded in a bone and they have to be pulled off

by main force. The Gila monster, on the other hand, hangs on and gnaws and chews with a bite far more tenacious than any bulldog. Once he has seized hold he is more difficult to remove than the treacherous abalones of the Pacific which often trap the Japanese and Mexican divers and condemn them to a watery grave.

"Now, the most interesting thing about the Gila monster is that, unlike all other venomous reptiles and all other poisonous animals, he is not equipped with any poison sacs whatsoever. In addition, his alimentary passage is not provided in its upper reaches with any digestive juices. His stomach and upper gut are extraordinarily resistant to all toxins. You could feed this little animal a half ounce of pure prussic acid and it would have no effect on him whatsoever. His digestive processes are unique in the entire animal kingdom. After he has ingested a rodent or other reptile, he retires to his burrow, usually an abandoned gopher hole, and lies in a somnolent position while the food slowly rots. After it has become an amorphous, putrid mass, it passes on into his middle gut where it is absorbed by a peculiar chemistry of his cold reptilian blood stream. Now the venomous effect of the bite of the Gila monster is due entirely to the fact that he regurgitates a small part of this appalling mess into the open wound of his victim. There is no poison more deadly, and it is composed exclusively of food which had decayed in the beast's alimentary passage. Ladies and gentlemen, I know, just by looking at you, at your lackluster eyes, at the pimples on your foreheads, at your pale hanging lips and thinning hair, that you, too, like most of the inhabitants of the United States, suffer from exactly the same conditions as are beneficial to the Gila monster but which cause you untold harm— rheumatism, nausea, habitual colds, hot and cold flashes, back pain, swelling feet, bad breath, acne—conditions which not only afflict you with these minor diseases and discomforts but which weaken your resistance and leave you the prey of fatal diseases and epidemics.

"Like the Gila monster, ladies and gentlemen, your innards are a compacted mass of decaying food which moves slowly out of you like glaciers move down the valleys of the mountains of

Greenland. Cathartics are of no help. They only blast a narrow passage like a tiny tunnel through the surrounding abomination."

At this moment I squeezed another orange peel into the candle flame. By that time it was dark, and the spurt and the flame were very impressive.

"However, ladies and gentlemen, just as poison kills poison and thieves catch thieves, food, properly used, can cure the conditions which are the result of its abuse. In the most ordinary foods are hidden tremendous powers of which the average person knows nothing. You have seen the fireworks display which resulted from a gentle squeeze of an orange peel. In the skin of an orange is a small quantity of oil of orange, mixed with water and other substances. Oil of orange is potentially more explosive than nitroglycerine. The only reason that it is not used to blow open safes is that it cannot be extracted. It must be used fresh, and its power starts to decay the minute it leaves the skin of the living orange. Now I do not advise you to go about munching orange peels, they will only make you sick. In fact, as you might have noticed, if you've ever left an orange peel along the trail, they are so violent in their effect that every animal, no matter how wild, instinctively knows better than to eat them. However, there are many perfectly normal foods which, if properly prepared and eaten in balanced meals, will cure you, in a matter of a couple of weeks, of the constipation which has made all your life miserable. Not only that, but there is no part of the United States so remote or in such wild or desert country that some of these foods cannot be obtained. Many of them are things you eat every day; they only have to be properly prepared. Furthermore, they are far more delicious than soggy, hot bread, flour gravy, and meat fried till it is like leather, which, as I know, having grown up in this country, is what most of you eat three times a day.

"On a visit to Colorado I was employed by the Foundation for Natural Health, a nonprofit organization financed by one of the world's most famous philanthropists. I am traveling through the Southwest, distributing a little book of healthful recipes and menus which will teach you the proper way to eat. There is nothing freakish or cranky about these foods. They are all perfectly ordinary American vittles, but this book will teach you the proper way to prepare and serve them. And after two weeks of following their menus, planned by one of the greatest living dieticians, all your constipation will pass away in more senses than one; your petty, nagging illnesses will leave you and you will discover the world of radiant, robust health. Now the Natural Health Foundation could easily afford to pay my salary, and for livery for my stock, and in addition, give these little books away. If we did that, you would have no respect for them. In a couple of days they would be out hanging on a hook alongside last year's Monkey Ward catalog and Dr. Mile's Almanac. So we are charging a small pittance, only a fraction of the cost of printing alone—two bits, twenty-five cents, a quarter of a dollar."

The only trouble with this pitch was that after I'd made three or four towns I ran out of books. In the course of the summer I managed to connect with a couple more shipments here and there in the intermountain country. Each time I sold them out in a few days. I imagine I did a lot of good.

I spent the rest of the summer drifting up and down the west side of the Rockies, from the San Juan to Jackson Hole. For several years I was to work here every summer. It was still pretty undeveloped country with thousands of square miles of unfenced range. I picked up jobs for a week or two, mostly as relief cookee and wrangler. This is an easy job to get if you're trustworthy. The regular fellow seldom gets a chance to go to town. I suppose in many ways this is the best of all cowboy jobs. It isn't anywhere near as hard as driving or gathering cattle and there are short periods in the day when you don't have to work. Furthermore, you're up before anybody else, and it's wonderful to start the fire and to go out and chase the cavy in the early dawn. Sitting on a horse in the midst of illimitable miles of sagebrush and rock under the paling stars is an experience like those described by the mystics—the smell of greasewood and juniper smoke, the strong smell of horses as you come on them in the chill air, the stringent smells of the land itself, the sound of thrashers and wrens waking up the country, the sharp aseptic smell of mountain streams in the night.

There's only one trouble with this work—most cowboys are not interesting people. From Nebraska to the Sierra Nevada they tell the same jokes, and respond to all of life's situations with the same limited number of reactions. Still, the particular part of the country I had chosen did in those days offer the widest variety of people and customs in the West.

In many ways the nicest people to work for were the Mormons. Southern and eastern Utah were in those days still strongholds of practically unreconstructed Saints. Big stone ranch houses surrounded with their "wife houses," great barns, neat outbuildings, and barnyards that were raked every morning, all set under a clump of Lombardy poplars in the midst of an irrigated meadow. It's not just the neatness and efficiency of the Mormons; they have built a genuine culture in the anthropological sense, one of the most integrated in the world. Mormonism is a farmers' and working-class version of the radicalism of the pre-Civil War America, in which it was born, an Oneida Community held together by religious sanctions. Certainly it is very unlike the Puritan tradition of the rest of rural America. Possibly the long struggle over polygamy gave the Mormons a more wholesome attitude toward sex. Most Gentiles think that this has resulted in clandestine promiscuity. It hasn't, but it has produced an American community which takes sex as a natural and fundamental determinant in human relations. And it's permissive enough. Drinking coffee and smoking cigarettes are considered more harmful sins than a few premarital and extramarital relationships. Every Mormon church has weekly socials which are among the most enjoyable get-togethers of any kind in America, and in spite of the anti-Mormon literature about the Mormon debasement of women, the spontaneous and easy relationship between girls and boys can be compared only with the French Auberge Jeunesse Laïque or similar activities in modern Scandinavia—there just are no symptoms of the American sex war. Whatever the demerits of polygamy, it should not be forgotten that thousands of women, alone and vol-

untarily, crossed thousands of miles of desert, in very inconven-
ient conveyances, to take part in it.

I made the most of my introductions and spent as much time
as I could with Indians. Nowadays, wandering hitchhikers are
hardly made welcome. In those days it was still possible to "live
on the mesa," as they say, and I spent a week at Oraibi treated
like one of the family by an Indian artist on whom I simply
walked in. I had looked forward to a week or more at Zuni, but it
was too much for me. There are limits to togetherness. I would
say that within an hour anyone of the slightest sensitivity would
begin to feel the oppression suffocating. It's like being in the midst
of a boxcar stuffed with pillows. I discovered in talking about this
to the Hopi and Navajos and Apaches that they are well aware of
Zuni group dynamics, and joke about it. Today I believe it is quite
impossible for a white man to live in any of the pueblos. Nowadays, of course, in their bitter struggle to preserve every jot and
tittle of their way of life, Zuni is far worse than it was then. Every
cholera vibrio in the water is as important as the most important
kachina.

I'm not opposed to togetherness as such. Some of the most
socially happy hours I have ever spent were with the tiny Havasupai tribe deep in their canyon among their peach trees. The
Havasupai were at least as well integrated as the Zuni, but they
were not so damn compulsive about it. In fact, they weren't compulsive at all. They just seemed to thoroughly enjoy being with
one another, securely locked away from all the world. In those
days the trail to the bottom of the canyon constituted a minor
mountaineering feat.

Toward the end of the summer I worked my way up to
White Rocks, the Ute reservation in the southeast foothills of the
Unitas. I don't want to sound prejudiced, but, although they
treated me royally, I believe the Northern Ute in those days were
the most disagreeable people outside the island of Manhattan in
the Western hemisphere. They were pretty savage. Many men
were still alive who had taken scalps, but they were in the first

shock of reservation demoralization and withdrawal. They were dirty, cruel, drunken, and promiscuous is too nice a word for their sexual habits. The moral atmosphere, I imagine, was something like that of a Puerto Rican gang of delinquent kids in New York today—for obviously much the same reasons. The Anglican missionary at White Rocks was a friend of many Anglo-Catholic clergy whom I knew in the East, and I went to Mass and Sunday school and listened to rocky-faced old warriors sing with the kids:

> Washing and wiping the dishes,
> Mending the baby's clothes,
> Working and praying for Jesus,
> Yes, there is room for us aw-ull.

Father Grant had a couple of little kids who showed up years later in San Francisco and became close friends of mine. One of them, the artist Richard Ayer, gave me his Missal, and my daughter Mary still carries it to church.

Father Grant died years ago in California. But a far more extraordinary man, one of the most remarkable people I've ever met in my life, was the missionary in the San Juan country. An aged man, he is still active, traveling over the deserts on horseback and saying Mass in the open air on altars of piled rocks. His vestments had been made for him by the Indians: leather chasubles ornamented like Navajo sand paintings, and albs of heavy cotton woven on Navajo looms and decorated with rainbows, clouds, terraces, and phallic symbols. Some Chicago musician had written for him a "Mass of Father Jogues." The Indians sat around and beat on drums and sang the Gloria and Credo and Sanctus to tunes that sounded a little like "Indianola" when they didn't sound like "Dardanella." It was most impressive.

At the end of the summer I was up in Jackson Hole and I headed east for the fall gathering on the Crow Indian reservation. By this time I was a fair horse wrangler and competent cook, so I got a pretty good job. In those days this was the last of the great, spectacular roundups. There were all sorts of cattle being driven in from what I guess was the largest single chunk of unfenced good range left in the country. This was real Wild West show cowboying. Part of the time I worked as a circle rider at night. Roping and even efficient driving were beyond me. I never really tried to learn. I just don't like cows. If forced to choose, I'd rather be a sheepherder. Most of the time I cooked: sourdough pancakes and steak for breakfast; steak and potatoes, canned tomatoes and canned peaches; sourdough bread at noon; steak, potatoes, canned tomatoes, canned peaches, sourdough bread for supper; boiled coffee, boiled tea, and always extra saleratus bread for those who didn't like sourdough. With few exceptions the steaks had to be thoroughly burned through and through, but I and one or two others ate rare meat and were kidded about it at every meal. It was the hardest work I have ever done but it was continuously exciting. The atmosphere was one of unrelieved melodrama, a little like living in the midst of a revolution. Away from the noise and the milling men, horses, and cattle, I suppose due to the scope of the job, it had tremendous exultation. Thoroughly worn out, dark as a Ute Indian, and trained down like a boxer, I headed back to Chicago, riding in the crummy behind a trainload of cows.

This job was a thorough nuisance. I got no pleasure out of running along the top of cattle cars, least of all in catching my meals on the fly. We never stopped long enough in towns to eat a proper meal, and then we'd lay over, waiting for a highball or passenger on some siding for hours in the midst of the prairie. Every time the train stopped I had to run alongside with a rod and pry loose horns and hoofs caught in the slats, and sometimes risk my life getting a beast up that had fallen down. Feeding and watering them, at least, was not my job.

Someplace in Nebraska we were held up for a long time outside a little town on a siding just off a trestle over a creek. It was early evening, and there was a campfire under the cottonwoods on the bank of the creek. I went down to visit. It was a jungle, and the bums were cooking up slum gullion in a ten-gallon oilcan.

They invited me to have some. There were carrots, turnips, potatoes, sweet corn, peas—a conventional mulligan except for the
meat, which was pigs' tails.

"Where'd you get all the pigs' tails?" I asked. "Is there a
slaughterhouse in town?"

Nobody said anything for a minute, and then the old man
who was doing the cooking said, "You don't work for the railroad,
do you, nursing them cows?"

"No," I said, "I'm just a workaway. I've already been paid off
by the cattle outfit."

"Well," he said, "that being the case, I guess we can tell him.
Before your cows were parked on that siding, there was a load of
pigs there, most of the morning. I hope they didn't bleed to death
before they got to Omaha."

18

Big Head
Obituary for a Junkie
Interview by Charles Hayden

Charles Hayden conducted a number of "inside" interviews over the years for Pacifica. What follows is one of the most famous.

HAYDEN: I understand you're familiar with the narcotics scene, not only in New York, but in other parts of the country as well. For the purpose of this interview, let's choose a pseudonym for yourself.

BIG HEAD: I know a junkie who was murdered a few months ago in the Tombs by the bulls. His name was Big Head. A really pathetic character. So you can call me Big Head.

HAYDEN: O.K. Big Head. Could you give me some idea of the narcotics scene in New York, just a general description of things as you would describe them to a newcomer?

BIG HEAD: I don't know. I was aware of narcotics when I came to the city. I was introduced to narcotics in the army on my own hook. Had a cough once while I was a medical technician running a dispensary in Korea. I had been drinking turpenhydrate with codeine for my cough and I remembered that morphine was an excellent cough suppressant. The inventory left us with seventy-six extra morphine surrets. Cured me of alcoholism at that point.

HAYDEN: But it led to other things.

BIG HEAD: It led to morphine . . . and more morphine . . . and more morphine.

HAYDEN: Actually your discovery of narcotics came quite accidentally then while you were serving in the armed services. Is this a very common way for someone to be introduced to narcotics?

BIG HEAD: Yes it is. Most addicts who are introduced to it in this way, however, never become publicly known. There are an unknown number of doctor and nurse addicts in this country. The Narcotics Bureau estimates 1 per cent of those involved in the medical professions are addicted, but it's probably higher than that. The medical associations sort of regard addiction as an occupational hazard. When the Federal Narcotics Bureau does catch someone, they don't want to make trouble. They just tell them they either have to go to Lexington or to jail. If they go to Lexington, there isn't any prosecution.

HAYDEN: Well, now you tried morphine. What was your initial drug experience like? What was it, for you, about a shot of morphine that was so exciting or captivating? What caused it to become so important to you?

BIG HEAD: At first it was merely something to relieve tension as well as relieving my cough. It relieved all the tensions I had and after a while I began to take it, cough or no cough. But it was no sudden revelation.

HAYDEN: Then things evolved slowly. How long did it take? Did you actually become addicted to morphine?

BIG HEAD: Yes, but it took about three months.

HAYDEN: And at what point did you realize you were hooked? Was there a certain moment when you suddenly realized that you had to have morphine?

BIG HEAD: I never did. While kicking my first morphine habit, I did get sick on a troopship. But it hadn't been a very heavy habit and I didn't really want to recognize it. It was only when I came to New York City and started using heroin that I realized what had happened. I had been using it for a month. I had not come down. I had used an average of twenty dollars' worth of heroin a day for about a month and one day I just decided to stop. Within twenty-four hours I really wanted to put my head in an oven. Then I recognized that this was the same feeling I had had on the troopship except now it was greatly intensified.

HAYDEN: But how did you move from morphine in the army to heroin in New York? When you came to New York had you gotten to know people who fooled around with narcotics?

BIG HEAD: Morphine's not available in New York, so one has no choice.

HAYDEN: Well, how did you know where to find heroin in New York? How did you manage to find out where to get it?

BIG HEAD: Oh, I don't know. It just seemed, it just seemed that the air was saturated with it.

HAYDEN: In other words, you had gotten so you could spot someone who was using narcotics and therefore could always find out where they were available?

BIG HEAD: You can walk down any street just jammed with people. For blocks and blocks you won't see a God-darned soul, nothing. Except for a junkie; you can see him from five blocks away, like he was waving a flag.

HAYDEN: Then another junkie is obvious to you. But just how is a junkie obvious?

BIG HEAD: Well, it's almost impossible to say. It's small things. The carriage of the head, the expression, the ease of movement.

HAYDEN: And these are the people that the average guy on the street would never spot as being different from anyone else?

BIG HEAD: Well, a junkie would tend to look a bit poorer than most people. He doesn't usually look like a bum. He's clean-shaven. He's wearing clean clothes, but he doesn't usually strive for a good appearance. He only pays enough attention to his appearance so that he won't be conspicuous.

HAYDEN: There's literally a whole subculture in the city based on heroin use, isn't there?

BIG HEAD: Well, it's not a subculture as much as it's a separate culture. At no point is it at all integrated with the economic or social life of the city. You take a doctor and an itinerant laborer and they'll both be aware of the same international issues of pressing importance, of the same public scandals and perhaps will talk about going to the World's Fair. But a junkie isn't interested in any of that at all. Most junkies don't follow the baseball scores or even bother to read the headlines.

HAYDEN: Their whole world centers around narcotics?

BIG HEAD: When you have to spend from twenty, to sixty to one hundred dollars a day and you have to get that twenty to a hundred dollars a day you haven't got the time to be interested in anything except getting that.

HAYDEN: Now, you said addicts constituted a culture apart. What kinds of places do junkies choose to congregate in and meet each other? Coffee shops? Areas of town? Is there much social interaction among junkies as a group?

BIG HEAD: No, the type of place a junkie would use—I guess I can name this place because it's been shut down. There was a place on Delancey Street near Eldridge that was open twenty-four hours a day. It was a natural central place in an area where there were a lot of junkies and people who came to make meets.

HAYDEN: What do you mean, "make meets"?

BIG HEAD: Well, originally it all started when some dealer said to his customers, "Well, I'll be sitting in such and such a luncheonette if you need anything."

HAYDEN: Did the luncheonette know what was going on?

BIG HEAD: At first, no. Then about the middle of this past winter it got so bad that you could walk in there at almost any hour and people would be nodding out, falling into their coffee, everything. People were dealing openly, trading their money back and forth, handling books of matches with bags in them and things like that. One of the countermen was a junkie too. If there was no one there you knew, you could ask him to cop for you. He always knew who was dealing there.

HAYDEN: What about the ownership of the luncheonette? By this time did they know what was going on?

BIG HEAD: They'd set up a quarter minimum at this place. Every fifteen minutes they'd run around, twenty-five cents was the price of staying in there. Every fifteen minutes they'd go around and make you spend another quarter.

HAYDEN: So they looked at it just as a way to get money out of you while you used their luncheonette to score in.

BIG HEAD: Yeah.

HAYDEN: Now, when it comes to supporting a habit that takes twenty, fifty, a hundred dollars a day, do junkies sometimes face intense problems when it comes to getting money in the beginning. In other words, do they feel bad or are they frightened to death the first time they rob an apartment?

BIG HEAD: It wasn't a matter of fear. It was a matter, for me anyway, of just being dragged and having to go through this. It was a drag to have to do something like that, but there was no moral equivocation.

HAYDEN: How did you feel the first time you set out to rob an apartment? What is a second-story man?

BIG HEAD: Well, a second-story man is just a term that means what it implies, a man who climbs through your window. But usually I was a step-over burglar. That was my specialty.

HAYDEN: What's a "step-over burglar"?

BIG HEAD: Well, people don't lock their windows, except the ones on the fire escapes. So you just hang over the edge of the fire escape and reach out and open one of the windows near the fire escape. And "step-over" into the pad. But most times you crack a pad just by forcing the door open.

HAYDEN: How proficient did you get? In other words, did you find crime became something of an art—to be able to enter an apartment quickly, find the valuables, and leave quickly?

BIG HEAD: No. I think I was more leisurely after a while. When I was less nervous about it.

HAYDEN: Why? Isn't it dangerous to rob apartments in Manhattan?

BIG HEAD: No, it's not. There's only about a 23 per cent conviction rate for burglary; only 23 per cent of all the burglaries in this town are ever brought to any sort of legal conclusion.

HAYDEN: What per cent of the burglaries are supposedly done by people on narcotics?

BIG HEAD: Oh, I . . . I wouldn't know.

HAYDEN: It's supposed to be 50 to 75 per cent, according to the Police Department.

BIG HEAD: I would say it was more like 90 per cent.

HAYDEN: Well, now you go into an apartment and you get goods of value. . . . I had a robbery in my own apartment ten days ago. An electric typewriter was taken, a tape recorder, a gold watch, a Polaroid camera. But anyway, let me get back. So you enter an apartment and take things of value, then what do you do with what you've taken?

BIG HEAD: Fence it.

HAYDEN: How do you go about that?

BIG HEAD: Depends on what you've got.

HAYDEN: What items are the best to take?

BIG HEAD: Depends on what kind of fence you've got. I know people who steal antiques. Others specialize in things like typewriters, some steal clothes. I know one chick who does nothing but steal meat.

HAYDEN: Steal meat?

BIG HEAD: Meat out of supermarkets, the choicest cuts.

HAYDEN: How could you steal enough meat to support a habit?

BIG HEAD: She steals seventy dollars' worth. She realizes seventy dollars' worth a day, stealing meat. She's that good a shoplifter.

HAYDEN: So now, is the fencing operation in New York City a very large operation? Is it centralized, or are most fences independent?

BIG HEAD: It doesn't seem like the type of thing that would easily lend itself to centralization. (*Chuckles.*)

HAYDEN: Well, the fences know where the goods are coming from, don't they?

BIG HEAD: Sure they do.

HAYDEN: And for one hundred fifty dollars' worth of items, how much does a junkie get? What percentage of the value?

BIG HEAD: No more than 35 per cent.

HAYDEN: Thirty-five per cent of what the fence could sell them for, really?

BIG HEAD: Yes.

HAYDEN: Are any of these items sent outside the city?

BIG HEAD: Certainly, certainly. All over the less urbanized areas of the country they have auctions where people come and buy damaged—supposedly "damaged" merchandise, or merchandise "unclaimed in freight." That's the front for it.

HAYDEN: And this is the way some fences get rid of the merchandise they've gotten. Well, tell me, have you ever been caught, or have you ever known anyone who's been caught in the act of robbing an apartment?

BIG HEAD: Yes, I've known people who've been caught. I've been caught myself.

HAYDEN: By tenants or by the police?

BIG HEAD: No, I've never been caught by the police.

HAYDEN: What happened when you were caught by the tenants? Could you describe the situation?

BIG HEAD: I talked my way out of it. I had cracked a pad and I was inside. I had gotten a typewriter and a television set, taken them out and come back for some more stuff. And the people came in on me. I just told them, "Well, the door was open and it looks like you've been took off." They went for it.

HAYDEN: In other words, they didn't know that you'd been the thief. Does this very frequently happen? That a thief caught in the act will be able to talk his way out of it? . . . The point I'm getting at is I caught a thief two days ago on the fire escape of my building. He was breaking in a neighbor's apartment. I leaned out the window and confronted him. I said, "I see you up there." He began climbing to the roof. Then I said, "O.K., Buddy, but we're going to get you in the hall." Well, personally I was scared to death. After I pulled back in the window, the first thing I did was lock my door because confronting a thief for me was a frightening experience. Apparently though, it must have terrified the thief more. We never did get him by the way. When we finally went on the roof, he had gone. But do people usually react aggressively or timidly when confronting thieves?

BIG HEAD: There's no standardized reaction. For one thing, it depends on whether they know the thief or not. And it also depends on how much they've been took off for. It depends on a lot of things really. I find that most people don't want to believe they're confronting the man who did them harm. So it's easier than you would think to convince a person you've robbed that you haven't done it.

HAYDEN: Is this a very frequent thing, that the people a narcotics addict will rob first are his friends?

BIG HEAD: Yes, very frequently.

HAYDEN: Does this cause those friends to break off their relationship with him? Does this also lead him into final isolation in the world of addiction?

BIG HEAD: Well, not necessarily. Some people that I know who are on the fringe of narcotics society have a kind of philosophical attitude about it. You know, "Well, I shouldn't have tempted him." There are some people like that. But after a while you find you're not welcome any more. Then it becomes acquaintances that you rob from. You always have enough acquaintances to rob from.

HAYDEN: People that don't know you're hooked or what have you?

BIG HEAD: They know, but they just . . . you just go in there. You're introduced to them once in their pad and case the place, split, and then you come back a couple of days later.

HAYDEN: Let me hasten to tell you that my pad has been cleaned out. (*Laughter.*)

HAYDEN: Can you give me an idea of how heroin traffic runs generally? In other words, you're a pusher now. What size lots do heroin pushers usually get their heroin in, how do they dispose of it? What's the mark-up?

BIG HEAD: Well, the lower East Side is my scene. The only difference is that on the lower East Side usually the prices are a dollar higher per bag to the user. They cop in seventy-five-dollar bundles, a bundle makes 25 five-dollar bags. So uptown, if I were dealing uptown, I would be making fifty dollars profit. Downtown you make a seventy-five. It's 100 per cent profit. But nobody begrudges you, nobody feels that a pusher is taking too much profit. Not the junkie, nobody. And there's never any protest like that because it's really a hassle to be in action nowadays. It used to be you could be in action for a couple of years and nobody would get hip to you. But now, there are rollers on every block.

HAYDEN: What do you mean, "rollers"?

BIG HEAD: Police. Police.

HAYDEN: How are your relationships with the police generally? I take it you have been busted several times. By now they must know your face at least as a suspect face.

BIG HEAD: Well, once you get known, like when I got known on Avenue C, you get rousted all the time. You're walking down the street and suddenly—Well, it doesn't matter now. There were two detectives who were working down there as a team a couple of years ago. Let's call them Smith and Johnson. You'd get to know them, you'd know their car, you'd know their habits. Some detectives prefer to watch you from a doorway. Others go through elaborate changes trying to conceal themselves, driving a taxicab or something. Some of them just stand around. Some sit in their car and watch. You get to know how they operate. These two guys used to sit in the car, maybe they'd pretend to be fixing the engine or something. I'd spot them and clean myself.

HAYDEN: What do you mean, "clean yourself," get rid of the narcotics?

BIG HEAD: Yeah, stash it. Put it in an empty cigarette pack and throw it in an alley, leave it somewhere.

HAYDEN: And then go back and get it later on?

BIG HEAD: Yes.

HAYDEN: But isn't stashing a bit risky? If a junkie is watching you, wouldn't you lose——

BIG HEAD: Yes, but you're generally pretty careful about where you stash. You make sure nobody sees where you've put it. Then, when they toss you, they grab you, throw you in a doorway and search you. It's a game. You know, it's their job to catch you dirty and it's your job to make sure they always catch you clean.

HAYDEN: Well, are they nasty or are they friendly?

BIG HEAD: It depends on the policemen. I've been beaten and robbed by a police officer. Once I was thrown into a doorway and handcuffed to a radiator and robbed of seventy-five dollars. I was going to score. He knew I was going to score, he thought I already had.

HAYDEN: He took your money?

BIG HEAD: That's right.

HAYDEN: Rather than your dope?

BIG HEAD: That's right. I didn't have any dope. He thought I had scored and he was going to catch me with a bundle. He didn't catch me with anything. He was teed off so he took it out on me by slapping me around for a while and then taking my bread.

HAYDEN: Is this exceptional?

BIG HEAD: Yes, it is exceptional.

HAYDEN: How does the average narcotics officer——

BIG HEAD: There is no average narcotics officer. There are no more idiosyncratic police in the world than the narcotics squad. Especially New York City's Narcotics Squad. They are all rather odd individuals. None of them really fit in. They don't fit in the Police Department, and they don't fit in society at large. They're all very, very individual. They have tics and mannerisms that are very gross and exaggerated. I know one detective who has to have his mouth hanging open all the time. If he doesn't he'll burst out laughing. That's his attitude, his actual attitude.

HAYDEN: He says this, or this is the way you read him?

BIG HEAD: I watch him. Every time he starts to say anything, if he has to close his mouth while he's talking, he smiles. To make a "w" sound you have to compress your lips. He just comes right up, he'll burst right out laughing in the courtroom and will have to leave.

HAYDEN: Some of these questions you may not be able to answer and others you might not want to answer, but is heroin traffic highly organized in this city? Or in the United States?

BIG HEAD: It's highly organized down to the ounce level. Once the ounces are broken up, it becomes less of an organizational thing.

HAYDEN: You mean heroin is sold wholesale by the ounce?

BIG HEAD: If you're copping by the ounce, that's the highest level at which you can be a junkie. Junkies don't deal in weight because it's just too big to blow. They just won't let you. The man who brings it in won't let somebody who's using deal for them on that level. It's just too much involved.

HAYDEN: Do narcotics necessarily stretch into a variety of other worlds? It's said that most of the prostitutes, female prostitutes, in this town are junkie women, women who are hooked that have to prostitute themselves to supply their habit. Is this true, or is it a myth?

BIG HEAD: Well, you see, it's harder for a chick, in one way, to avoid prostitution. I'd say 60 per cent of male addicts are burglars. Then there are smaller percentages who are forgers, there are shoplifters, etc. There are very few violent criminals among the junkies. In fact, I've never seen a narcotics officer pull a pistol.

HAYDEN: You were telling me about being busted. Go ahead and finish your story, but then I'd like you to describe the way a narcotics officer busts somebody.

BIG HEAD: Well, a chick can only make it in three ways: she can deal in junk, she can be a shoplifter, or she can sell herself. By far the easiest way to take is prostitution. Women just don't go in for burglary for some reason. Maybe it's lack of physical dexterity, I don't know.

HAYDEN: What about marijuana? How does marijuana figure in the so-called narcotics scene generally?

BIG HEAD: Well, it's an entirely different thing. Marijuana is completely unorganized. There are no syndicates bringing in grass. It's impossible to import in great quantities without detection which you have to do to support a syndicate-type operation. A pound of marijuana would fill, oh, I don't know, but a shopping bag would only hold ten pounds. Ten pounds wholesale represents about a thousand dollars, maybe only five hundred dollars, depending on how much you sell at one time.

HAYDEN: Then these figures we hear quoted in dope raids are based on retail prices?

BIG HEAD: When you hear that fifteen thousand dollars worth of marijuana has been seized, they probably found thirty pounds.

HAYDEN: Which would only be about three thousand dollars wholesale.

BIG HEAD: Much less than that. It would bring two grand, maybe only fifteen hundred.

HAYDEN: Well, something which is very interesting is that marijuana is not addicting. You do have a group of people which are in no way addicted, the so-called "potheads." You were telling me that junkies, people on heroin, very rarely will touch marijuana. Could you give me some of the background on this?

BIG HEAD: Well, marijuana contains several active principals. It's a great mystery, marijuana, although it's been known for about three thousand years. It's been used by the human race, by the medical profession, and to this date nobody is sure of the physical action of marijuana. No one knows what happens after you smoke it. Where does it go in your system? What effect does it have? It seems to have a purely intellectual effect, and it has a slight depressing effect, but it also contains one drug called synhexal which has stimulant properties. Smoking marijuana produces an introspective state, a state of heightened awareness regarding that occurring around you. It slows down your time sense, so that minutes will sometimes seem like hours. A heroin addict is looking for exactly the opposite effect.

HAYDEN: Then this is the reason the two groups are basically incompatible. The pothead is actually getting an exhilarating effect, coming closer to life in a sense, while the heroin addict is attempting to escape life and reality.

BIG HEAD: Well, I wouldn't say attempting to escape life and reality. He's filtering life and reality. He's saying, this part of life and reality I dig, and this part of life and reality I don't want any part of. For instance, if you're nervous, if you're a junkie and you're nervous and up tight and you take a shot of stuff, it will calm you. But if you smoke marijuana you will become more nervous and up tight. Marijuana doesn't change the nature of your sensations, it merely heightens them. But when you use heroin, all of your bodily processes are depressed, including physical perception.

HAYDEN: You become very sluggish, and very——

BIG HEAD: No, not necessarily. There are personality types, and physical somatypes which, due to some imbalance in metabolism, or in their psyche, are liberated by heroin. The depression of one area, say a person has intense sexual repressions, for instance, and he uses heroin, then all his anxiety about it will disappear. Heroin depresses the sexual function in the body, and so it is no longer important to him.

HAYDEN: The positive aspect of this is that a junkie never commits a sex crime.

BIG HEAD: Well, that's true, of course.

HAYDEN: Yet, one of the things thrown at people by the mass media is the image of the dope fiend. Have you any idea where the image of the dope fiend came from?

BIG HEAD: Sure, it comes from the period during the 19-teens when everybody was a snowbird.

HAYDEN: What's a "snowbird"?

BIG HEAD: It's an antiquated term for a coke-sniffer.

HAYDEN: That's cocaine?

BIG HEAD: Cocaine, which is a central-nervous-system stimulant.

HAYDEN: I understand cocaine is very uncommon today.

BIG HEAD: Very rare. Nobody uses coke. It's mainly a curiosity drug. People who use it do so only occasionally as a special great treat. I don't enjoy cocaine at all. It makes me very nervous.

HAYDEN: Give me, as best you can, a description of what it's like to take a shot of heroin. A physical, subjective description which the average person will be able to understand.

BIG HEAD: Oh, oh, it's like trying to describe something for which you have no senses to perceive. The physical sensation is simple to describe; it's just a feeling of warmth and relief. Everybody has little aches and pains. You know, your right great toe twinges you a little, the spam you had for breakfast is a little anxious in your stomach, and maybe you got a little eyestrain. With heroin, all this is gone. It's just wiped away like with a cloth. It's as if someone has poured warm water in all your veins, every minor discomfort and major discomfort, everything physical is just gone, pfft. You're left with this feeling of warmth, this feeling of control.

HAYDEN: You were telling me about an experience where, mentally, I think you were on heroin. No, it was a different drug. You went to Times Square and started directing traffic.

BIG HEAD: No, that was psilocybin.

HAYDEN: I think we'll get too far astray if we go into too many narcotics. I take it you have a general——

BIG HEAD: Psilocybin is not a narcotic, it's a psychomometic. Its action is totally unrelated to the action of known drugs of intoxication up to the last ten years. It doesn't present any problem, and the police aren't the least bit concerned about it. It's not a repetitive experience. There are very few people who would take hallucinatory drugs continually day after day. The hallucinogenetic experience is a catharsis. Sometimes it takes months before you're interested in taking them again.

HAYDEN: These experiences are similar to those caused by LSD-25 which got enormous publicity about a year ago. Leary and Alpert at Harvard and what have you.

BIG HEAD: Yes.

HAYDEN: In your opinion, what do you feel the LSD movement, if we can call it that, represents in this country?

BIG HEAD: Well, I don't know what it represents but I know its magnitude. There's less LSD available right now than there has been at any time in the last four years, and less psilocybin. In fact, I don't know of any psilocybin right now. Mescaline is not very hard to get; neither is peyote. The hallucinatory drugs that are available are going like hot cakes. People all over the country are becoming interested. Almost every academic community has a group of hallucinogen fanciers who take peyote once. . . .

HAYDEN: You said that you hid some heroin in a matchbook. It must be a very small amount of heroin that's taken in each dose.

BIG HEAD: Yes, it's small in comparison to the amount of, say, alcohol.

HAYDEN: Would you say it was half a teaspoonful, or a few grains?

BIG HEAD: Oh, no. A few grains would kill the average junkie. The amount of powder that a heroin addict receives in a bag of heroin is usually about 250 milligrams. Narcotics are measured in grains. A grain is 60 milligrams, so you would think you were getting a little over four grains of heroin when you cop a bag. But you're not, you're getting about 3 per cent heroin, the rest is milk sugar and quinine.

HAYDEN: Who does the mixing, the people who bring it into the country?

BIG HEAD: Yes, they do part of it. Then it's cut a little more everywhere it goes. If you sell an ounce, it's generally about 20 per cent heroin by volume, but by the time it reaches the street it's down to about 3 per cent.

HAYDEN: And this is the reason you hear of overdoses, and people dying of overdoses?

BIG HEAD: Yes. Some, either intentionally, but usually unintentionally, will give an addict a bag much stronger than he's used to. Actually, overdoses don't generally happen to addicts because an addict's daily maintenance dose is much smaller than his tolerance. You develop an enormous tolerance.

HAYDEN: Who's prone to the overdose? The first-time user?

BIG HEAD: The chip-eater, the guy who gets off once a week, or every other day or so.

HAYDEN: There are a great number of these people around too?

BIG HEAD: He has no tolerance. See, it takes about a month to get addicted to heroin. That means serious use of heroin, you have to shoot at least three times a day for a month. Sometimes, only for two weeks, sometimes for as long as two months, but never less than two weeks of serious, daily, three-times-a-day shooting such that you're high all the time, before you can become addicted.

HAYDEN: Do you ever have problems with diseases gotten from dirty hypodermic needles? Hepatitis?

BIG HEAD: Well, I've gotten hepatitis, that's standard. Also maybe once every month or two, you'll get a blood reaction from a trace of somebody's incompatible blood on the spike.

HAYDEN: Well, what are the occupational hazards? In other words, what are the tragedies that befall a junkie?

BIG HEAD: His man gets busted and he can't score. Or he has a hassle scoring. Or he gets himself busted. The main tragedies that befall a junkie are connected with society. There is no hazard at all in being a junkie except for the fact that people are going to bother you for it.

HAYDEN: Well, isn't one of the reasons they bother you because of the crime elements connected with addiction? Do you feel this is——

BIG HEAD: Which came first now? In 1914, when they passed the Harrison Narcotics Act, they had a group of people who were indistinguishable from the general population. They have them in England now; they have some seven hundred heroin addicts who are kept on heroin by the English government. They have no crime problem. A junkie is much less prone to crime than other people are because he hasn't got the interest in it. You know, he hasn't got the ambition to own automobiles, to impress women, to have beautiful clothes.

HAYDEN: They have found that some heroin addicts work very well under drugs, were jobholders, and that the drugs in some cases actually seemed to benefit those using them. They agreed that without drugs some people could not function as well in society.

BIG HEAD: Well, according to Lexington, 93 per cent of addicts show an increase in efficiency on intelligence tests, on tests of emotional maturity, on physical dexterity, and so on, under the influence of narcotics. Meanwhile, the controlled nonaddicts, people they experimented with, dropped in efficiency. There is an addictive personality that is benefited by heroin.

HAYDEN: What is your own personal feeling or what are the general attitudes of narcotics users? I'll limit it just to the narcotics user, when he looks at something like Narcotics Anonymous, or Dr. Baird's Haven House Clinic in Harlem where addicts can go and voluntarily withdraw.

BIG HEAD: There's Synanon also. There's Manhattan General Hospital where you can go and they'll give you methadon pills. Every junkie wants to kick and he wants to kick, not because he doesn't like junk, but because it's such a hassle to keep going. When you're going to get sick if you don't have thirty dollars, and you gotta have thirty dollars every day, rain or shine, 365 days a year, it's an enormous burdensome hassle. So everybody wants to kick. But nobody wants to live without junk either. So when an addict is offered a program like the program at Lexington he is likely to accept it. The only reason a junkie doesn't want to go to Lexington is that they make you stay four and one-half months.

HAYDEN: Are you sure of that? I spoke with one boy and his father, at Dr. Baird's clinic and the father said his boy only stayed in Lexington for three days.

BIG HEAD: He signed himself out. Well, they can get vindictive at Lexington and have, at times. They call up the local authorities and as soon as you walk out of the gate, the local police pick you up. You can get two years in Kentucky, just for being an addict.

HAYDEN: You mean that the Lexington people turn you over to the Kentucky authorities?

BIG HEAD: Right.

HAYDEN: For just being an addict, or for having heroin?

BIG HEAD: For being an addict. You can go to jail in California for having a needle mark on your arm, or for internal possession of heroin. They give you a naline test, they give you a shot of anamorphine hydrochloride.

HAYDEN: That isn't the law in most states of the Union? Having internal possession of heroin, having it in your blood, is not illegal in most states, is it?

BIG HEAD: No, it's not. But——

HAYDEN: Is it in New York state?

BIG HEAD: No. In New York the drug itself and hypodermic needles are illegal. You can go to court completely blasted, and sit and nod out in the courtroom and they're not going to bother you.

HAYDEN: In other words, they're very lenient in New York state?

BIG HEAD: Well, they're not lenient at all. They just never bothered to pass a law that punishes the state of being. That's rather absurd to punish someone for not committing a crime but just for being.

HAYDEN: One thing which stands out very much in my mind is the talk I've heard about stiffer penalties for pushers. Now, you're someone who pushes heroin, what about these very serious charges that anyone who sells heroin to someone is a destroyer of human life, a destroyer of lives?

BIG HEAD: All junkies are pushers.

HAYDEN: Are you a junkie now?

BIG HEAD: Yes, of course. Once you're a junkie, you're a junkie. There's no way out, really.

HAYDEN: The point I'm making is, will all pushers turn to new people in order to get new customers?

BIG HEAD: No, most drug addicts in this society are very much opposed to that. If someone asks him, "Can I taste the stuff?"

and you know they don't use stuff, you say, "What? Are you nuts? You want heroin? You're crazy!"

HAYDEN: Can you say then the average junkie-pusher will not turn out new people?

BIG HEAD: Certainly he will. The only criterion I have when I deal is: do I know the guy and is he cool? If I think that he's not the kind of cat that when the man stops him and says, "Where do you get it?" he'll point him the way, I'll sell it to him, of course.

HAYDEN: Is there any chance that you might stop living if you were to point out all the people you know in narcotics, the pushers I mean?

BIG HEAD: Of course. Somebody'd cowboy me, or slip me a hot shot, or——

HAYDEN: "Cowboy you"? What's that?

BIG HEAD: Jump on me and slit my throat.

HAYDEN: What are some of the other terms? Hot shot, I take it, is an overdose.

BIG HEAD: No, hot shots are usually strychnine, battery acid, or something like that instead of stuff.

HAYDEN: And this is the way one junkie can eliminate another?

BIG HEAD: It looks like stuff. It cooks up like stuff. I don't know if it's very commonly used. Actually the most common hot shot now would be an overdose; someone would give you 20 per cent stuff instead of your 3 per cent stuff. If you're using a bag at a time, you throw the bag in the cooker and before you've got it half way in, you've turned blue.

HAYDEN: Is there any way to save a guy? The moment you've taken an overdose, do you know it? I mean, is there anything an addict can do to save himself?

BIG HEAD: Save himself? No, usually not.

HAYDEN: How about a junkie's friends, will they usually try to save him?

BIG HEAD: Sure.

HAYDEN: Can you take an overdosed addict to a hospital in this city and get medical treatment quickly?

BIG HEAD: No. No, you can't. But that's an academic question any-

way, because if a man's really taken an overdose, it's very un-
likely that he'll be alive by the time you get him to the hospital.
You have to give him artificial respiration right away. If you
have some naline around, a dose of naline, if you can. If you
don't have any naline——

HAYDEN: What is naline?

BIG HEAD: Naline is anamorphine-hydrochloride, which is an an-
tagonist for opiates. It directly counteracts heroin.

HAYDEN: Do most junkies know all this? I see you have a great
number of medical books around here; you know these things
to do in case of an overdose.

BIG HEAD: Most junkies would give a shot of table salt, and artificial respiration, and cold compresses.

HAYDEN: What are the chances of pulling a guy through?

BIG HEAD: I never had anyone die on me. Well, I had one die on
me once, but it wasn't really my fault. I wasn't really in control
of the situation. I imagine there would have been cases where I
couldn't have done anything.

HAYDEN: What do you do when a guy dies on you? Where do you
put the body? What do you do with it?

BIG HEAD: Well, it depends on your area. You can dump it out the
window if you live on the lower East Side. You're on the sixth
floor, you dump him out in the courtyard, there're a lot of pads.
The cops aren't going to bother looking around; he's a junkie.

HAYDEN: They think he fell off a fire escape, or jumped himself?

BIG HEAD: He overdosed, they don't much care what happened to
him. It's generally put down as suicide.

HAYDEN: Is that what they do, they claim that these are suicides?

BIG HEAD: Sure. Well, the very fact you see, there is the Freudian
contention that as soon as a guy sticks a spike in his arm, he's
suicidal anyway. So when he's finally kicked by it, it is a suicide.
I don't go along with that, but there is some basis for their
thinking.

HAYDEN: Some of the junkies I've talked to insist that there're
some cops who confiscate narcotics only to sell them back to
others. Are these isolated instances, or is this rather common?

BIG HEAD: No, it's not too common. But there are a couple of narcs on Riker's Island right now who were caught dealing up in Harlem.

HAYDEN: And they got caught by other narcotics agents?

BIG HEAD: Right, by the Pepsi Cola Squad probably.

HAYDEN: What do you call the "Pepsi Cola Squad"?

BIG HEAD: Well, in this town you have a system. All towns have shoefly cops who run around and check on other cops. In this town there's a squad of police who check on other squads of police. They keep them on their toes and make sure there's no hanky-panky.

HAYDEN: And these are called the Pepsi Cola Boys?

BIG HEAD: Yeah, because they've got a lot of fizz and energy.

HAYDEN: Are most addicts young? Are most addicts from impoverished areas?

BIG HEAD: Now that's funny. In 1942, at Lexington the average age of addicts was around thirty-five. Right now the average age is twenty-six. There's definitely been a move downwards in age and a shift in the ethnic groups involved. The Italians still control the traffic downtown but it's moving over to Negro control now. From Chinese to Jewish to Italian to Negro.

HAYDEN: You apparently have this concept of narcotics having been around all these years such that you see sociological changes in it.

BIG HEAD: Oh, definitely. Junk used to be sold like, I've worked for old-time schmeckers——

HAYDEN: What are "schmeckers"?

BIG HEAD: Junkies. It is kind of esoteric, isn't it?

HAYDEN: No, that's the kind of stuff I like to know. It adds to my general knowledge.

BIG HEAD: For instance, there's a guy I know who got busted in January and who's now doing five to fifteen. He's used stuff for about thirty-five years. When he started coppin' heroin was thirty dollars an ounce and came with brand names and labels.

HAYDEN: In drugstores?

BIG HEAD: No. It was illegal, but it had things like that.

HAYDEN: I understand there is a flourishing counterfeit traffic in marijuana. The beatniks take catnip, which looks and smells like marijuana, and sell it to tourists in Greenwich Village as the real thing.

BIG HEAD: Oh, sure. I've done that myself. You go over to Washington Square and pick a handful of grass, shred it up fine, and throw it in a bag. You can sell that. You can sell catnip, oregano too.

HAYDEN: How do people react when you go up to them? You don't know anything about them; do you say, "Hey fella, you wanna buy some marijuana?" How do you do it?

BIG HEAD: Oh, it isn't that way. Some weekend hippie from the Bronx winds up in the Rienzi. He strikes up a conversation and you mention marijuana. He seems to want to go along with it; you just burn him, that's all. You whip the bag on him. I've sold quinine for mescaline, talcum powder for heroin.

HAYDEN: Is this very common? Does a junkie have to be careful about the stuff that he's buying?

BIG HEAD: Very careful. Very careful. You don't have to worry about getting killed usually because if someone's going to burn you he generally does it with milk sugar or talcum powder.

HAYDEN: I can't picture the world of the junkie in one respect. I gather that it's very much a one-man world, that you're a junkie and you have the problem of supplying your own habit, but while there are places to go to see and meet other junkies, it remains an outlaw world. In other words, if you have any money, won't the others possibly be contriving to get your money to supply their own habits?

BIG HEAD: I had a partner once, we had a partnership dealing in drugs. Things went along very well. We both had habits that cost us sixty dollars a day apiece and we were supporting them very easily selling marijuana, cocaine, and mescaline. But business went bad. My partner just became incapacitated for a couple of weeks; he lost all urge to function, something happened to him and his end of the business fell off. We lost capital and lost capital until we finally didn't have the bread to recop. Then I was stuck with a sixty-dollar habit.

HAYDEN: Your outlook upon narcotics throughout your conversation is strictly business.

BIG HEAD: Of course, it's business. It's the business of staying alive. It's a total need. Because junk depresses hunger, depresses sexual appetite. It depresses your need for social acceptance; it depresses your need just to be warm. All the energy you usually devote to those needs are devoted to heroin. All the mental concentration, all the time you usually spend thinking about food, or sex, you spend on junk. Junk supplies everything.

HAYDEN: Why do you feel most people become junkies? I mean, is there any pat reason?

BIG HEAD: I love junk. I love dope, and so does everybody I know.

HAYDEN: Then it's the drug itself, rather than broken homes, or the need to escape frustration, or an inability to deal with life.

BIG HEAD: Most people, most junkies, do come from that sort of background. They have had problems before they have had problems with junk. But I feel the reason these people are junkies while Joe Blow on the street isn't is because junk is illegal. If junk were legal, like liquor is, and was sold freely and without stigma, then there would be an enormous percentage of addiction in this country. As long as you leave it on the street where it's available, where a guy's gotta sell a bag in order to make enough money to keep his habit going, then there's going to be just more and more addicts.

HAYDEN: This is the argument for the——

BIG HEAD: The reason that most junkies are like me is that Joe Blow would never think of doing anything illegal, basically, so Joe Blow never gets his first taste of stuff. Someone who's been in trouble all their life anyway, it's nothing for them to make some more.

HAYDEN: I'm getting off a little, but something I've been personally very interested in is how criminality begins small, then grows. It's the first little wrong thing. I mean people seem to violate one taboo and this would lead to violating other taboos. Criminality is something, in a sense, that becomes a way of life, doesn't it? You would admit that this is criminality, when a guy becomes hooked on junk and begins robbing apartments?

BIG HEAD: Of course, it's criminality by definition. A criminal does something that is prohibited; it is prohibited, so naturally you're a criminal. But don't forget in 1914 there were 500,000 known narcotics addicts in this country, 500,000 suspected narcotics addicts anyway. These people, by act of Congress, became criminals overnight. The day before they were just citizens on the street, completely legit. All of a sudden they passed the Harrison Narcotics Act and these guys all became criminals. Then they went to doctors and got prescriptions. They had to bribe the doctors but then they stopped the prescriptions. Things got tighter and tighter until the prices went up. This idiot who wrote this book, who used to be Deputy Narcotics Commissioner, is proud of the fact.

"Our efficiency can be demonstrated by the fact that heroin is so expensive, that the percentage is so small, and therefore," he says, "there are no real narcotics addicts left in the country like there were when the Narcotics Act was passed, because the quantity you can use is limited now by its expense."

But then again, in 1960 there was no one spending sixty to one hundred dollars a day for dope. He's reasoning that you spend the same amount of money and you get less dope, but that's not true.

HAYDEN: Well, you've had a lot of talk recently about bringing the English system into this country. You were telling me before we began our interview that even the *Daily News,* one of the most conservative and reactionary newspapers in the country, had come out for the legalization of drugs.

BIG HEAD: They've run two editorials which have called for clinics dispensing narcotics to addicts. I'd like to think it is an enlightened step on their part but I don't think it's anything at all except an attempt to sell papers.

HAYDEN: Do you think this would eliminate drug addiction over a period of years or decades?

BIG HEAD: Nothing will ever eliminate drug addiction so long as there are drugs. But certainly the English experience demonstrates that it will end the social problems caused by addiction.

HAYDEN: You have a philosophy that comes through. I take it you don't consider drug addiction a problem in itself. You consider it's a problem only because the energies of society——

BIG HEAD: It's made a problem. It becomes very clear when you look at people like Anslinger, who was Federal Narcotics Commissioner until his retirement a couple of years ago, who say they don't believe in legalization of narcotics on moral grounds. He said any person who gave narcotics to an addict was helping to perpetuate a condition of slavery. It was a very Thomistic attitude, it was almost as if a Jesuit was saying this. He said he knew of no case in which it would be justifiable to give narcotics to someone addicted except where the law allowed it for incurable cancer patients, and so forth. He had made two exceptions, one of them was a Congressman. He said the reason he supplied the Congressman with narcotics was to prevent a scandal in the Congress until this man left.

HAYDEN: In his book, Anslinger speaks of a Congressman who was a narcotics addict?

BIG HEAD: Right. The medical profession also knows of thousands of cases where doctors have lived to the age of eighty-five or ninety with distinguished practices and after they died it was discovered that they'd been addicts.

HAYDEN: How do they discover this, needles in their drawers, or what?

BIG HEAD: You discover it in an autopsy, an analysis of the man's blood, or just by looking at his arms. You find his arms are full of holes and you realize he's a junkie.

HAYDEN: Doesn't heroin addiction physically destroy someone over a period of years?

BIG HEAD: No, not at all. There's no evidence for that at all.

HAYDEN: Not even by decreasing the addict's appetite such that he doesn't eat properly?

BIG HEAD: So you might become slender. In fact, most junkies are kinda skinny, but there's no harm in that. There're two reasons you become skinny: (1) because your hunger is not pressing and (2) because you neglect food. You may be hungry but getting food's not as important as getting stuff.

HAYDEN: I've seen ex-addicts on programs like David Susskind's show. I've also heard ex-addicts on radio, on discussion programs——

BIG HEAD: Addicts are a bunch of sanctimonious phonies. Every time you're in the Tombs, or in Manhattan General, or anywhere where people are withdrawing from narcotics, those who are freshly withdrawn preach at you. "What? Heroin?" they'll say. "Don't speak to me of evil! I'll never." You know, it's fine until junk's accessible again. If you're in jail, and can't get junk, you just put it out of your mind—you can't get junk. But all the time you're wanting it, you're dreaming about it.

HAYDEN: But how about those people who leave jail and resume functioning again in society? They apparently have reformed, at least in the social sense of the word.

BIG HEAD: Junk supplies a purpose. Junk is a built-in system of reward and punishment. Somebody who has no real reason to live, who has no goals, no aims that are pressing, starts using stuff and enjoys stuff because it gives him these things. It's a knife in your back that keeps you moving. At the same time when you do well it rewards you. When you do well, you cop. Your values become centered on junk; it is your purpose in life.

HAYDEN: Well, what's wrong, what is your real objection to the reformed addict, the person who has dropped narcotics, has kicked the habit, gotten himself a job and rejoined everyday life?

BIG HEAD: Not "rejoined life." He has rejoined massness. He has rejoined what Joe Blow does but he hasn't rejoined what I've done. He hasn't rejoined what you're doing. He's got his own stick, and I've got mine. I object to people who moralize, who say because they dig herpetology and now can be with snakes all the time in the Bronx Zoo, they won't use stuff any more. I'm supposed to develop a consuming passion for herpetology? Or Christianity? Or women?

HAYDEN: In other words, you feel that they've found individual solutions to their problem, then they turn on you because they've worked out their own hang-ups?

BIG HEAD: Yeah. Here's a guy who been a stone junkie like me for years. All of a sudden he has a revelation, real or not—it doesn't matter. He finds something else is more important to him, that something else can satisfy him like junk can. Then he turns around to me and says, "Stop using stuff, I'm satisfied."

HAYDEN: Have you known any of these people?

BIG HEAD: I've only known one guy who's a true cured junkie. I've only met one in my life.

HAYDEN: What did he say to you; how did you happen to meet him?

BIG HEAD: He hangs around with junkies. He can go out and cop for you. He can sit in the room and watch you take off, and yet he hasn't had a shot of stuff in years, nine years, I believe.

HAYDEN: He still socializes with junkies?

BIG HEAD: Yeah, he hasn't developed any kind of moralistic attitude toward junkies.

HAYDEN: Do you feel you'll probably be dealing drugs the rest of your life?

BIG HEAD: If it's necessary I will. I know I'll be using drugs the rest of my life. If it's necessary, I'll be dealing drugs the rest of my life.

HAYDEN: Because you use drugs and you intend to use them the rest of your life, do you feel your life may be shorter, or more violent, or more horrendous, or better than the average person's?

BIG HEAD: If present conditions prevail, it will certainly be much more violent. It gets broken up into little chunks all the time.

There's a week of being straight, a day of being sick, a month of being in jail, four months of being action-heavy, then two months of tight hustling. It's——

HAYDEN: But you fit here. You fit here as a person?

BIG HEAD: I fit with drugs as a person. I don't fit on the scene. I mean the scene is more acceptable to me than various civilian occupations.

HAYDEN: Junkies as a group don't particularly, you don't have a very high regard for the average junkie?

BIG HEAD: I have a higher regard for the average junkie in some respects than I have for most people. For one thing, the average junkie is ruthlessly honest about himself, always. As they've discovered at Lexington, it gives you this vantage point of emotional maturity; you're very objective about everything on stuff.

HAYDEN: You know what you're doing and why you're doing it?

BIG HEAD: You know exactly what you're doing. You know your motivations. You'll make admissions about yourself to another person that you would never make if you were out on the street as a truck driver. You would never say the things to another truck driver that you would say to another junkie.

HAYDEN: Yes, but what the people at the other end of this microphone are never going to be able to understand is how someone could understand what was happening, claim to have a full awareness of it, and yet feel there was no better life for them in some other field.

BIG HEAD: If all of my interests were centered on junk. You see, there have been times in my life when I've paid attention to nothing else but junk, only because of necessity. I'd be sick if I didn't do it, and things were so tight that I had to be on the hustle twenty-four hours, literally, twenty hours a day, with no sleep. I've gone without sleep for two or three weeks. The only rest I'd get was when I'd sit down and nod out. Everywhere I'd sit down I'd nod out for a few minutes; that was the only sleep I'd get.

HAYDEN: When you're fighting so hard to keep your habit supplied, do you manage to keep an apartment and things like that?

BIG HEAD: Sometimes. I haven't had my own place now for a year and a half. Before that, I had my own place, certainly at times. I expect to have one again pretty soon.

HAYDEN: Some people join a drifting population. In some areas, they just hang out in pool halls, they——

BIG HEAD: Well, I hang out in people's pads. I'm an ornament. There are several people similar to me. My interests aren't only junk; I'm fairly competent in one of the arts. I don't want to mention which one, I just don't want to pinpoint myself. I'm not making any claims to being one of the Cervantes of the century, but I'm fairly competent.

HAYDEN: You're in a creative art?

BIG HEAD: Yes. I'm also an excellent nurse. I can't practice though.

HAYDEN: In conclusion, are there any final ideas you'd like to throw out? What would you say to anyone if they were offered a shot of heroin? Honestly.

BIG HEAD: Honestly? Don't mess with it.

HAYDEN: Why?

BIG HEAD: It's too much of a hang-up, really. I would say to them that if they were absolutely desperate about their condition as it is at present and feel that there is no need to continue living, if they are locked in a nonproductive cycle where there are a million things that they would sort of like to do but they can't get organized to do them, well then take a taste of stuff, sure.

HAYDEN: We were saying that after you get along in life, or you like an unusual life such as you have lived, there doesn't seem to be any—how did you put it? You express it.

BIG HEAD: Well, you've already thrown me into a bad context. I said nothing of the sort. I said that in anybody's life. The message that I was trying to get across (*pause*). Maybe he didn't put it right either. So I'll just give you my message, my message, baby. The great fault of the liberal, and of the well-meaning, enlightened individual of today, the person who is all for the legalization of junk, clinics, registration of addicts and all that, is that they have chucked the moral sense. They have thrown away the idea that there is an absolute right and there is an absolute wrong, which is an advance that was made by Blake hundreds of years ago when he said, "The one law for the lion and the ox is oppression." He recognized it, and people are starting to recognize that now generally. The general tone of the world intellectual community is that of course it is absurd to think of things in terms of right and wrong. Let's instead set up our scientific measuring instruments and determine what is real and what is unreal. Let us set up a standard of objective reality. But there is no objective reality.

HAYDEN: But when you tear down—

BIG HEAD: If you eat an apple, you get stoned, baby. Those chemicals just course through your body and completely change your outlook, your mood, your metabolism, your attitude. Because I throw stuff into my system and perceive things a little differently owing to its metabolic effect, I'm living in an unreal world? When you're eating an apple, you're living in a real world? That's not fair. My world is just as real as yours, and just as objective as yours. There're three billion universes on this planet——

HAYDEN: But when you throw away the standard values and the conventional approach to life, aren't you lost in a sea; aren't you really lost in a drifting sea?

BIG HEAD: Not at all. You've got freedom for the first time. You're no longer drifting with objective standards of reality. This sea of common perception—the sun is round and so many miles across; the hell with that! One hundred and eight million people know that. I know things that nobody knows but me, and nobody ever will know them but me, that's reality.

19

Guerrilla Warfare—
Not to Worry
by Emile Capouya
(1962)

Emile Capouya is the New York writer, editor, and critic.

Many of us feel a quite vulgar and underbred resentment for the
men who may be in a position to put an end to the history of
mankind by helping to bring about atomic war. Politicians, generals, technicians, scholars, scholar-propagandists—such people are
the natural objects of our plebeian distrust. We are all Falstaffian
cowards in that regard. We say privately, "Honor—what is that
but a word?"—referring, of course, to the honor of generals, politicians, etc., that often seems to us to be quite unconnected with
our own honor as two-legged creatures that love the light and
would like to live in it a while longer. Of the politicians and generals East and West who threaten one another and all of us with
atomic sanctions, we say, "They are mad," or, to put it in American, "They're crazy," and we hope that they will go away. But if
we were fairer to those people in our own minds, we should see
clearly that they won't go away. The truth is, I am sure, that many
of them are most superior people, motivated not solely by garden-
variety lusts and ambitions but also by the purest, most uncom-
promising ideals. Even in their murky ghost-written speeches we

can catch the gleam of the unregarding absolute that impels them to sacrifice everything for what they conceive to be a great cause, to seek out occasions for heroic self-discipline, martyrdom, immolation. No, they won't go away. They have enough of the divine madness, the political leaders, the generals, and the public poets of East and West, to set fire to the world.

But while we wait for a sign to tell us whether the race is finally doomed or provisionally ransomed, there are lesser men and smaller notions competing for our attention. We can't always be thinking of the great big soul-satisfying bang and its advocates. Here and now, we have guerrilla war.

On the one side are bandits, warlords, revolutionaries, and liberators, determined to snatch while they can material goods and a little human dignity. They write manuals of guerrilla war that are as sober and appalling as Caesar's *Commentaries,* concentrating on a few chief heads of strategy and tactics. On the other side are the police forces of the West that have to cope with something new under the sun—dark-skinned men carrying modern firearms. The theoreticians of the West enjoy pleasant working conditions, and they are very short on practical experience of guerrilla war. To deplore the fact would be uncivilized. I feel gratified that military men in easy berths and civilian lecturers at the War College are our leading experts on the subject. I shall be just as happy if the day never comes when field-grade officers of the United States armed forces have enough practical experience of guerrilla war to write something useful about it. It would be perverse to feel otherwise. But naturally this happy state of affairs has its drawbacks when it is a question of making sense of guerrilla war. Among the guerrillas, Mao Tse-tung and Che Guevara write their own treatises on how to fight the armies of great powers and live to tell of it; their books are perspicuous, dogmatic and, if you'll forgive the blasphemy, written as by men having authority and not as the scribes.

In our own country, guerrilla warfare has become the basis of a scholarly industry. It is a new academic discipline, and the schoolmen are hard at it, inventing distinctions, drawing conclusions, shedding great quantities of ink. The authors among the guerrillas are men who are accustomed to shooting and being shot at. They did their research in the field—it is said that Mao Tse-tung ate grass during the Long March. The books they produce amount to straightforward manuals of murder. With us, the academic mills are grinding exceeding fine. Most of what they turn out is too finely bolted to have any connection with a form of warfare that is only a step removed from hand-to-hand combat. And then the self-possession of our writers is impaired because they are in a false position—official democrats exploring ways of suppressing popular revolutions. On the moral side, the result is Creeping Jesus crossed with two-bit Machiavelli; on the technical side, I doubt that guerrillas and guerrillas-to-be the world over have any cause for alarm.

Now, here am I, a civilian to my marrow, addressing an audience that probably includes very few fire-eaters and no professional soldiers, on the subject of guerrilla war. In a way, that fact epitomizes what is wrong with American theorizing on the entire question, and explains how we can arrive at such grotesque notions as that of fighting *their* guerrillas with *our* guerrillas. Except that I am not an expert, and presumably you are not experts, and there is some promise in that. We can discuss the matter on a higher level that can be achieved by experts, for it is written, "Except ye become as little children," and there is no doubt that we are a lot closer to the state of innocence than the experts are. For one thing, our only vested interest is in our skins. That means that in the intervals of being dazzled by expertise, we know very well what Blake was getting at when he said,

> To Mercy, Pity, Peace, and Love,
> All pray in their distress.

Any fool can find out the essentials of our subject; only an expert, perhaps, thinks he can find out more. But we promised to keep the discussion on a high level, and not spin the thread out of our own guts like the spider. The essentials, then, are these:

Guerrilla warfare is a means of armed struggle that allows

the weaker force to assume the strategic initiative. The chief tactic
is pecking the enemy to death by harrying his advance guard, his
rear, and his line of communications. Exploiting to the full the
advantages of mobility and surprise, the guerrillas concentrate
their forces to overwhelm a static, weaker enemy, and disperse
before a mobile, stronger enemy. Attrition of the enemy's will and
resources is their object. Their auxiliary weapons are terror and
propaganda, directed indifferently at the armed enemy or the civil
population as the case may appear to require. Guerrilla strategy
necessarily envisages the eventual building up of the guerrilla
force into a regular army for the decisive, pitched-battle phase of
the war.

Until the final phase, which is conventional warfare, the
guerrillas employ what amount to hit-and-run tactics. When do
such tactics work? When you can count on the support of the
population—moral and physical, but particularly physical—when
the enemy exposes himself in units weak enough to be hit with
impunity, and where there is room to run away from an enemy
strong enough to hit you successfully.

I am afraid that is all there is to the theoretical aspect of
guerrilla war.

I don't mean that any disaffected colonial, armed only with
these principles, can become the father of his country. That takes
talent and luck. What I do mean is that, if they wish, our experts
may cease from troubling, while the rest of us are free to draw
what Paul Goodman calls dumb-bunny conclusions from these
observations.

Practically speaking, then, guerrilla warfare is effective
against modern states because the latter, for very good reasons,
are not willing to make a countereffort commensurate with that of
the forces of revolution. Such a countereffort, however, is almost
always theoretically possible. It calls for patrolling the foreign
borders in force so that guerrillas cannot escape to sanctuary, setting up heavily manned forts at small distances from one another
all over the country, and advancing in strength, never permitting
a weak salient to develop. Difficult terrain that allows the guerril-

las to set up ambushes also restricts them to relatively few avenues of approach, and air reconnaissance can discover what
those avenues are. If tanks cannot negotiate gorges and preci-
pices, aircraft and artillery and mortar fire frequently can command them. All in all, from the purely military point of view,
there is absolutely no tactical problem raised by guerrilla operations that cannot be solved by concentrating sufficient troops and
matériel, and by generous use of barbed wire, forced relocation of
civilians, and polite counterterror. What! You can say that after
Dienbienphu, after the Algerian war, after the Cuban revolution
that overthrew a government armed and advised by the United
States? Yes.

In all these cases it was possible for the great powers to concentrate sufficient force to do the job. For many reasons, they
were not willing to do so. The level of sacrifice demanded was too
high. The rebels, for their part, were willing to give up everything. Individual soldiers in the armies of the powers may have
been in the same frame of mind, but their governments did not
agree with them. If it is the soldier's business to die bravely, it is
the politician's business to go on minding the store. The soldier
always says the same thing: "Give me enough men and weapons,
and I'll take any objective you like. Name it, I'll take it." And
that's no boast. The intangibles—such as morale, for instance—
are significant only when the forces are evenly matched. When
there is a good margin of strength on one side or the other, and
that strength is deployed without gross ineptitude, then the intangibles do not count and God is on the side that has the biggest
battalions. So the soldier always says, "Give me the wherewithal
and I'll do the job." But the politician always says, "What kind of
fool do you take me for? Mobilize the entire nation, put all our
lives into your hands, ration gasoline and chocolate? Fat chance.
Listen, it's a poor workman that finds fault with his tools. You can
be replaced, you know. Now get in there and fight."

That little vaudeville turn has been going on since there were
states and armies, and it is going on now about our intervention in
South Vietnam. Sooner or later the responsible soldier there will

ask for more support than the government is willing to let him have. And that is doubly sure because of a new addition to the act—the dialogue between the Statesman and the Muse of History. Clio says, "You know, the active military phase of the Chinese revolution took twenty years. Are you willing to struggle that long against the rebels?" The Statesman says, "Well, actually, no, actually." And adds to himself, "Not even if we were going to win, let alone if we are going to lose." But when the Muse of History makes the same observation to a guerrilla leader, he replies, "My dear, I've got nothing but time."

And it is very nearly the literal truth. Such a man speaks for multitudes that have little more to lose than their lives. That is the best reason for doubting that we can train Americans as counterguerrillas, ship them out to the swamps and mountains of the world, and with a final word of encouragement, unleash them to destroy the rebels. Men who have nothing to lose are a low form of life. They can eat young Americans for breakfast. I don't mean to echo those aging soldiers of ours who periodically exclaim over the softness of American youth. To toughen our youngsters to the requisite hardness, we should have to raise them from a tender age under the conditions of moral and physical deprivation that the guerrillas themselves have enjoyed—and who can say for sure that they would be appropriately grateful when they reached fighting age? No, even in official circles the myth of the American counterguerrilla is being dissipated. Official doctrine now inclines rather to recruiting counterguerrillas in the troubled countries themselves, saying in effect, "Let's you and him fight."

But what kind of inducements can we offer *our* guerrillas to rouse them to the pitch of military efficiency displayed by *their* guerrillas? Can we offer them those blessings to secure which their brothers have already taken the field against us? I say against us since we customarily assume—rightly, I think—that any revolt among the wretched of the earth is a revolt against us. And isn't it a disconcerting fact that of those vast territories that we now refer to as underdeveloped lands, hardly a square foot was not at one time the property of some Western nation that by common consent was licensed to underdevelop it? The resentment generated by that fact ensures that our conscripts and mercenaries cannot be as good as the genuine article. Counterguerrillas are nonsense. If we want to keep down the rebels, it will take conventional forces employed on the grand scale. Recall that guerrilla strategy envisages the eventual organization of a traditional army to engage the enemy in traditional pitched battle. At that point, at least, the rebels are exposed to the fortunes of war and no longer enjoy the special advantages of guerrillas. Why don't our strategists propose to wait out each new guerrilla movement until it is strong enough to dare the kind of warfare we best understand and are best equipped to wage? Well, besides the fact that we cannot afford to have our tail twisted and do nothing about it, besides the fact that guerrillas take their war aims with them, expropriating foreign investors and parceling out the land wherever they go, pitched battles invite atomic intervention—the last hurrah. So that is another reason why nations—our own nation—will not commit sufficient force to any theater to suppress the guerrillas effectively, for to do so invites rockets.

Now, we have said that guerrilla warfare is the choice of the weaker force that elects to harass the exposed points of the enemy courageously, ingeniously, inflicting the greatest possible damage at the smallest cost to itself in men and matériel. The guerrilla leader hopes that the price of suppressing him will be more than the opposing government is willing to pay and, especially in terms of time, he is likely to be right. All the chances are against a great nation's mobilizing the necessary force to crush a guerrilla uprising swiftly and decisively, and the fear of starting a general war, out of all proportion to the immediate objective, is a real stumbling block to the military policy of great states in the atomic age. Imagine cremating half of Russia and the United States for the sake of our objectives in Vietnam, a place about which we do not give a damn. Of course, in human affairs one word does lead to another, and our government has assumed embarrassing commitments in that exotic country. But failing a John Foster Dulles, that stern daughter of the voice of God, there are few people around really ready to risk atomic war for *ad hoc* principles. Berlin, now, is another matter. There we are anxious to act up to the high standards of courage set for us by the West German generals. And while we worry about the good opinion of those fountains of honor, the way is being smoothed for our providing them with atomic weapons. And if we don't, before long they'll make their own. And if Russia concludes a peace treaty with East Germany, the West Germans will get their atom bombs all the sooner— either openly, from those unteachable recidivists the Americans, or clandestinely, out of their own resources, as they got their Luft-waffe, their Reichswehr, their Panzer divisions the last time, with the consent of the Western powers because, after all, Hitler was against Russian Communism and no doubt the German general staff still is.

Now, if an American happens not to be a soldier facing tech-nological unemployment, nor a politician seeking, after the man-ner of his kind, a diversion from the real political and social issues of the age, why in the world—that world in which Germany is about to acquire atomic weapons—why in the world should he take guerrilla warfare seriously? Of course he should not. By and large, the guerrilla outbreaks are the work of men who are tired of being hungry. What really legitimate, avowable reasons do we have for being against that? Only one, that I can see, a very slim one. Because Russia encourages them, the revolts are, as Joseph Heller would say, a black eye for us and a feather in the cap for the Russians. And it is presumed that those black eyes and feath-ers in caps have some cash value in the game of power politics. All right, then. Let us encourage the revolts too. That is not just flip-pancy. Mr. Moscoso honestly reports, on the anniversary of the Alliance for Progress, insufficient results to warrant an anniversary celebration. But the Devil reports naval revolts in Venezuela, Pe-ronista riots and anti-Semitic outbursts in Argentina, a military junta attempting to seize power in Chile, a struggle between the military and civil power in Brazil, and throughout Latin America more mouths to feed this year than last and less to feed them with. Now, Latin America is going to revolt, and what a black eye that will be. The idea that Latin Americans will continue to starve docilely is like the idea that Negroes will continue docilely to play their traditional role in the United States. Both assumptions were reasonable for a hundred years, and suddenly they are no longer reasonable. Because of this and that, American Negroes are now acting like men, and so will the Latin Americans.

So the saints and seers dream of pre-emptive atomic strikes that will not wholly pre-empt, since they are scheduled to cost our own side, say, sixty million dead, and the humbler professionals talk about guerrilla war. The two groups are almost equally unrealistic. But the atomic strategists, and guerrilla strategists, and even disarmament strategists, are, I suspect, mere window-dressing for a very realistic government that is pursuing a policy equidistant from that of all three groups. The government is advancing toward an international ban on atomic weapons at about the same pace that the South is integrating its schools. Taking advantage of our deliberate speed, the Germans will borrow or build the bomb, as will the Chinese. Then we can resign the cares of empire to two virile races that love making decisions. Why do I call this policy realistic? Because the real is fact, is history, and this little sketch is about to become history.

It seems to me that if we are going to allow our government to be realistic in this way, and I suppose we are, then there are two things that reasonable men can concern themselves with. One is, in the short time remaining, to throw roses, roses riotously with the throng. The alternative is to enlist in a religion that demands a lot and promises a lot. But what we don't have to do at all is worry about guerrilla war.

I should like to knock this subject on the head, so that honest citizens won't be diverted from their proper concerns by it any longer. All that can profitably be said about guerrilla warfare falls within the compass of an ordinary military field manual. It is a tactic of weakness, practiced upon the squad, platoon, and company level by movements that aspire to act upon the regimental, brigade, corps, and army level, but do not as yet have the necessary troops and equipment. What they do have is time, and the bitter strength of the destitute. The rich nations are attached to their wealth, and rightly reckon time to be a dimension of their wealth. Accordingly, more often than not, guerrilla movements that have sufficient motive will succeed in making their revolts against the rich nations stick. As a subject for study, guerrilla warfare has a very narrow scope. It is no more than a department of infantry tactics—indeed, it *is* infantry tactics adapted to a low technological level. It is a technical specialty like glass-blowing, and it has no particular place in a liberal education. Neither is it the ground of political philosophy, whether pro or anti. It is the great new field for military scholarship, but that kind of scholarship has about as much to do with warfare as theology has to do with God.

There are two ways of dealing with guerrilla uprisings, and I hope we are agreed that stripping down to moccasins and breech-clout is not one of them. Landing a large army is one of them, though that method is likely to precipitate atomic war. The second way consists of four easy steps. First, if the aims of the rebels are legitimate, as they frequently will be, recognize them as such, aloud. Second, send them a military mission, and some of our obsolete tanks and aircraft. Third, grant them long-term credits so that they can indemnify the owners of expropriated land and industrial establishments. Fourth, agitate openly for the admission of the rebels to the United Nations.

That four-step program is the guaranteed foolproof self-cocking double-action hammerless equalizer for dealing with guerrilla uprisings. The rest, as Céline says, is bla-bla-bla. In fact, if our government really had an intelligent interest in Henry Luce's American Century, in Manifest Destiny, in dreams of a thousand-year Reich made in U.S.A., that is the policy it would be pursuing. But there is this odd thing about government: If you send a lot of professors to Washington, it doesn't make Washington more intelligent; it makes the professors less so. Necessarily, because they become organs of government. We Americans at one time were put to a lot of trouble—we had to make a revolution—in order to change our form of government and achieve one somewhat less offensive than the average. I take it that we have since declined from that condition of reasonably anodyne government. When the poet says, "Shine, perishing Republic," we know what republic he has in mind. But because of the struggle we went through to get our government, and because of the praise it lavishes upon itself, we tend to forget that its sole justification lies in promoting life, liberty, and the pursuit of happiness. To achieve those ends, says the Declaration of Independence optimistically, governments are instituted among men. By now it should be obvious that the role of our own government has become far more oppressive than benevolent.

In our private lives, when we apply for a pistol permit or a driver's license or unemployment insurance, and the organs of government are discourteous, when we are drafted or volunteer into the army and the sergeant calls us dirty names in his robust, manly way, or we notice that our passport is not valid for such countries as the State Department may be annoyed at now—generally the countries that it would be most instructive for us to visit—then we feel keenly enough that we are the government's property, and that whatever we may have instituted it for, its business is to administer us. In our public lives, of course, the government is out to get us killed. As men of the world, we ought to remember that governments all around the terraqueous globe stand in precisely that relation to their subjects. They have their respective populations backed up against the wall, and bully and wheedle them as seems most opportune. That ought to lessen our enthusiasm for whatever course of action our government chooses to take about rebels in the poor countries. Whether it follows its present realistic policy of drift, or intervenes in force against the guerrillas, we, the citizens, shall suffer. If it chooses to follow the intelligently Machiavellian policy I have outlined, it won't be for our sake but for its own. Indeed, the point is always the same. We are in terror of our government, whereas our government should, like Alice Ben Bolt, tremble at our frown. Our government, which we neither own nor control. To get control of our government is for us, the citizens, the first order of business. Do you remember

President Eisenhower's saying that if the governments of the world did not make peace, the peoples of the world would make peace for themselves? How about that? Is Eisenhower to remain the most radical and visionary of our thinkers?

An Indian Tale
by Jaime de Angulo

*Jaime de Angulo became a legend long before his death in
Berkeley, California, in 1951. Stories about his feuds with D. H.
Lawrence in Taos, about his spectacular existence in Big Sur
long before Henry Miller brought it new fame, about his life
among the Pit River Indians of California have been told and
retold in books and tales. In the early days of KPFA, Jaime came
each week to the small studio to record* Indian Tales, *a brief
manuscript he had written about the prehistoric dawn of mankind and the animal people who first inhabited the earth. When
the manuscript had been read, and he was persuaded that it was
unthinkable to end the series, he made up new stories every week,
singing the Indian chants and keeping time with a matchbox,
which made marvelous drum sounds into the microphone. Here
is one of the stories that he told in 1949 to the delight of as many
adults as children.*

I am going to tell you about the adventures that happened to the
little boy Fox, and his sister Quail, and their mother the graceful
Antelope, and their father Bear, who was very strong, but sometimes he was grumpy. All these adventures happened to them during a long trip they took, long ago, when they left their home in a

little valley in northern California and went to visit some relatives who lived on the other side of the mountains, near the coast.

Of course, all this happened long, long ago—long before the Americans today came to California, a long time, even, before the American Indians were living. All this happened in the long-ago time when the people on this earth were animals. And that's why Mr. Bear's wife was Antelope, and their children were the little Fox and his sister Quail.

And now don't ask me if these stories are true. Of course they are true! I tell you I heard them when I was living with the Indians, and became a sort of Indian myself. They used to tell all these kinds of stories in the long evenings, and we used to lie on our backs near the fire and watch the smoke curl up and out through the smoke hole—because you must remember that in Indian houses there is no chimney. The floor is the earth and there is a big hole in the roof for the smoke to go out. And that hole in the roof also serves as a door: people go up and down the ladder against the center-post and in and out of the house through that smoke hole in the roof, just as on board ship you go up and down a companionway and in and out of a hatch onto the deck.

I lived with the Indians, here and there, in northern California, and I tell you I became a sort of Indian myself. I was a young man then, twenty, thirty years ago. So don't ask me if these stories are true. Of course they are true. And don't ask me again how it is that Bear and Antelope and the others talked and acted like people. I tell you that in those days of long ago, all the animals were people, and all the people were animals. I became an Indian myself, so I know.

Well, now . . . It was just at dawn, when the trunks of the trees begin to show dark against pale gray, and you see maybe an owl going home through the tops of the pines, and the woodrats and the fieldmice are scurrying home also—it's hard to see them, because the ground is still so dark under the trees, but you can hear them scurrying under the dead leaves—and if you can see a patch of sky between the treetops maybe there is an early vulture already soaring way up in the silver-blue of the sky. That's the

dawn—and Fox-boy was already awake and lying under the rab-
bitskin blanket and peering at everything: you could just see his
head and the end of his tail curled around his neck . . . and he
heard Old Man Coyote, who had made his bed just a few feet
away, singing softly to himself:

> I am coming, I am coming
> With the daylight I come home
> Over the mountain I come home
> I am coming, I am coming
> From the East I come home.

"Why! Grandfather, do you also call your shadow home in
the dawn?"

"Sure I call my shadow home in the dawn! Everybody does,
everybody who has any sense! Suppose your shadow does not find
you, after gallivanting around all night, and gets lost? WHERE
are you, then? Are you going to go around living without a
shadow?"

"But Grandfather, I didn't think you had a shadow, you too!"

"Why of course I have a shadow."

"But I thought you were Marum'da, who made the world!"

Coyote laughed. "Who told you I was Marum'da? I am just
an old Coyote, I am Coyote Old Man!"

Fox thought a while. Then he said, "Does the Kukusu have a
shadow?"

"How do I know if the Kukusu has a shadow? I have never
seen the Kukusu!"

"Oh, Grandfather, I think you are fibbing! I think you know
the Kukusu very well, and I think you are Marum'da, but you
won't admit it. You and the Kukusu made the world . . ."

"No, no, no. In the first place the Kukusu didn't make the
world, it was Marum'da who made the world. He just went to his
elder brother, the Kukusu, to ask his advice about making the
world, because he was lonesome. The Kukusu wasn't lonesome.
He didn't care whether there was a world or there was no world!
He sat in his cloud-house and he smoked his long, straight pipe,

and he thought and he dreamed. But he gave some wax from his armpits to Marum'da, and he loaned him his pipe which had a lot of carvings on it and then Marum'da made the world."

"Does anybody ever see the Kukusu?"

"Yes, some people say they have. Maybe . . . Some people say they have seen him in the woods, hiding behind a tree . . . and some people say they have seen him at noontime sitting on a rock, thinking . . . and some people say they have seen him floating in those round clouds that rise into the sky beyond a ridge."

"Grandfather, if I should see him, will he hurt me?"

"Why, of course not! *Why* should he hurt you? He doesn't care about you."

"Doesn't he take care of the world?"

"No indeed! The world takes care of itself . . . well, maybe not always. They say Marum'da destroyed the people three times, because they didn't behave properly. And every time he made a new kind of people before he got them just right. And each time he went to visit his brother Kukusu, to ask his advice—but he never destroyed the world itself, he could not destroy it after he had made it—he only destroyed the people. Marum'da is always worrying about the people, and whether they behave properly, but Kukusu doesn't care. He goes around sometimes, they say, leaves his home in the south world and travels around, but he never visits anybody. He is always thinking and dreaming—and if you find him and ask him any questions, he won't answer you. He just squints and smiles and disappears."

Soon they were going along the trail, and that day Little Fox got lost. It was about at sun halfway down. They were going along the trail, following the top of a ridge, tras, tras, tras, and Fox was looking for rabbits to shoot with his little bow and arrows. He lagged behind the others, and nobody noticed he wasn't along. Very soon he couldn't find where they went, he couldn't find their tracks. They must have left the ridge somewhere and gone down. Little Fox was running back and forth everywhere looking for their tracks. Little Fox was losing his head. Little Fox was getting very scared. He was running back and forth on the ridge, crying. Nobody answered. There were plenty of valleys, and ridges, and other valleys must be beyond those other ridges all blue in the distance. "Where did they go? Where are you? Ye-ye, where are you? You are mean! You are mean people! You left me! Ye-ye-ye . . ."

Then Little Fox saw several men coming along the trail. They were very small, just about his own size, or even a little smaller, some of them were. But they looked like grown-up men just the same. And they looked mean. They each carried a spear, and they all had a hat with two long feathers sticking out, one on either side of the forehead. They were coming along fast ta-ka-ta-kata-kata-katakatakata. . . . Little Fox turned around and ran. And then another bunch of little men with spears sprang out of the bushes in front of him. Little Fox stopped short and turned to run down the hill to the south, but another bunch of little men jumped out from behind the bushes there. And another bunch came up from the north side.

Little Fox wasn't crying any more. He put down his bow and arrows on the ground. Then he opened his sack of flints. Then he arranged the flints all around him in a circle, all pointing outside. Then he started to sing the Hawk War Song. The little men were watching him.

"What shall we do with him?"

"Kill him with our spears."

"No, he is cute, let's keep him for a pet!"

"Ask him who he is."

"Look at him: he is crazy!"

"No, he isn't crazy. He is dancing for us. What's the matter with you? Haven't you got any sense? Don't you see he is performing the dance of the giants? He is bigger than you are, anyway."

"No, I tell you that's the acorn soup dance. That's the way they dance it in the east. They always dance it that way when they eat roasted fox with acorn mush."

"Oh, you talk too much. I am going to kill him with my spear and take him home. I don't like pets. I have to feed my family."

"Wait a minute. You talk like a fool. How do you know but maybe he is some medicine-man. Maybe his father is a medicine-man, and the little one is learning his song. How do you know but maybe his father's medicine will hear him and come flying back."

"My father is not a medicine-man," cried Fox, "but my grandfather is one. My grandfather is Coyote Old Man!"

All the little men roared with laughter. "Haha-ha, Coyote Old Man is *my* grandfather, too. Coyote Old Man is everybody's grandfather. I guess you must be our cousin. Ha-ha-ha."

Little Fox got mad when he saw them laughing at him. He stamped his foot. "You'd better not make fun of Grandfather Coyote. He is not far from here. He will be coming back around here with everybody else as soon as they miss me. He'll surely be coming back looking for me, and if he sees you, he'll kill all of you."

"What is he talking about?" they said.

"Yes, if you look around, you will find the tracks of my people. We are traveling west to visit our relatives and Grandfather Coyote is with us. That's what I am telling you."

"He is crazy. He is crazy. He is crazy. He is raving. Grandfather Coyote closed the door of his house and destroyed the center-post a long, long time ago, long before my grandfather was born. He is there yet, sleeping away. Maybe he is dead. Nobody ever could get into his house to wake him up. One little man said that's what the old people all say."

"You had better ask him again. I did see the tracks of several people along the trail over there. And there was a coyote all right, traveling along with a bear, and another track like those of a deer."

"That's my mother Antelope."

"There he goes, raving again. What's an antelope?"

"That's my mother, I tell you. And Bear, he is my father. And Coyote he is Grandfather Coyote Old Man. That's his name, and you had better not make fun of him."

Then another party of little men arrived. They had seen the same tracks going down off the ridge. Then they all started to follow the tracks. Everybody was talking. They forgot Little Fox. They all started, going very fast, takatakatakatakata . . . "Hey, there, wait for me!" cried Little Fox, gathering up his flints and bow and arrows.

Down there in a little valley they found Coyote Old Man, and Bear, and Antelope, and Quail-baby. The little men said, "That's Grandfather Coyote, all right. Where have you been, Grandfather? We thought you were dead in your house."

"Why, children! Why, here are all the warriors of the Ant Tribe. I had forgotten that you live near here. I have been asleep so long. I had forgotten."

"Oh, Grandfather, you ought to be ashamed! What would our chiefs say if they heard you went by and didn't stop with us? You had better come along right now. We had better start right now. Our village is not far. We have plenty of grub. You know, our people always have plenty of grub stored away. We'll soon have a big dance going on."

Tras, tras, tras, takatakatakatakatakataka, they all went. The people of the village heard them coming. All the ants came out of their big house under the ground.

"They must be bringing guests here. They must be bringing some big chief. Hey, you women, start a big fire, cook a lot of things. Get ready. Come on, girls, get ready, get on your beads, we are going to dance all night. A big chief is coming with his family."

They danced all night in the big Hall of the Ant People. The children were asleep in heaps everywhere but the old people kept on starting fresh dances all the time. They didn't stop 'til morning.

The sun came out. Nice clear morning in the hills. The grown-ups were asleep in the big hall. The children were running around outside shouting. Little Fox boy had a gang following him. They wanted to see him shoot his bow and arrows. They all tried it, but they didn't know how. Fox tried to show them, but the Little Ant boys didn't know how. Then Fox wanted to see if he could throw a spear. But he could only throw it a little distance and all the Ant boys were teasing him. They had a fine time. Then they had races and Fox almost won in one of them. Then they played gambling games and Fox won nearly all the time.

When the grown-ups came out it was near noontime and Fox had already traded his bow and arrows for a spear and a hat with antennae.

The Bear party was all ready to travel on. All the chiefs of the Ant people, all the old men came out to say goodbye. "Goodbye, Chief Bear. Goodbye, Mrs. Antelope. Come through here on your way back. Goodbye, Grandfather Coyote. We are happy now that we have seen you again."

"Fine dance! Good dance! Good old-time dancing!" said Old Man Coyote, "I enjoyed it. Made me feel young again. Nice dancing, nice girls, pretty girls. I like to dance with pretty girls when they stand behind me and hold my hips and I sing He, He, Ha-Ha, He, He, that's the way, that's the way," and Old Man Coyote stamped on the ground to show how. Everybody laughed.

Then he started swinging down the trail and kicking at the pebbles with his stick. They all followed after him, Little Fox boy first with his new hat with the two long feathers streaming back, and Antelope with the cradle-board on her back, then Bear shuffling behind with the heavy pack of provisions which he carried on his back, hanging from his forehead with a hemp-line. Antelope turned and teased him: "Now is the time to give us a little lively dance. All the Ant girls are watching you from the top of the hill!"

"Never mind that hill," growled Bear, "all the Ant boys are on that other hill to the south, watching for the end of your shadow!" Antelope laughed and didn't say anything more.

Tras, tras, tras, they went along the trail. Tras, tras, tras.

III

PACIFICA'S
LICENSE-RENEWAL
CONTROVERSY

1

The Federal
Communications
Commission Decision

Late in December, 1962, and in early January, 1963, newspapers
throughout the United States headlined the news that the three
Pacifica radio stations were being investigated by the United
States Senate Internal Security Subcommittee. At the same time it
was reported that the Federal Communications Commission had
not renewed Pacifica Radio licenses "pending final determination." It was rumored that a large volume of complaints about
Pacifica Radio was being investigated by the FCC.

Five witnesses from Pacifica Foundation were heard before
the Senate Judiciary Subcommittee on Internal Security in early
January in executive [closed] sessions. Pacifica's Board of Directors chose to tell the subcommittee about Pacifica and its policies
and programs, and asked that the hearings be open to the press
and public. They also requested permission to tape-record and
broadcast the entire proceedings. Under the subcommittee's rules
both requests were denied.

Critics of this position expressed to Pacifica's Board the view

320 / THE EXACTING EAR

that cooperation with the subcommittee was improper because they believed this kind of investigation had no real legislative function and no purpose other than harassment and attempted intimidation. Pacifica responded in a publicized statement including:

> Our broadcasting philosophy has been publicly declared and practiced for fourteen years. The past broadcasting history of these years is readily available in program logs. We can be heard and evaluated by anyone with an FM receiver. Such radio stations could not exist under a Communist or Fascist government—nor under any government which cannot abide freedom or anything but the official position in matters where it counts. Such freedom—or its absence— marks the difference between governments. The only way to preserve this freedom is by practicing it. This Pacifica stations do every day of the year.
>
> We might also question the propriety of this legislative hearing. However, we choose not to do so, not because we conceded the right to compel testimony in these matters, but because Pacifica's policies and programs are open to everyone. No subpoena is necessary to secure that kind of information. Those responsible for making and administering Pacifica's policies will discuss these policies and our programs with anyone, including the senators.
>
> Of course we also respect the rights of an individual compelled to speak under subpoena to respond to purely personal questions in the light of his own conscience and understanding of his constitutional rights.

Just prior to the hearings, U.S. Senator Thomas J. Dodd, of Connecticut, who is vice chairman of the subcommittee, issued a seven-page statement to the witnesses, and later to the press. In his reference to the Pacifica investigation he stated,

> Our world has become so vast and complex that the average person is completely dependent upon mass com-

munication media—the press, radio, television and films—
for his knowledge of the outside world. Communist control
over these media would present the gravest threat to our
national security. Any substantial Communist infiltration of
these media, which would give influence to agents of a foreign totalitarian power seeking to poison the well-springs
of public opinion in the United States, would be of concern
to this Subcommittee. But let me make it clear right here
that we are not inquiring into the question of who said what
over the air. We are not concerned here with the program
content of any station nor even with the question of whether
programming has been influenced or controlled by Communists, but rather with whether there is any such infiltration
as might make Communist influence or control possible. . . .
Recently there have come to the attention of the committee
reports of possible Communist infiltration or penetration of
an important radio chain, the stations of the Pacifica Foundation. We are here today to seek information, from witnesses
whom we believe to be in a position to supply it, respecting
facts which may shed light on the question of how much
substance there may have been to these reports. This is our
major objective. . . .

In response to this widely publicized investigation, and the
investigation begun earlier by the FCC, thousands of protesting
letters were sent to each of Pacifica's stations, and to the FCC.
Prominent citizens in northern and southern California formed
"Friends of Free Radio" committees and placed advertisements in
newspapers. Subscriptions and contributions to the stations in-
creased markedly.

On January 22, 1964, the Federal Communications Commission issued a historic decision which clarified and strengthened
the responsibilities of radio and television as media of free speech
and free expression. It renewed and granted licenses to the three
stations and issued an opinion about the stations owned by Pacifica Foundation. Here are relevant excerpts from that opinion.

1. *Programming Issues:*

Its [the FCC's] very limited concern in this type of case is whether, upon the overall examination, some substantial pattern of operation inconsistent with the public interest standard clearly and patently emerges. . . . It would thus appear that there is no substantial problem, on an overall basis, warranting further inquiry. . . . (we have examined the licensee's overall showing as to its stations' operations and find that those operations did serve the needs and interests of the licensee's areas.) . . . We recognize that as shown by the complaints here, such provocative programming as here involved may offend some listeners. But this does not mean that those offended have the right, through the Commission's licensing power, to rule such programming off the airwaves. Were this the case, only the wholly inoffensive, the bland, could gain access to the radio microphone or TV camera. No such drastic curtailment can be countenanced under the Constitution, the Communications Act, or the Commission's policy, which has consistently sought to insure the "maintenance of radio and television as a medium of freedom of speech and freedom of expression for the people of the Nation as a whole. . . ."

2. Communist Party Affiliation Issue:

Under the public interest standard it is relevant and important for the Commission to determine in certain cases whether its applicants, or the principals of its applicants, for broadcast licenses, are members of the Communist Party or of organizations which advocate or teach the overthrow of the Government by force or violence. . . . Because of information coming to the Commission's attention from several sources, the Commission requested information from Pacifica Foundation on this score. On the basis of information obtained from Government sources, the Foundation, and our own inquiry, we do not find any evidence warranting further inquiry into the qualifications in this respect of Pacifica Foundation.

In the view of the foregoing, IT IS ORDERED, this

22nd day of January, 1964 that the above-entitled applications of Pacifica Foundation, ARE GRANTED as serving the public interest, convenience and necessity.

Reference to this important decision by the Federal Communications Commission was made by its Chairman, E. William Henry, at a conference of the National Association of Broadcasters, April 7, 1964, in Chicago. Newspapers reported that Mr. Henry's outspoken criticism of the radio and television industry's complacency and lack of courage "stirred shock waves in the industry." Mr. Henry told the radio and television men at the conference that their reaction to two recent FCC proceedings "cast a disturbing light on the basic motivations of an industry licensed to do business in the public interest." Mr. Henry reminded the broadcasters that they raised a storm of protest when the Commission proposed to issue a rule limiting the number and length of radio and television commercials. He contrasted this to the industry's silence in the case of Pacifica Foundation, which involved broadcasting's right of free speech.

Mr. Henry candidly told the NAB convention in effect that in his opinion the FCC was at fault in postponing action on the Pacifica licenses, but that the broadcasting industry bore the greatest part of the blame.

> Which state [broadcasting] association sent delegations to Congress charging that the FCC had deferred the Pacifica licenses for an unwarranted period and was operating outside its jurisdiction? [he asked]. Which of you wrote me a letter urging the commission to dismiss these charges and to reaffirm the commission's time-honored adherence to the principles of free broadcasting? Where were your libertarian lawyers and their amicus briefs, your industry statesmen with their ringing speeches?
>
> If broadcasters felt involved in this issue, there is no evidence in our records to indicate these feelings. Apparently not one commercial broadcaster felt obliged to make his views [on the Pacifica case] known to the FCC. When you

display more interest in defending your freedom to suffocate the public with commercials than in upholding your freedom to provide provocative variety, when you cry "censorship" and call for faith in the founding fathers' wisdom only to protect your balance sheet, when you remain silent in the face of a threat which could shake the First Amendment's proud oak to its very roots, you tarnish the ideals enshrined in the Constitution and invite an attitude of suspicion. You join the forces of crass complacency—in an industry and at a time in the history of this nation when complacency of any sort is both misplaced and dangerous.

Thus after the ordeal of investigation, of time-consuming defense, Pacifica Foundation's case led to a decision which challenges the broadcasting industry to exercise its freedom as media of free speech and free expression.

Many thousands of listeners to Pacifica Radio who wrote to the Federal Communications Commission sent copies of their letters to each of the radio stations. The following were selected from a few of these which were readily available at the New York station, WBAI.

2

Letters from Listeners

Mr. Newton Minow, Chairman
Federal Communications Commission
Washington, D.C.

Dear Mr. Minow:

Being a person of sound mind, I resent being told that I cannot hear, see, taste, smell or feel something because it will corrupt me. Don't you trust my judgment on this matter?

On this basis I am very enthusiastic about WBAI. They make it their business to present any and all sides of an issue. Can you explain to me how such freedom of presentation can corrupt the minds of the American public? Are you so contemptuous of our minds, of the basic traditions of the United States itself, that you would attempt to prevent our contact with certain thoughts? And do you dare to say this censorship is for my own and this country's good?

How does the number of complaints against WBAI compare with the number of people who pay money to hear the station—the subscribers?

On this station I am able to hear extreme leftists, extreme

rightists and perhaps wiser, calmer men and women speak on what is closest to their hearts, all of which is of vital interest to me. There is constant broadcasting of new music and ideas, of discussions of these, and of new ways of programming itself. The children's programs are fresh with colorful stories, often full of poetry and are beautifully narrated. They are stimulating to children and refreshing to adults.

I look upon WBAI as a miracle, and am proud to know of it, and to know that it grew from my culture. Let me judge what is good or bad for me to hear—and give this station its license so I can have some choice in what I hear on radio.

Sincerely,

J.S.
A WBAI subscriber

Dear Mr. Minow:

I have heard recently that the licenses of the Pacifica Foundation FM radio stations (KPFA, KPFK and WBAI) are now before the Federal Communications Commission for consideration of either granting or denying these stations a permanent license to operate on the air. That there should be a possibility of a license for these stations being denied comes as a shock to me. I have been a subscriber to the Pacifica stations since 1955 and some 8 years of acquaintance with the programs of the stations has left no doubt in my mind that these stations are one of the most important and enrichening events in the cultural life of the country. They are also far and away the best radio stations on the air not only in the United States, but possibly even in the world. (People who have heard the BBC regularly, for example, rate the Pacifica stations higher in overall quality of programming.)

The principles of operation of the Pacifica stations are a rare excellence at a time when the quality of much radio programming is dictated and modulated by the needs of the advertisers who make the programs possible. The Pacifica stations, on the other hand, are paid for by the people who listen to them, and, consequently, offer a genuinely democratic opportunity for a mass medium to reflect the interests and tastes of its audience (or audiences). A glance at any of the Pacifica program folios will amply and accurately demonstrate the results. Poetry readings, continuously excellent and varied musical offerings, first-rate drama, discussions and lectures by authorities and scholars on a wide range of social, political, economic, philosophical and psychological subjects—in which all points of view receive an airing—are just a portion of what the Pacifica stations offer. It amounts to more than superior entertainment; it is a mode of education for adults to whom education and cultivation is a life-long process. It is also a richly educative medium for children.

More deeply, the principles and programming of the Pacifica stations are an aspect of the essence of democracy in action—the free interplay and exchange of ideas and experiences and opinions. If there is one force which keeps a country free, vigorous and great, it is just this sort of exchange and interplay. Thus the Pacifica stations genuinely function as bulwarks of democracy, and they should be cherished and promoted. These stations have given my wife and me delight and stimulation for years, and, if they were to go off the air, one of the great powers in American cultural life would disappear.

For these reasons, my wife and I submit to your attention an urgent request that permanent licenses be granted to all the Pacifica stations.

Sincerely yours,

D.C.

Gentlemen:

As a devoted and appreciative listener of Pacifica Foundation Radio Station in New York WBAI-FM, I am seriously concerned at the turn of events in the investigations of Pacifica stations by the Federal Communications Commission concurrently with a separate investigation by the Senate Internal Security Subcommittee. This is one station that, in my opinion, fulfills the intents of a

radio communications service. Station WBAI-FM in New York
City presents programs of a wide spectrum, leaving to the individual listener the molding and forming of his own opinions by a
comparison and evaluation of majority and minority views.

Pacifica Foundation presents many public affairs programs—
some of them advocate PEACE. This, in some quarters, is considered irregular. For it is the Communists, too, who talk of peace.
So anyone who believes in advocating the cause of peace is suspect. The public affairs programs are presented intelligently and
in depth—the ticking clock does not stop a discussion in midsen-
tence and development, as it frequently does on highly advertised
public affairs and documentary programs of larger commercial
networks. We have full opportunity to contemplate, and weigh
the subject being presented by a professor or other specialist. One
may agree, or one may not. But we do have the opportunity to flex
our mental muscles. And this is virtually the only station in this
vicinity that does not utter the stock, readymade phrases—and
word-for-word emissions of news and viewpoints—that are heard
generally on larger networks.

Radio Station WBAI-FM, and its sister stations, moreover,
give opportunity for presenting divergent views. They do give
time to minorities. Each has his day. In this way the discerning
listener can get in on many matters ranging from domestic affairs,
foreign affairs; domestic and foreign views; on sociology, psychology, science, medicine and education.

In addition to public affairs programs of a wide scope, Pacifica Radio offers cultural programs of poetry, famous old plays,
new plays, music of the Renaissance which we can hear very
seldom in concert programs, avant garde music, standard music;
we have had the great privilege of hearing music of one famous
international musical festival after the other. Recently, on George
Washington's birthday, for the third consecutive year they have
programmed in one consecutive 17½-hour day's program, the entire Ring of the Nibelungen, consisting of four opera dramas by
Richard Wagner, presented to listeners on tape from the famous
Bayreuth Festival. To hear the entire Ring Operas in even a two-

week period is a rare event. But to have the joy as a music-lover, to be kept in the mood in a concentrated, homogeneous continuous presentation, is an unforgettable experience, and thoroughly uplifting to the spirit. The intermission programs of these four operas were in themselves well-thought out, diverting, informative and relaxing.

In the realm of children's programs, an intelligent and imaginative service is given. By contrast with the caliber of programs offered by larger networks in this field, the real public service given by Pacifica Radio is a revelation. You have but to look at the "Folio" issued by Pacifica to see the range and literacy of programs for young people between 4:45 and 5:45 P.M. every day, and on Saturday mornings.

Every listening hour on WBAI-FM is an experience. One never knows when a whole new world will be opened up. The people who plan and research and present these programs must be truly dedicated to public service; for the kind, volume, and quality of the programs taken as a whole cannot be produced haphazardly. For this dedication and idealization, it seems now that there are some complainants. These people who dedicate themselves to public service, sans commercial sponsors, depend entirely on individual, voluntary listeners who are glad to pay a nominal amount for the privilege and pleasure they are given, and to make token payment as their way of showing their gratefulness.

To get the volume and diversification of information offered regularly on WBAI-FM, one would have to pore through countless magazines and periodicals, domestic and foreign. In fact, it would be very difficult to research individually that which is here presented to us, giving both chapter and verse for those who might wish to research deeper in any particular vein. This is truly a PUBLIC SERVICE in the real sense. Today, when developments and changes occur so rapidly and unexpectedly—amidst vague backgrounds—both in domestic and in foreign affairs, there is greater need than ever for America to be an informed nation. An informed public is an intelligent public, as opposed to being kept in ignorance, or spoonfed, regarding what is going on in this

world of ours. We need, more than ever, to know the facts of life.
We need to hear the bitter as well as the sweet. We need to hear
the truth, if even—in the proverbial sense—it hurts!

The day when Americans MUST, BY EDICT, be given
ONLY ONE VIEW—the DICTATED VIEW—is the day when
these United States of America will have died, freedomwise, and
we shall be no better off than the unfortunate people under Communism, Fascism, or any other *ism*. Those who object to minority
views or dissenting views—or to forthright ADULT programs for
that matter—are people who are afraid. They are wee people who
want to STOP THE WORLD and get off. . . . These mildewed,
roll-me-up-in-a-rug-and-put-me-in-moth-balls people are afraid of
letting in a little "mental air." Franklin Delano Roosevelt, our
President in the 30's, said: "WE HAVE NOTHING TO FEAR
BUT FEAR." And that is as true today, and more so, than when
he uttered these words to a nation at the crossroads of despair and
hope.

If we are to express our freedom and democracy only in
HATE, we are taking the negative way. We have more need to
express our beliefs in what we believe, rather. We do not want to
be treated as children and serfs and given the "party" line by the
wee people who would stuff our ears from hearing the minority
view, and hew to their "BE DUMB" line. *Managed* news, *managed* economy, *managed* thoughts. They result in damaged news,
damaged economy, and damaged thoughts. Where, in these, lies
FREEDOM or individuality? Truly, any censorship or curtailment of the range and depth of programs offered by Pacifica
Radio would be a disservice to the community, and to those of us
Americans who like selective programming. The others who do
not like these programs can switch on another station. Each to his
choice, without prejudice.

If we do not use our thinking muscles, we die. If we are not
permitted to listen to a dissenting opinion, we wither. This is a
dangerous method of thought control. By pursuing this line, we
lose our self-respect. We will all become automatons and George
Orwell's "1984" will be upon us—spied upon, listened-in on, bul-

lied, goaded, intimidated, fearful and untrustful of one another.

Americans should be trusted to think for themselves. If this freedom is abrogated by removal of freedom of press, freedom of speech, freedom of listening, freedom of assembly, freedom of dissenting, freedom of change, we are a *frozen* people, incapable of proclaiming we have a democracy in which the people mould opinion.

Your consideration of, and respect for, the value of a free, independent, unsponsored radio service is requested, in which all shades and colors of thought that are edifying are freely presented. This would be consonant with the greatness—present, that is—and leadership in freedom which the United States represents to the rest of the world. We want to have that which they think we have: FREEDOM.

Respectfully yours,

M.V.

Dear Mr. Minow:

The Pacifica Foundation has a right to be proud that they are free and responsible broadcasters. Who are these scared Americans who have complained that WBAI and its affiliates are broadcasting from far Left to far Right opinions of those who head such organizations as the American Nazi Party, the John Birch Society, Norman Thomas, Barry Goldwater, the National Review, I. F. Stone and a whole mixture of diverse opinions? Isn't this a healthy enough country to listen to the garbage as well as the roast-beef of political thought?

I don't think you can single out an FM station as a mass media outlet which caters to the ignorant. A study of the FM listener will reveal a higher income and college level listening to its stations. WBAI did a study of its listeners and it should be reviewed by the Senate Sub-Committee. An independent study of all FM listeners is also available, as you well know. The complainers are in the minority.

The whole problem here is that certain self-righteous American Firsters are beginning to witch-hunt again. I don't think the *New York Times* can be called a radical paper in their defense of the Pacifica Foundation (see editorial of early February, West Coast edition).

Let anyone say that Pacifica is not living to the letter of the First Amendment, and I'll show you a misinformed patriot.

Sincerely,

J.R.

Dear Mr. Minow:

As a listener and subscriber to Pacifica Foundation's FM station WBAI, New York, I am deeply disturbed by the Commission's withholding of the station's license, and by its failure so far to renew the license of its sister station, KPFA, Berkeley-San Francisco, whose programming I understand to be similar.

It is my opinion that no stations in history have ever so perfectly followed the Commission's criteria of "public interest, convenience and necessity" in the programming field.

Even in New York, with its multiplicity of stations, there is not one other single station—AM or FM—which a listener and his family can "live on" completely. If balanced programming is one of the FCC's criteria, WBAI should be awarded a medal for its complete coverage of public affairs, music, drama, culture, and children's programming.

In the single field of public affairs, there is no other station which approaches WBAI's diversity. Although there is little newspaper ownership of radio and television stations in New York City, most of the other stations might as well be owned by newspapers from the standpoint of variety of information and opinion. On WBAI alone does one hear the varying viewpoints which must necessarily be aired freely in a democratic society.

If there are pressures to force Pacifica off the air, I cannot understand them. I cannot conceive how anyone, regardless of his shade of politics, can fear the free expression of opinion and variety of information presented on WBAI. Can it be that they have not even listened?

In journalism, America has always had a tradition of freedom and diversity. Thus, *The Saturday Review* and *The Reporter* can exist alongside of *Life* and *The Saturday Evening Post*. Is it too much to ask that we be permitted to have the same freedom in listening? Or must government control and allocation of radio frequencies also mean conformity and sameness in programming?

A group of radio listeners feels strongly enough about WBAI's programming to contribute financially to its support. For my own part, my subscription and contributions are made for the purpose of helping to preserve, in a small way, the freedom of expression which made our nation great—in addition to the information and entertainment my family and I receive by listening to this unique station.

It has never occurred to me to ask the FCC to suspend the license of rock-'n'-roll stations. No matter what my distaste, I feel they have the right to operate—even on public frequencies—although they perform no public service that I can determine.

In the case of Pacifica's stations, however, the public service is explicit and implicit and rooted deeply in the heritage of our democracy. It will be a dark day indeed in this country's traditions if an agency of our government attempts to stifle what it is charged by our Constitution to uphold.

Sincerely,

D.L.

Dear Mr. Minow:

I am a WBAI listener and subscriber. I have heard that WBAI's license is in jeopardy. I, my family, and friends are anxious to do everything in our power to see that WBAI's license is renewed, and that their excellent programming is continued.

No other station on radio or television in our area offers programs which even begin to approach the caliber of those of

WBAI. It is the *only* station which consistently presents the very highest quality of literary, musical, social and political commentary.

I understand that the program is under attack specifically because views have been aired which are anti-government or anti-establishment. Is not the very presence of such a free forum of ideas the bulwark and the distinguishing characteristic of American democracy as prescribed by the Constitution? The real threat to our freedom in America is the silencing—or the censoring of unpopular or even heretical ideas. Communism, fascism, and all the other forms of totalitarianism thrive whenever and wherever criticism of government (political heresy) is no longer tolerated. Let it never be so in America!

At this moment WBAI is the only broadcasting station which attracts and continues to stimulate educated Americans—Americans who want to guard and foster the whole western tradition in art, music, drama, poetry, and political responsibility.

If it is really true that WBAI—the only station on the air which eschews soap operas, sensational murder-rape news stories, rock-and-roll "music," revolting commercials, a steady diet of the pop-classical music of the 19th century, and stereotyped news commentary—is found to be doing a disservice to the community, then our values have indeed become hopelessly topsy-turvy. It seems hardly necessary to say that, in fact, the demise of WBAI would deal a death-blow to any future attempt at educational broadcasting at an adult level. . . .

I look forward to hearing from you of the prompt renewal of the station's license.

Yours very sincerely,

Mrs. H.H.B.

Dear Mr. Minow:

My purpose for writing is to express my abhorrence for the investigations now being conducted against Pacifica radio stations. I wish to emphasize *against,* for the effect of such an investigation will be at best harmful, at worst fatal to one of those few eccentric institutions in the country which actually make Freedom of Speech something more than shallow mockery or empty flag waving. Freedom of Speech is for Pacifica its raison d'etre and the essential condition of its existence, and its being investigated as a result can only be surprising to those who have never heard of Galileo or Martin Luther.

The really sad thing about such an investigation is that it strikes a lethal blow to those whose faith in democracy is genuine and yet barely tenuous enough to withstand all the other onslaughts made against it; we can tolerate all the waste, hypocrisy and self-interest which cripple our democracy, especially our congress, if we can only believe that by the lack of efforts to clean house our main concern—Freedom—is somehow served. But when we see the usurpers of Freedom trying to abolish it, we may be driven either to blind rage or convulsive laughter, or both. (This letter is my expression of one on the brink of the other.)

It is no discredit to the institution at which I am studying when I assert that I have received greater intellectual stimulation from station WBAI (the Pacifica station in New York) while a graduate student than from any other single source. Indeed, the fact that such a station could exist, supported solely by its listeners, and appealing to the most diversified and esoteric interests, has been a source of continuous satisfaction to me, and has helped me believe that Thomas Jefferson was not merely visionary. The unhampered continuation of WBAI's excellent programming and broadcasting is thus of the most immediate personal concern to me.

That the international threat of Communism should produce a Senator McCarthy and a John Birch Society is only unfortunate, not difficult to comprehend. But when we not only cease to combat such deplorable symptoms of hysteria, but fall under their influence, then America is threatened by an evil more insidious and subversive than anything beyond our borders, and there are bound to be graver consequences than the harassment of a non-profit radio station. Nothing I have heard over WBAI ever jolted my patriotism like the announcement that this station was being investigated.

Sincerely yours,

R.E.D.

Dear Mr. Minow:

We are subscribers and regular listeners to radio station WBAI in New York City. We were recently surprised to hear of the Senate Internal Security Subcommittee investigation of this station and other Pacifica radio stations. We were even more astonished to hear that WBAI has been operating for the past three years on a temporary license and that there is a real danger a permanent license may not be issued by the FCC. In light of these two recent occurrences, we would like you to know of our feelings concerning this station and these actions.

We have lived in a number of large and small cities on the east coast. In none of them has there been as informative and stimulating a radio station as WBAI. We especially enjoy the station's public affairs programs which deal with a wide variety of subject matter always informative and thought provoking. The station's straightforward presentation of a variety of opinions and criticisms on a multitude of topics can not be matched on any other radio station or TV station we know. It was truly refreshing to hear Jack Levine's criticisms of the FBI on this station. Whether or not we agree with them is irrelevant. What is important is that such criticisms are honestly and objectively communicated and available for public digestion. Surely communicating this man's appraisal of a government agency can not be considered any more out of order than Senator Keating's widely communicated appraisal of this government's action (or inaction) in Cuba. Other public affairs programs we have enjoyed include a presentation of the feelings of people connected with the voter registration drive in Haywood County, Tennessee. It was good to hear views and feelings of tenants, landlords, and citizens alike. Also interesting was a heated discussion among several doctors representing a wide range of opinions on "socialized" medicine. We have also enjoyed hearing a variety of topics discussed and debated on the station's Opinion program.

We find WBAI's literary programs are of a quality rare on TV or radio today. We recently enjoyed listening to the BBC presentation of "The Doll's House" by Ibsen and a BBC presentation of W. M. Thackeray's novel, "Pendennis." The station's children's programs consist of especially delightful stories from different countries and times, as well as our own, and by a variety of well-known and unknown authors. They are pleasantly and intelligently told. WBAI's music programs are a far cry from the rock and roll heard on most other stations. They include intelligent jazz and musical comedy presentations, folk music, songs of social significance, and straight classical symphonic and chamber music.

This station really provides intelligent listening for the intelligent and interested listener. It is one of the few radio and TV stations that performs a most basic and important component for maintaining a democracy toward an educated and thinking populace. The only way to insure such a populace is through honest, educational, and thought-provoking communications media. Since the Senate Internal Security Subcommittee's role is to maintain a free and open democracy, it would seem more appropriate for the Subcommittee to investigate most of the commercial radio and TV stations to inquire why they are so inadequately informing and educating the public rather than to investigate one of the few stations taking this responsibility!

We would appreciate every effort that can be made to insure that this station remains on the air and obtains a permanent license while being *encouraged* to broadcast as it has been in the past.

Sincerely yours,

G.L.

Dear Mr. Minow:

As a subscriber to WBAI, a person actively interested in art and literature, and the wife of a psychologist, I would like to protest personally as well as on behalf of the other listeners, the investigations of the Senate Internal Security Subcommittee into Pacifica Foundation. Not only have I become greatly interested in the magnificent programming produced by this Foundation, but I have become in a sense indebted to it.

I have found the majority of their varied programs constitute a creative listening experience in that they act as a stimulus to creative thought and activity as well as being a vibrant source of pleasure and education. The diversity of the ideas set forth in their interviews and discussions and so forth, although not always to my way of thinking, and at times in extreme contradiction, is a challenge to the clarification and development of one's own thought which might otherwise lie fallow, as so often it does when numbed by the general mediocrity and repetitive blandness served up to the public by our mass media. Here is radio with dynamic enthusiasm and integrity, conscious of the need to exercise freedom and not just to emptily and stultifyingly mouth the word until it ceases to have meaning or takes on all too uncomfortably aspects of its antithesis.

And yet what is happening now? Possibly they are being denied license renewal and most certainly they are being investigated and denigrated. For what? I deplore the need of those few individuals who have been allowed to take command and seek to determine for me as a responsible citizen to whom and to what I should listen; to perhaps deprive me of the opportunity and right to evaluate ideas of others and formulate those of my own; to perhaps, if the Senate committee should succeed in their threat of censorship, intimidate the already somewhat timid "free" radio; and finally, to perhaps squelch Pacifica's listener-sponsored programming and all that it offers with intelligence and purpose in the various fields of literature, music, the sciences, etc., as well as in thoughtful programming for children. Is it not a shame, and something toward which investigation could be more productively turned, that in New York, the great and cultural city, there is no other station to which I can turn on my AM or FM radio (or TV for that matter) that offers or even seeks to satisfactorily offer me anything comparable?

Amid the wails of unending popular music, overplayed classical, repetitive news headlines, advertising jingles, disc jockey inanities, and only occasionally good programs, surely one channel could be permitted to continue to broadcast unmolested the ideas of man, past and present, in all his many facets, could be permitted to develop and aid certain mass communication in becoming a significantly creative interplay between the performer and listener as individual, and could be permitted to continue, with applause rather than with investigation, to inform about and display that which is dignified and heroic in man. In every respect one must honor the fact that Pacifica Foundation is a devoted public servant.

Sincerely,

A.W.